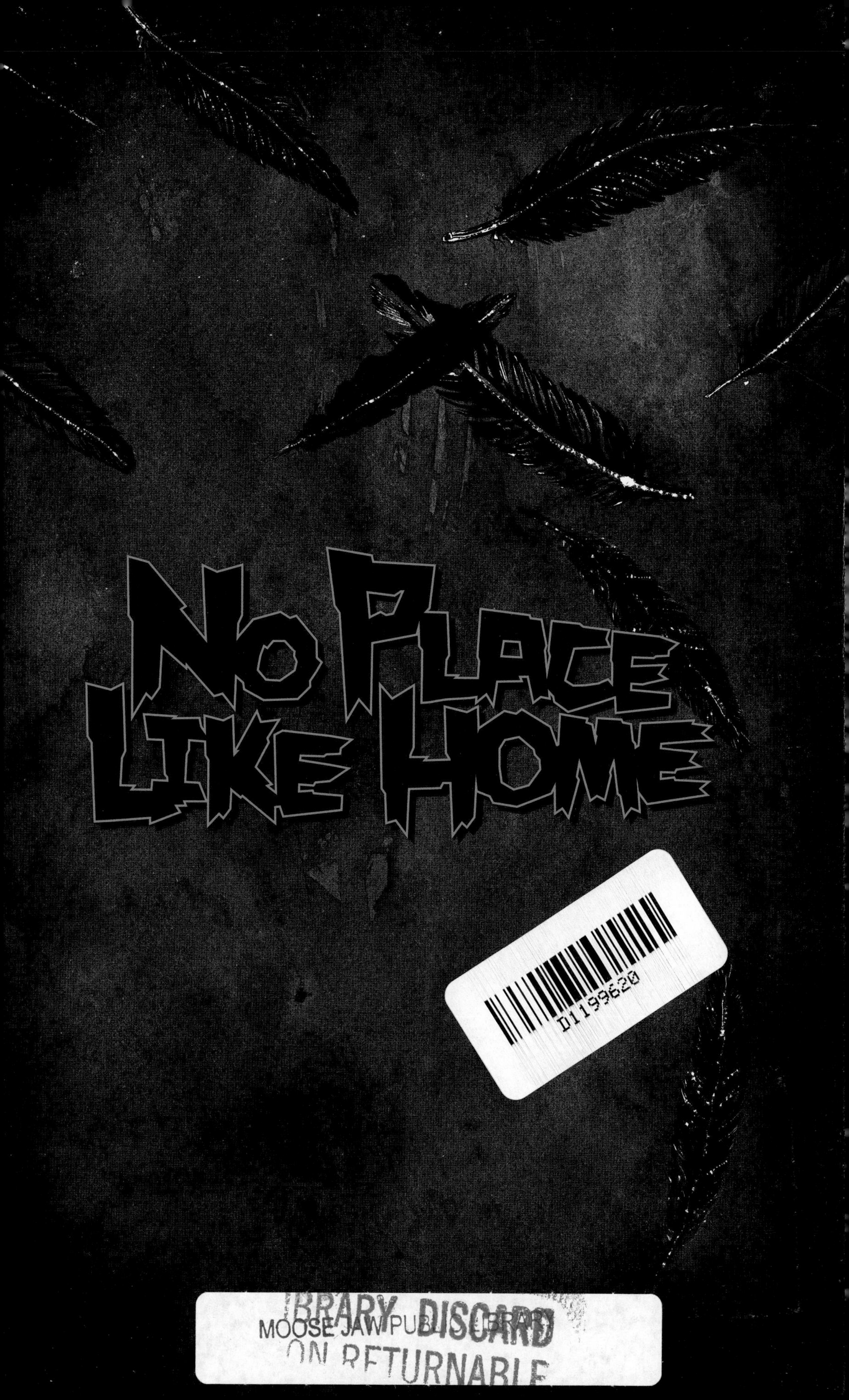
NO PLACE
LIKE HOME

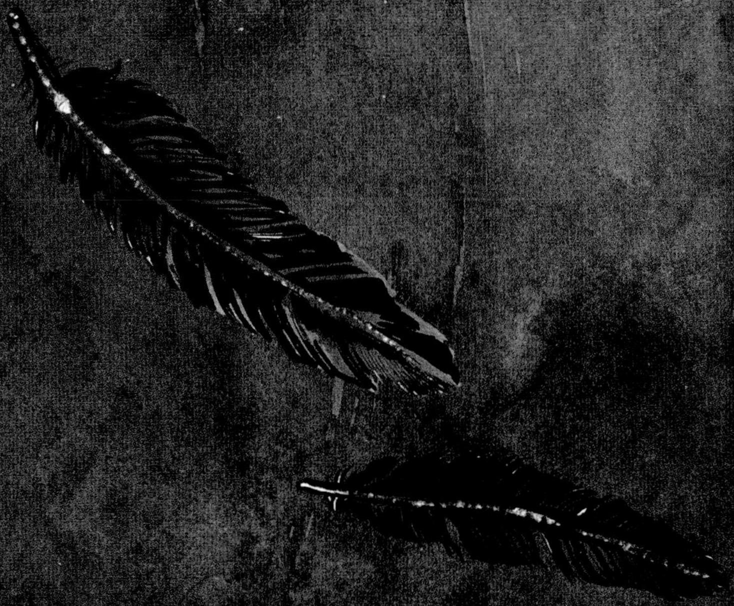

Dedicated to the memory of
Teresa Robinson

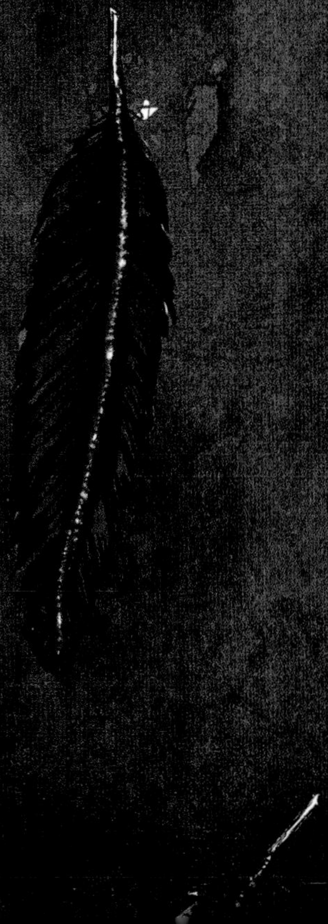

VOLUME ONE
HOME AGAIN

Written and Created by
ANGELO TIROTTO

Art
RICHARD JORDAN

Issue #1 Variant Cover
IAN CHURCHILL

Colors
PAUL LITTLE

Letters, Design and Logo
ANGELO TIROTTO

Everything Else
IAN CHURCHILL

Find out more about No Place Like Home at:
www.noonemournsthewicked.com
www.facebook.com/NoPlaceLikeHomeComic

IMAGE COMICS, INC.
Robert Kirkman - chief operating officer
Erik Larsen - chief financial officer
Todd McFarlane - president
Marc Silvestri - chief executive officer
Jim Valentino - vice-president

Eric Stephenson - publisher
Ron Richards - director of business development
Jennifer de Guzman - pr & marketing director
Branwyn Bigglestone - accounts manager
Emily Miller - accounting assistant
Jamie Parreno - marketing assistant
Jenna Savage - administrative assistant
Kevin Yuen - digital rights coordinator
Jonathan Chan - production manager
Drew Gill - art director
Monica Garcia - production artist
Vincent Kukua - production artist
Jana Cook - production artist
www.imagecomics.com

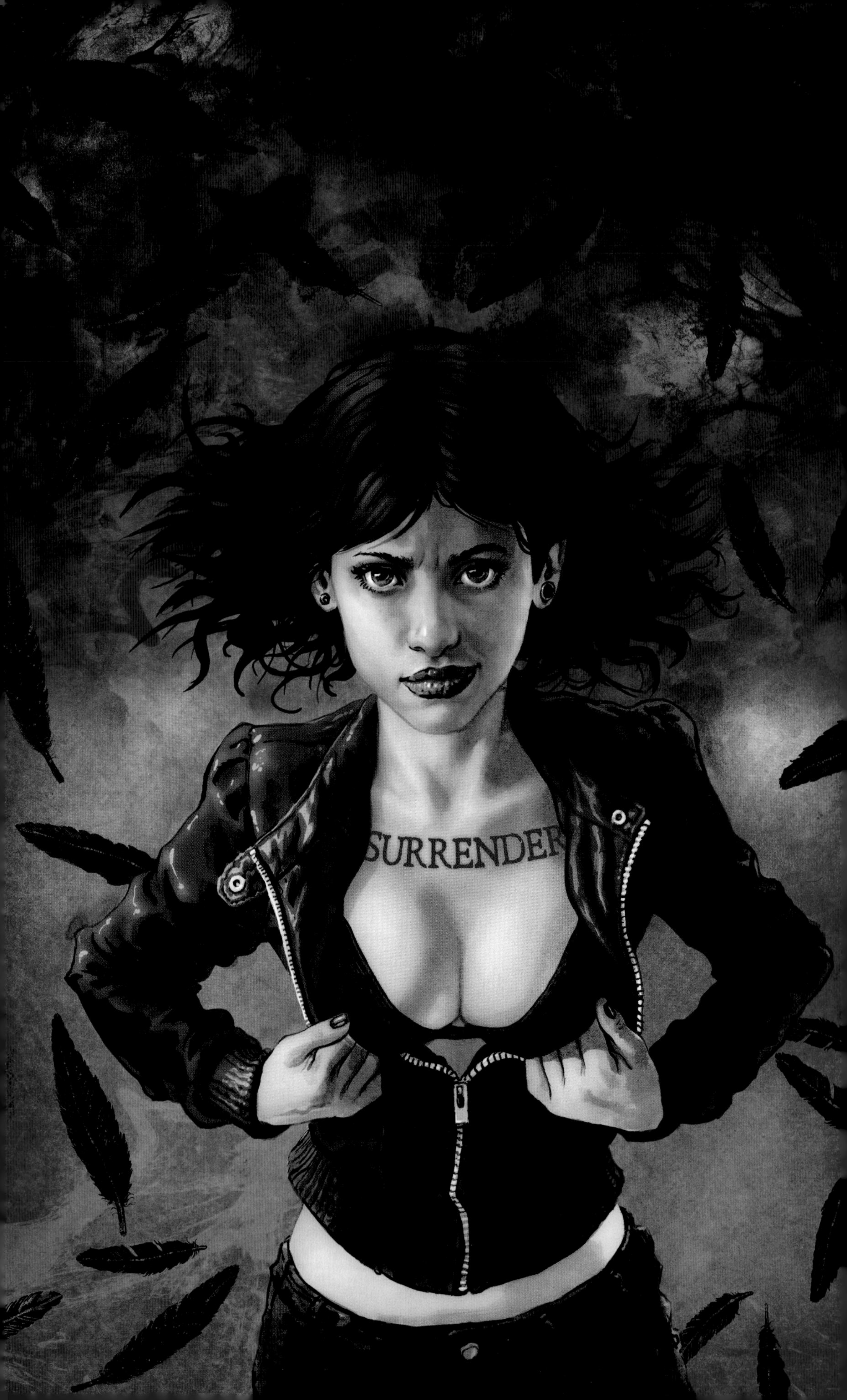
SURRENDER

Dorothy, you can never go home again.

SURRENDER.

I have a confession to make. I never saw THE WIZARD OF OZ.

Well, not until I was in my late twenties -- uh, a few short years ago -- when my homesick American girlfriend asked if we were going to watch the movie over the Thanksgiving weekend. When I told her I'd never seen it, her eyes popped out of her head and she rushed out and bought me a copy. We watched it over that weekend the way Brits used to watch the Queen's speech and the MORECAMBE AND WISE CHRISTMAS SPECIAL on Christmas Day... meaning I probably slept through most of it.

It wasn't until I lived in the U S of A a few years that I realized that American TV bank holiday traditions were just as important to them as DISNEY TIME, CHITTY CHITTY BANG BANG and DOCTOR WHO omnibus editions were to me and my British brethren. Up until a few years ago I hadn't seen more than a dozen episodes of THE TWILIGHT ZONE either, not until I'd spent a couple of Turkey Days in California bored toward the cathode ray tube which was generously spilling out twenty-four hours' worth of ZONEs as if it knew I desperately needed intelligent and entertaining distraction.

Another confession. For the longest time I confused Judy Garland with Joan Crawford and never wanted to see WIZARD OF OZ because I assumed Judy had been the dreadful MOMMIE DEAREST who abused her stepdaughter. I'd offer my apologies to Judy and her kids if I could, I'm sure they were and are perfectly normal parents and they enjoyed comforting and enriching family lives.

Okay, so NO PLACE LIKE HOME is not THE WIZARD OF OZ that sent me to sleep with half a bottle of wine. If it had been, I'd have reached for something much stronger. Something from Stephen King's liquor cabinet from the late 80's maybe -- a couple of six packs of Bud followed by an 8 year old bottle of Glenfiddich. Hm, no

something a little rougher, a whiskey more likely to burn the throat as you took a slug -- a scotch that gives you pain behind the eyes even as you reach for the bottle to refill your glass. Shit, NO PLACE LIKE HOME requires the kind of drink that'll make you think monkeys are trying to fly out of your butt the following morning.

When I met Angelo Tirotto at Ian Churchill's wedding in picturesque Chichester some six years ago, I'd never have pegged him as the kind of guy who'd take every American's favorite dream movie, douse it in kerosene and set light to it. He seemed so nice and polite. And Richard Jordan hails from Sheffield, home of GALAXY FOUR, my favorite DOCTOR WHO shop... and he worked on one of the DOCTOR WHO video games; a lovely lad, I'll bet. I'd trust any Yorkshire boy with my childhood heroes. I'd even leave a box of matches out as a measure of my trust.

But that's what Angelo and his collaborator, Richard Jordan have done here. They've set your cosy childhood on fire. And why not -- It was probably a dysfunctional childhood anyway, and if you really believe that any kid growing up in a state ripped apart by twisters had anything close to a normal upbringing, then you're following a yellow brick road straight to hell -- see that signpost up ahead?

So pull up at TWISTERS DINER -- I heard if the light is green, there's always coffee in the machine. Stay there all night and see what transpires. If Tirotto and Jordan sit at a booth near you, listen in. Surrender.

You can never go home again.

Why would you want to?

Richard Starkings
A Wondrous Land whose boundaries are that of the Imagination, Thanksgiving 2012.

Richard Starkings is the writer/creator of ELEPHANTMEN, from Image Comics, and the founder of COMICRAFT and comicbookfonts.com

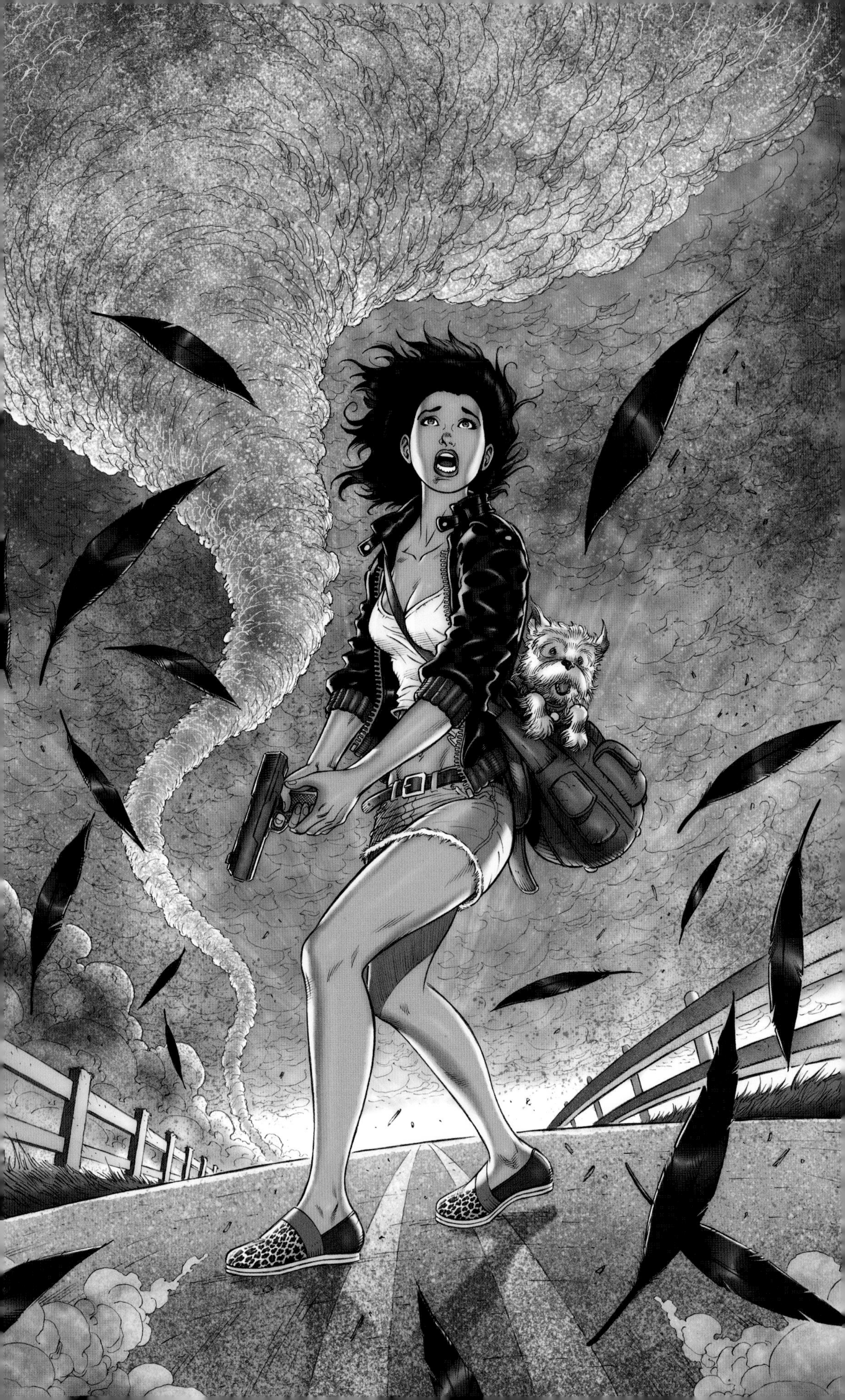

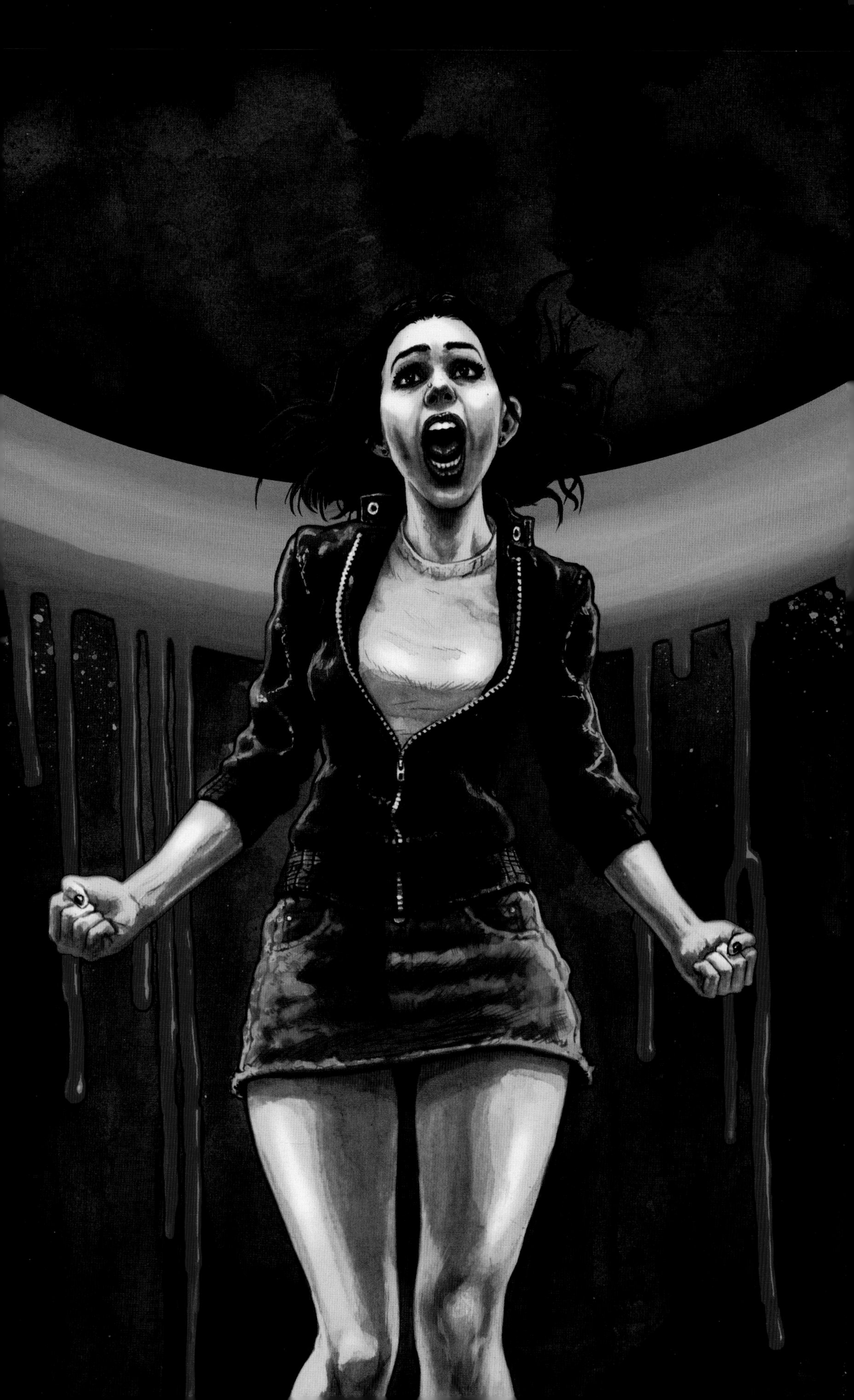

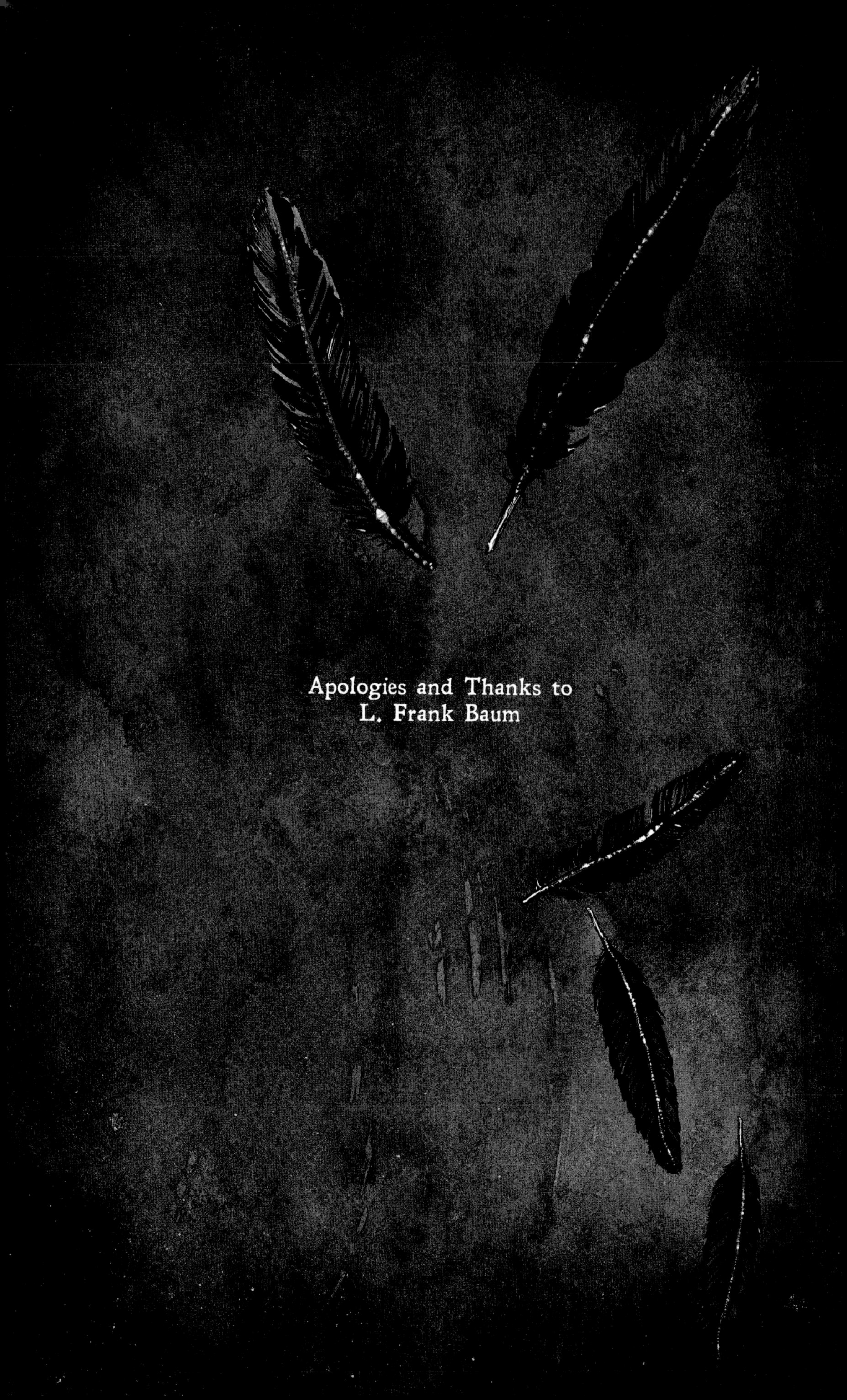

Apologies and Thanks to
L. Frank Baum

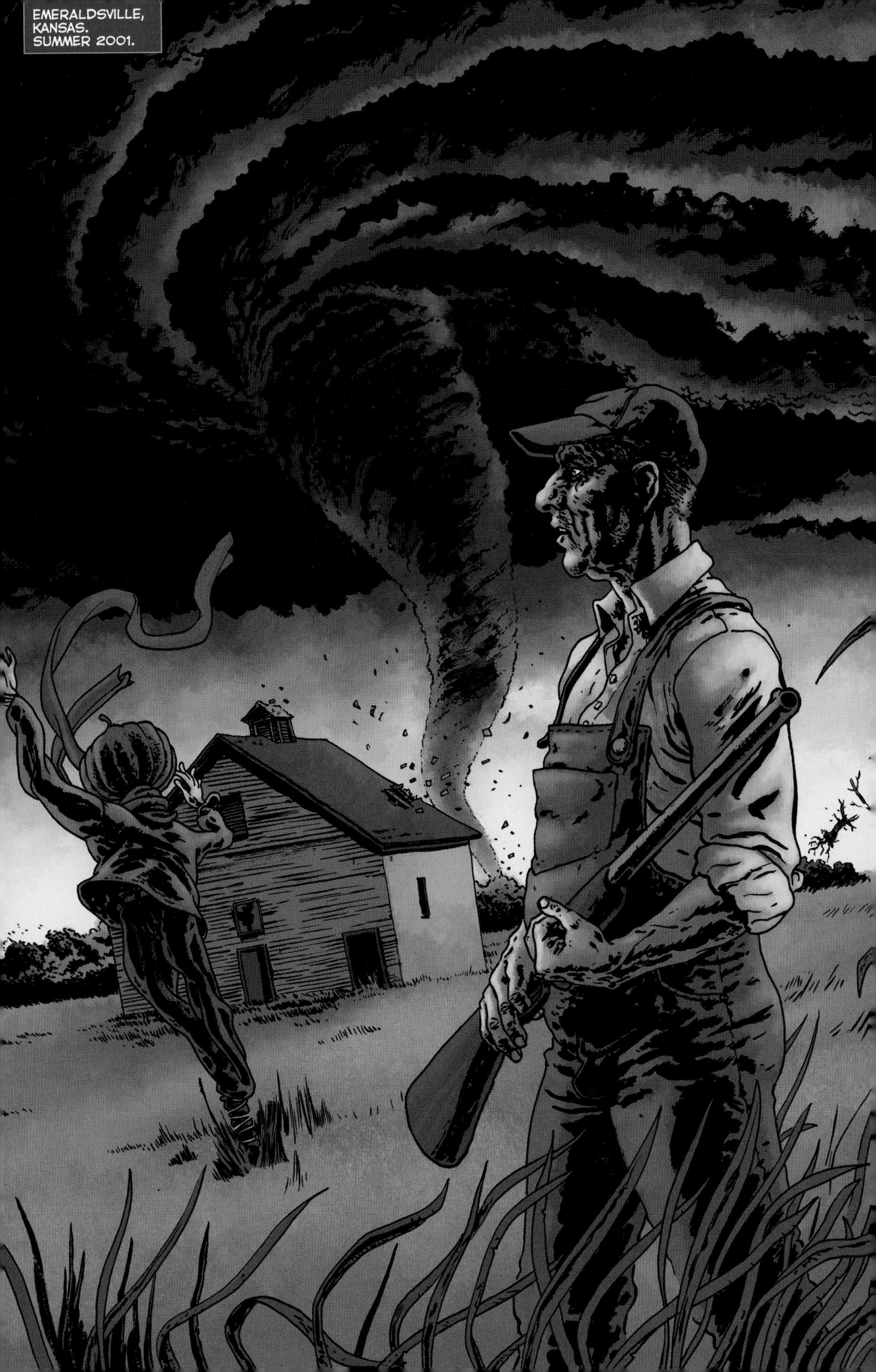
EMERALDSVILLE, KANSAS. SUMMER 2001.

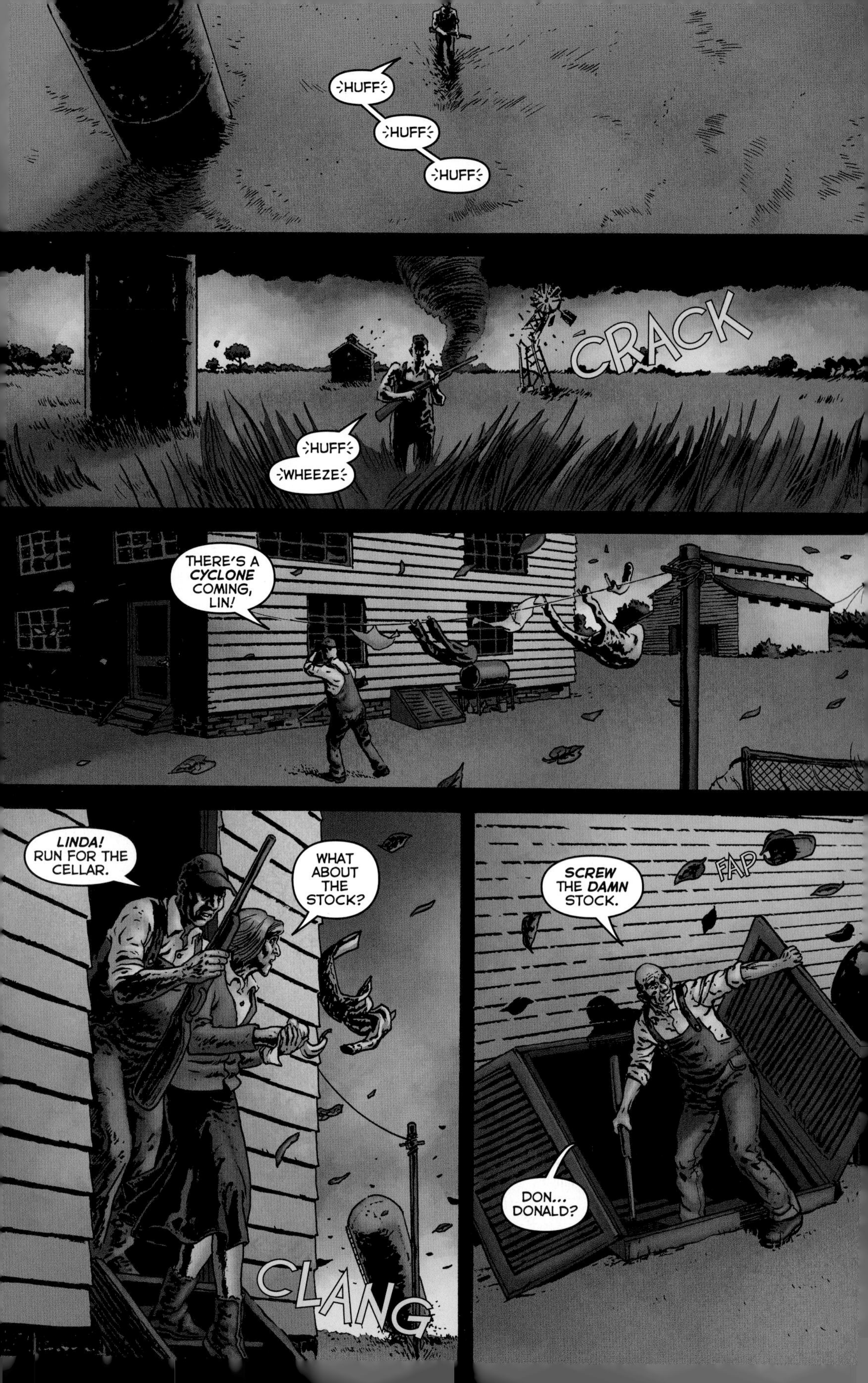

HUFF
HUFF
HUFF
CRACK
HUFF
WHEEZE
THERE'S A *CYCLONE* COMING, LIN!
LINDA! RUN FOR THE CELLAR.
WHAT ABOUT THE STOCK?
CLANG
SCREW THE ***DAMN*** STOCK.
FAP
DON... DONALD?

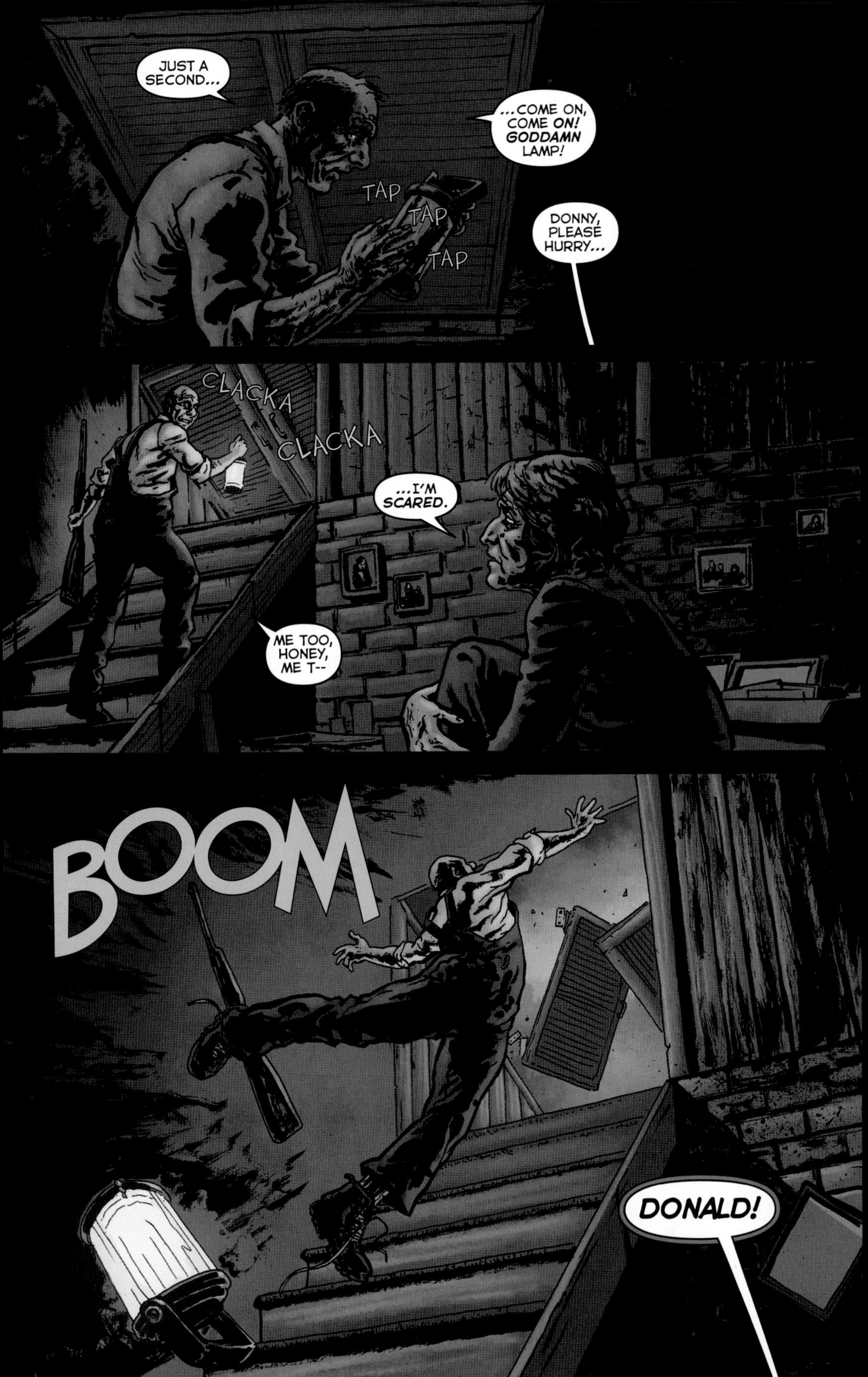
JUST A SECOND...
...COME ON, COME ON! GODDAMN LAMP!
TAP
TAP
TAP
DONNY, PLEASE HURRY...
CLACKA
CLACKA
...I'M SCARED.
ME TOO, HONEY, ME T--
BOOM
DONALD!

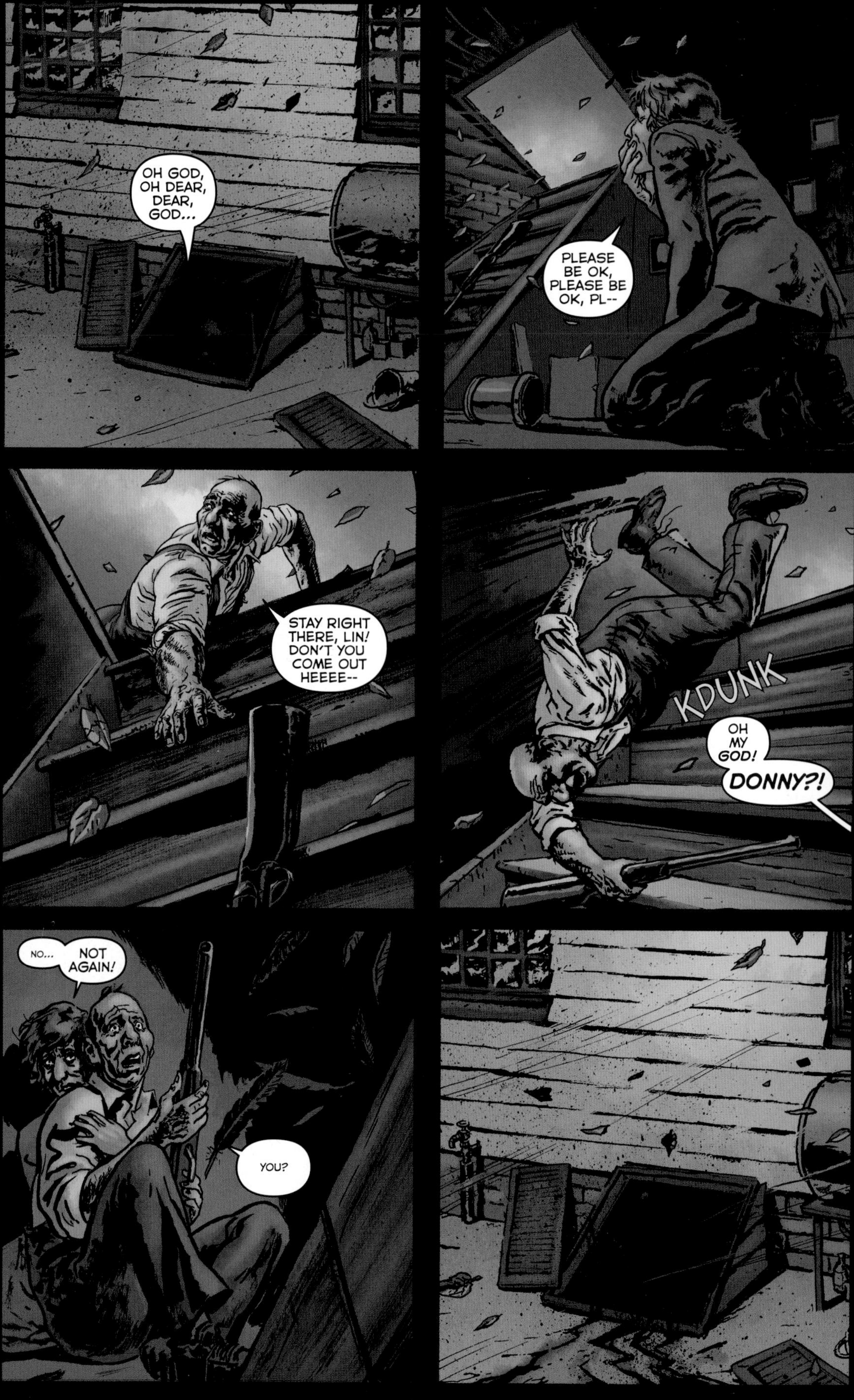
OH GOD, OH DEAR, DEAR, GOD...
PLEASE BE OK, PLEASE BE OK, PL--
STAY RIGHT THERE, LIN! DON'T YOU COME OUT HEEEE--
KDUNK
OH MY GOD!
DONNY?!
NO...
NOT AGAIN!
YOU?

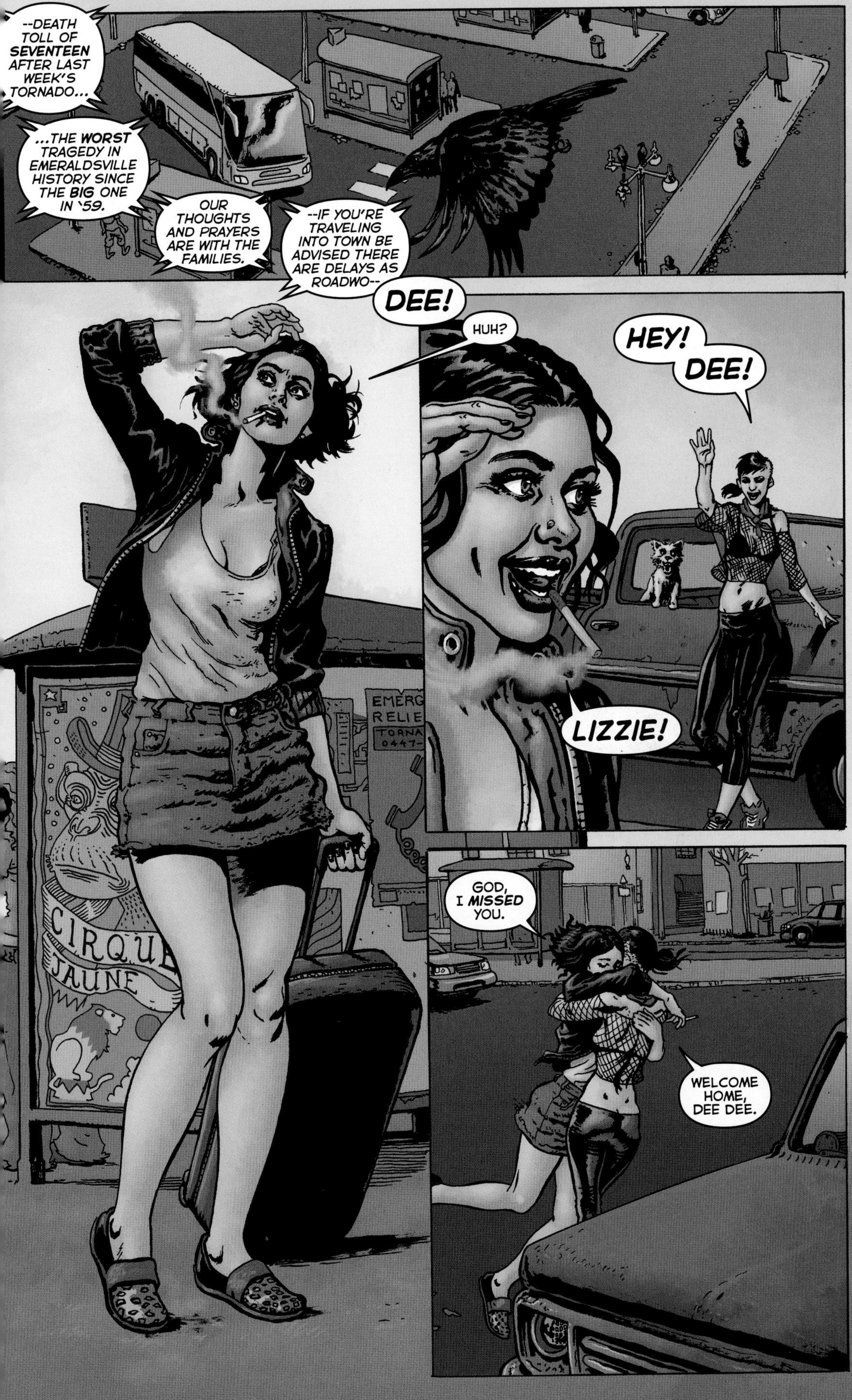
--DEATH TOLL OF SEVENTEEN AFTER LAST WEEK'S TORNADO...
...THE WORST TRAGEDY IN EMERALDSVILLE HISTORY SINCE THE BIG ONE IN '59.
OUR THOUGHTS AND PRAYERS ARE WITH THE FAMILIES.
--IF YOU'RE TRAVELING INTO TOWN BE ADVISED THERE ARE DELAYS AS ROADWO--
DEE!
HUH?
HEY! DEE!
LIZZIE!
CIRQUE JAUNE
EMERG RELIE TORNA 0447-
GOD, I MISSED YOU.
WELCOME HOME, DEE DEE.

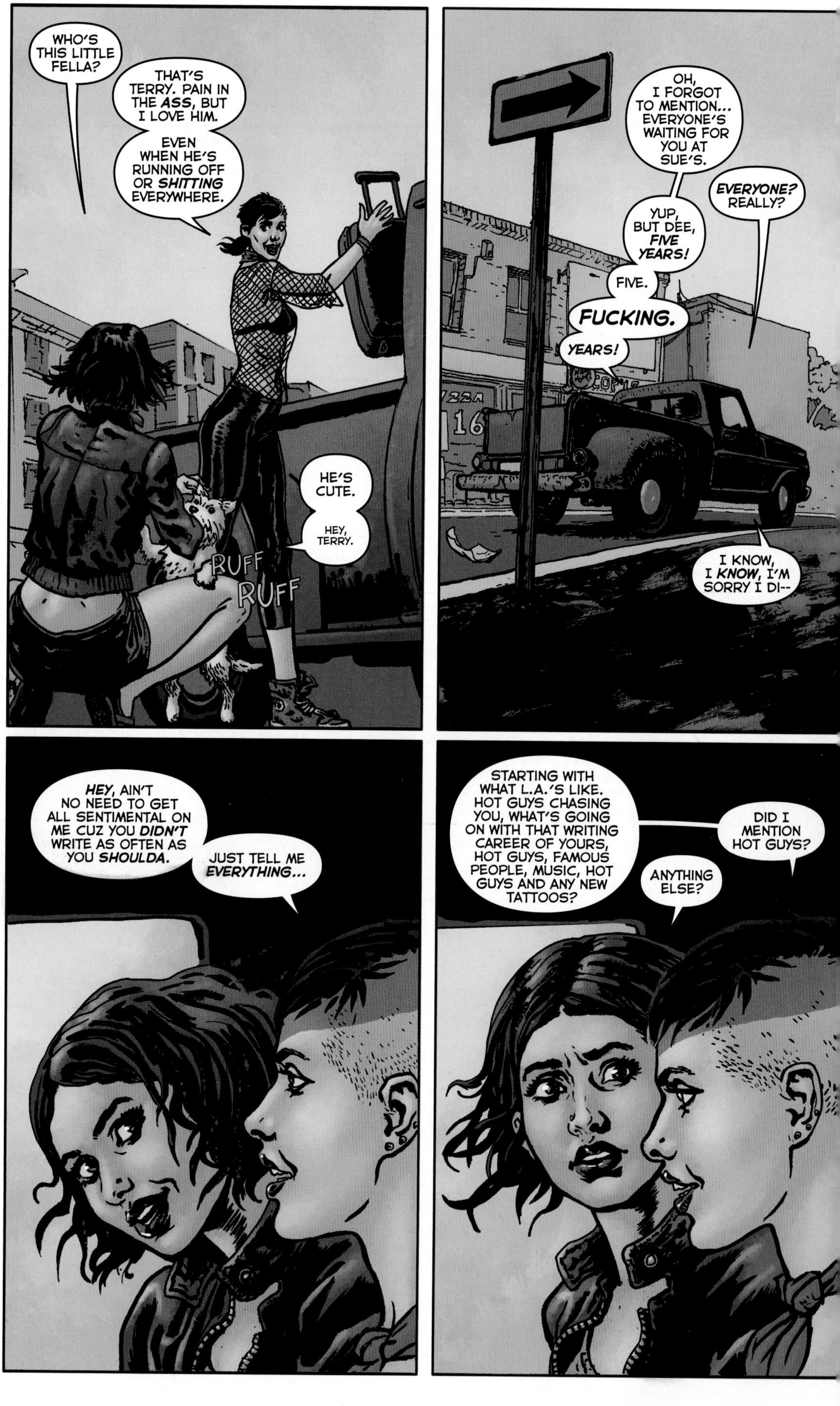
WHO'S THIS LITTLE FELLA?
THAT'S TERRY. PAIN IN THE ASS, BUT I LOVE HIM.
EVEN WHEN HE'S RUNNING OFF OR SHITTING EVERYWHERE.
HE'S CUTE.
HEY, TERRY.
RUFF
RUFF
OH, I FORGOT TO MENTION... EVERYONE'S WAITING FOR YOU AT SUE'S.
EVERYONE? REALLY?
YUP, BUT DEE, FIVE YEARS!
FIVE.
FUCKING.
YEARS!
I KNOW, I KNOW, I'M SORRY I DI--
HEY, AIN'T NO NEED TO GET ALL SENTIMENTAL ON ME CUZ YOU DIDN'T WRITE AS OFTEN AS YOU SHOULDA.
JUST TELL ME EVERYTHING...
STARTING WITH WHAT L.A.'S LIKE. HOT GUYS CHASING YOU, WHAT'S GOING ON WITH THAT WRITING CAREER OF YOURS, HOT GUYS, FAMOUS PEOPLE, MUSIC, HOT GUYS AND ANY NEW TATTOOS?
DID I MENTION HOT GUYS?
ANYTHING ELSE?

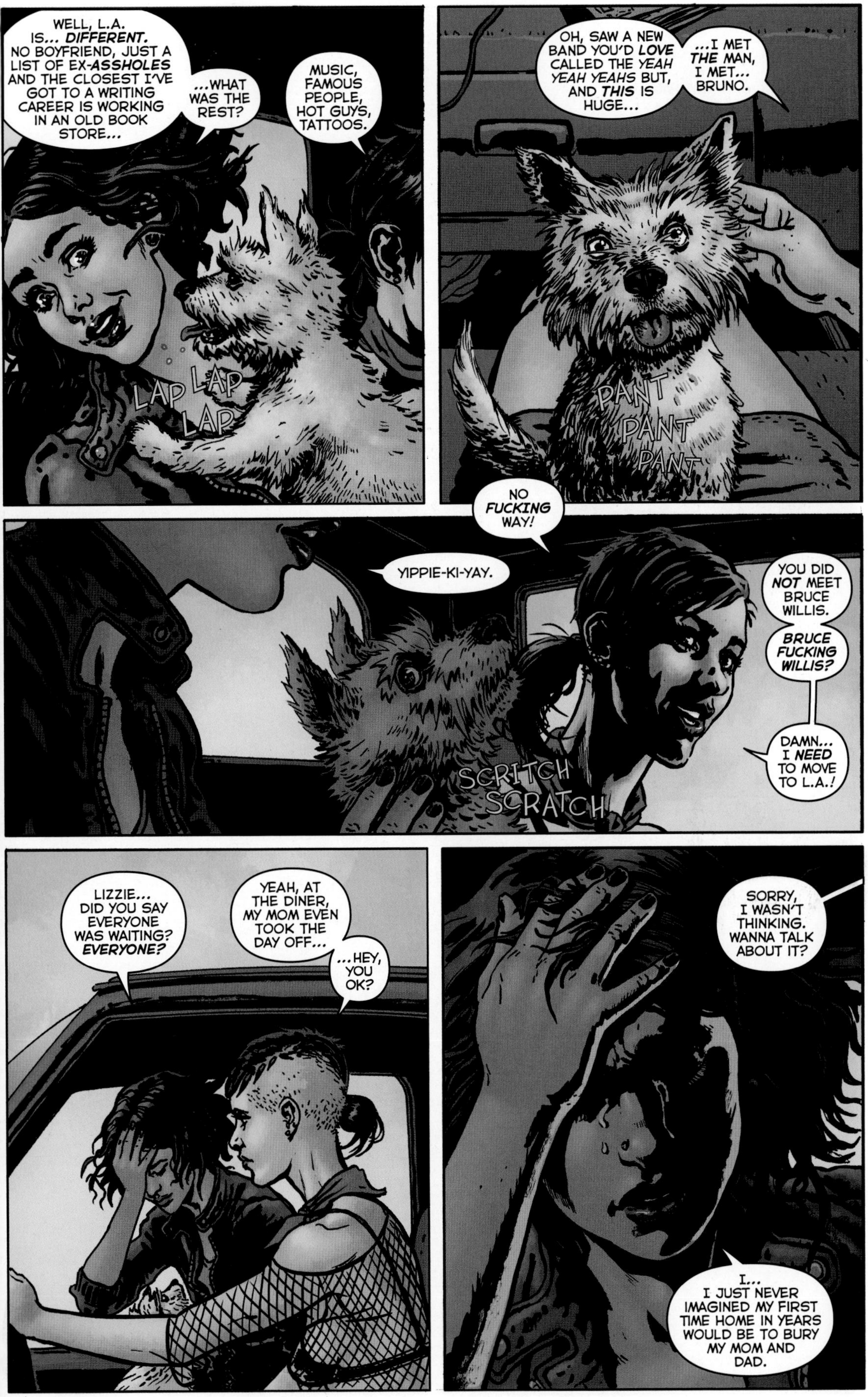

WELL, L.A. IS... DIFFERENT. NO BOYFRIEND, JUST A LIST OF EX-ASSHOLES AND THE CLOSEST I'VE GOT TO A WRITING CAREER IS WORKING IN AN OLD BOOK STORE...
...WHAT WAS THE REST?
MUSIC, FAMOUS PEOPLE, HOT GUYS, TATTOOS.
LAP LAP LAP
OH, SAW A NEW BAND YOU'D LOVE CALLED THE YEAH YEAH YEAHS BUT, AND THIS IS HUGE...
...I MET THE MAN, I MET... BRUNO.
PANT PANT PANT
NO FUCKING WAY!
YIPPIE-KI-YAY.
YOU DID NOT MEET BRUCE WILLIS.
BRUCE FUCKING WILLIS?
DAMN... I NEED TO MOVE TO L.A.!
SCRITCH SCRATCH
LIZZIE... DID YOU SAY EVERYONE WAS WAITING? EVERYONE?
YEAH, AT THE DINER, MY MOM EVEN TOOK THE DAY OFF...
...HEY, YOU OK?
SORRY, I WASN'T THINKING. WANNA TALK ABOUT IT?
I... I JUST NEVER IMAGINED MY FIRST TIME HOME IN YEARS WOULD BE TO BURY MY MOM AND DAD.

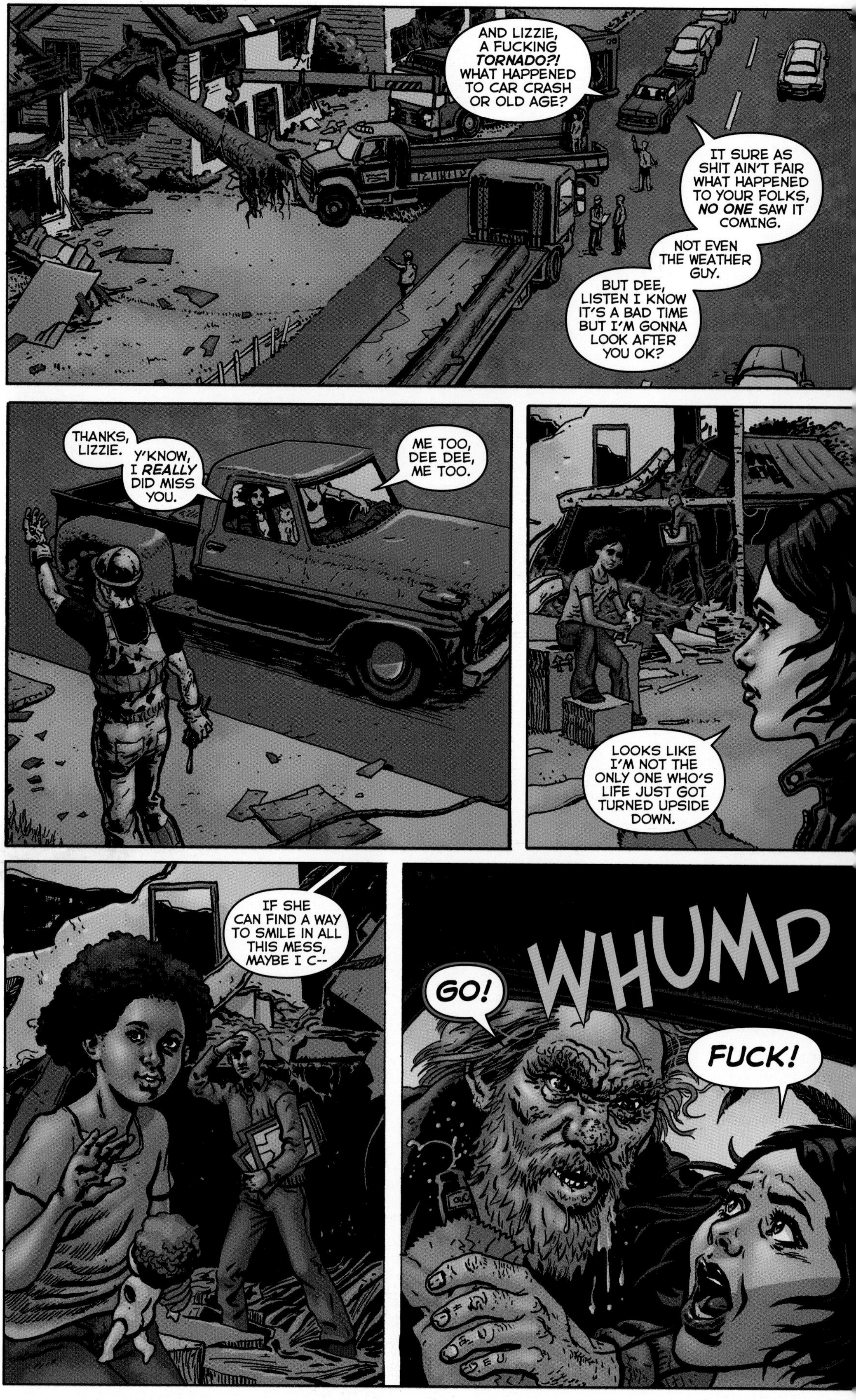
AND LIZZIE, A FUCKING TORNADO?! WHAT HAPPENED TO CAR CRASH OR OLD AGE?
IT SURE AS SHIT AIN'T FAIR WHAT HAPPENED TO YOUR FOLKS, NO ONE SAW IT COMING.
NOT EVEN THE WEATHER GUY.
BUT DEE, LISTEN I KNOW IT'S A BAD TIME BUT I'M GONNA LOOK AFTER YOU OK?
THANKS, LIZZIE.
Y'KNOW, I REALLY DID MISS YOU.
ME TOO, DEE DEE, ME TOO.
LOOKS LIKE I'M NOT THE ONLY ONE WHO'S LIFE JUST GOT TURNED UPSIDE DOWN.
IF SHE CAN FIND A WAY TO SMILE IN ALL THIS MESS, MAYBE I C--
WHUMP
GO!
FUCK!

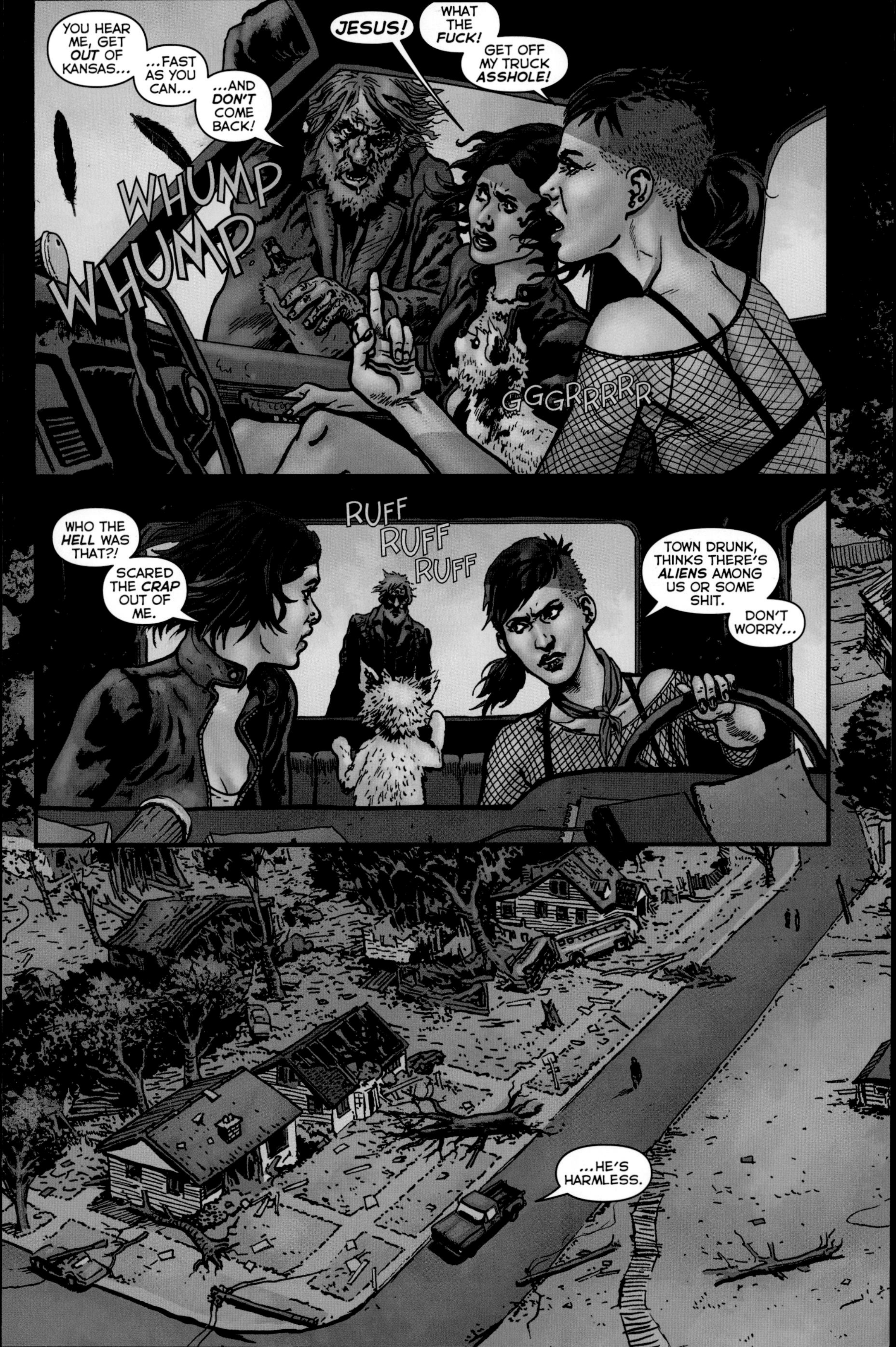
YOU HEAR ME, GET OUT OF KANSAS...
...FAST AS YOU CAN...
...AND DON'T COME BACK!
JESUS!
WHAT THE FUCK!
GET OFF MY TRUCK ASSHOLE!
WHUMP
WHUMP
GGGRRRRR
WHO THE HELL WAS THAT?!
SCARED THE CRAP OUT OF ME.
RUFF
RUFF
RUFF
TOWN DRUNK, THINKS THERE'S ALIENS AMONG US OR SOME SHIT.
DON'T WORRY...
...HE'S HARMLESS.

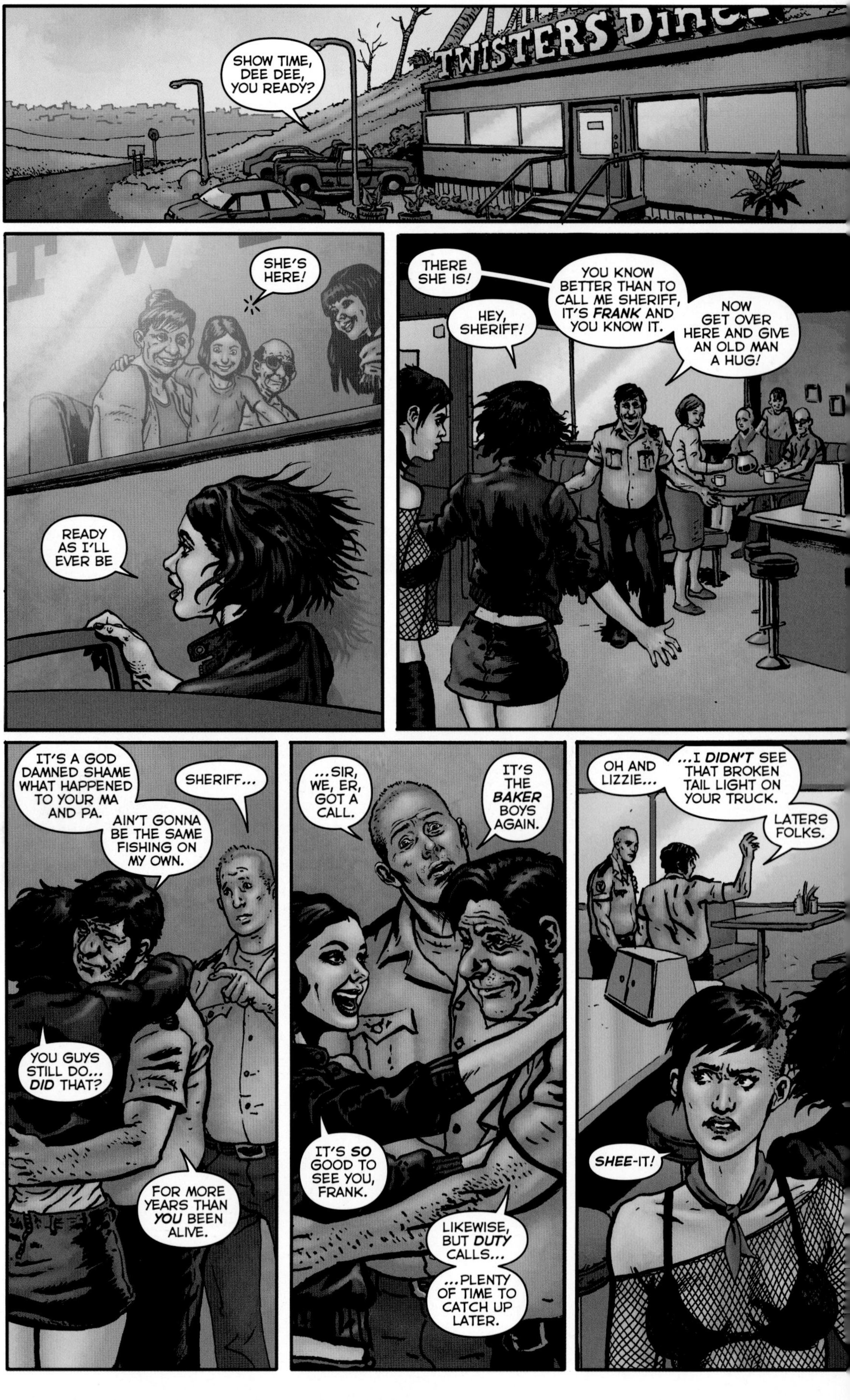
TWISTERS Diner
SHOW TIME, DEE DEE, YOU READY?
SHE'S HERE!
READY AS I'LL EVER BE
THERE SHE IS!
HEY, SHERIFF!
YOU KNOW BETTER THAN TO CALL ME SHERIFF, IT'S FRANK AND YOU KNOW IT.
NOW GET OVER HERE AND GIVE AN OLD MAN A HUG!
IT'S A GOD DAMNED SHAME WHAT HAPPENED TO YOUR MA AND PA.
AIN'T GONNA BE THE SAME FISHING ON MY OWN.
SHERIFF...
YOU GUYS STILL DO... DID THAT?
FOR MORE YEARS THAN YOU BEEN ALIVE.
...SIR, WE, ER, GOT A CALL.
IT'S THE BAKER BOYS AGAIN.
IT'S SO GOOD TO SEE YOU, FRANK.
LIKEWISE, BUT DUTY CALLS...
...PLENTY OF TIME TO CATCH UP LATER.
OH AND LIZZIE...
...I DIDN'T SEE THAT BROKEN TAIL LIGHT ON YOUR TRUCK.
LATERS FOLKS.
SHEE-IT!

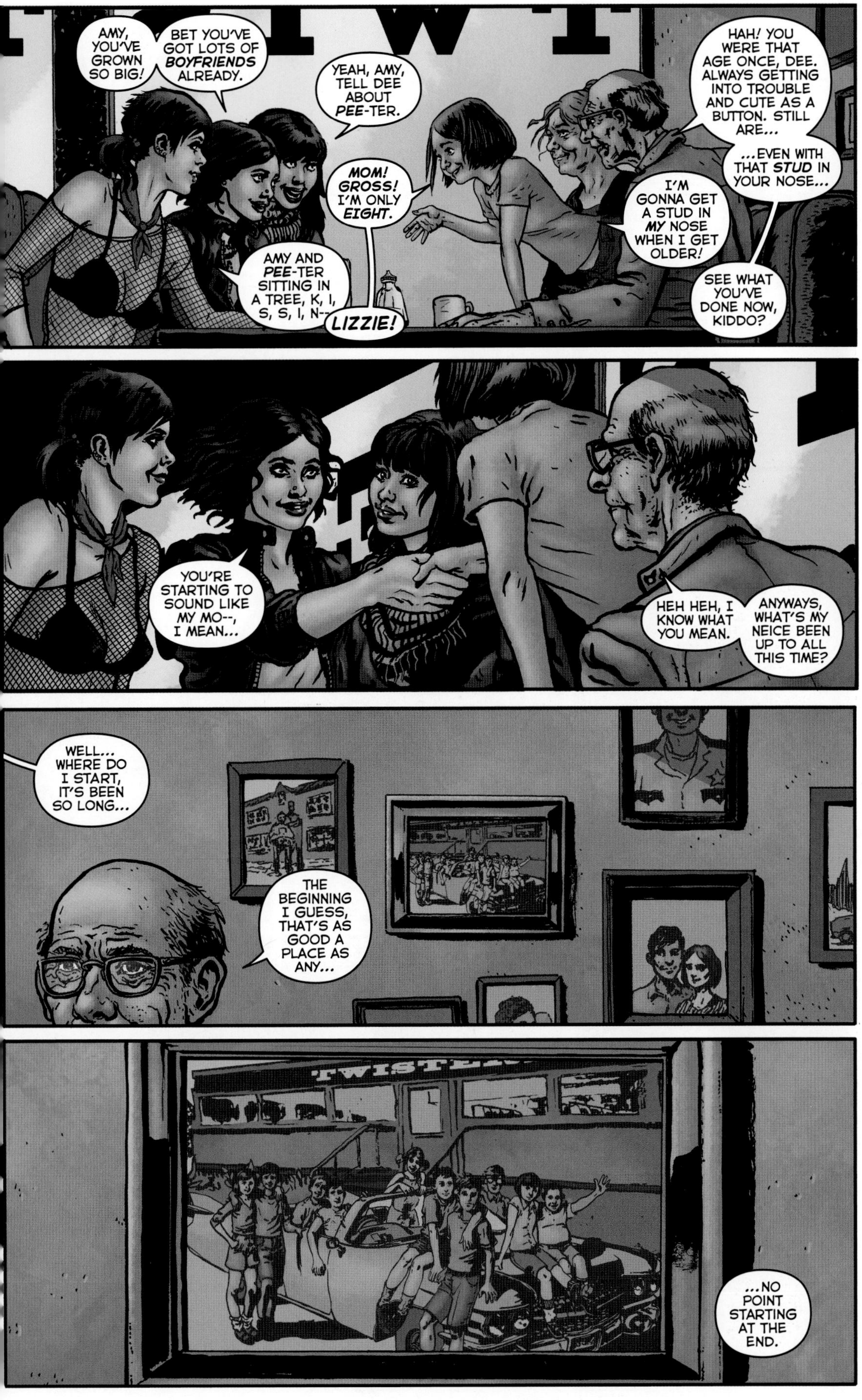

AMY, YOU'VE GROWN SO BIG!
BET YOU'VE GOT LOTS OF *BOYFRIENDS* ALREADY.
YEAH, AMY, TELL DEE ABOUT *PEE*-TER.
HAH! YOU WERE THAT AGE ONCE, DEE. ALWAYS GETTING INTO TROUBLE AND CUTE AS A BUTTON. STILL ARE...
...EVEN WITH THAT *STUD* IN YOUR NOSE...
MOM! GROSS! I'M ONLY *EIGHT*.
I'M GONNA GET A STUD IN *MY* NOSE WHEN I GET OLDER!
AMY AND *PEE*-TER SITTING IN A TREE, K, I, S, S, I, N--
LIZZIE!
SEE WHAT YOU'VE DONE NOW, KIDDO?
YOU'RE STARTING TO SOUND LIKE MY MO--, I MEAN...
HEH HEH, I KNOW WHAT YOU MEAN.
ANYWAYS, WHAT'S MY NEICE BEEN UP TO ALL THIS TIME?
WELL... WHERE DO I START, IT'S BEEN SO LONG...
THE BEGINNING I GUESS, THAT'S AS GOOD A PLACE AS ANY...
...NO POINT STARTING AT THE END.

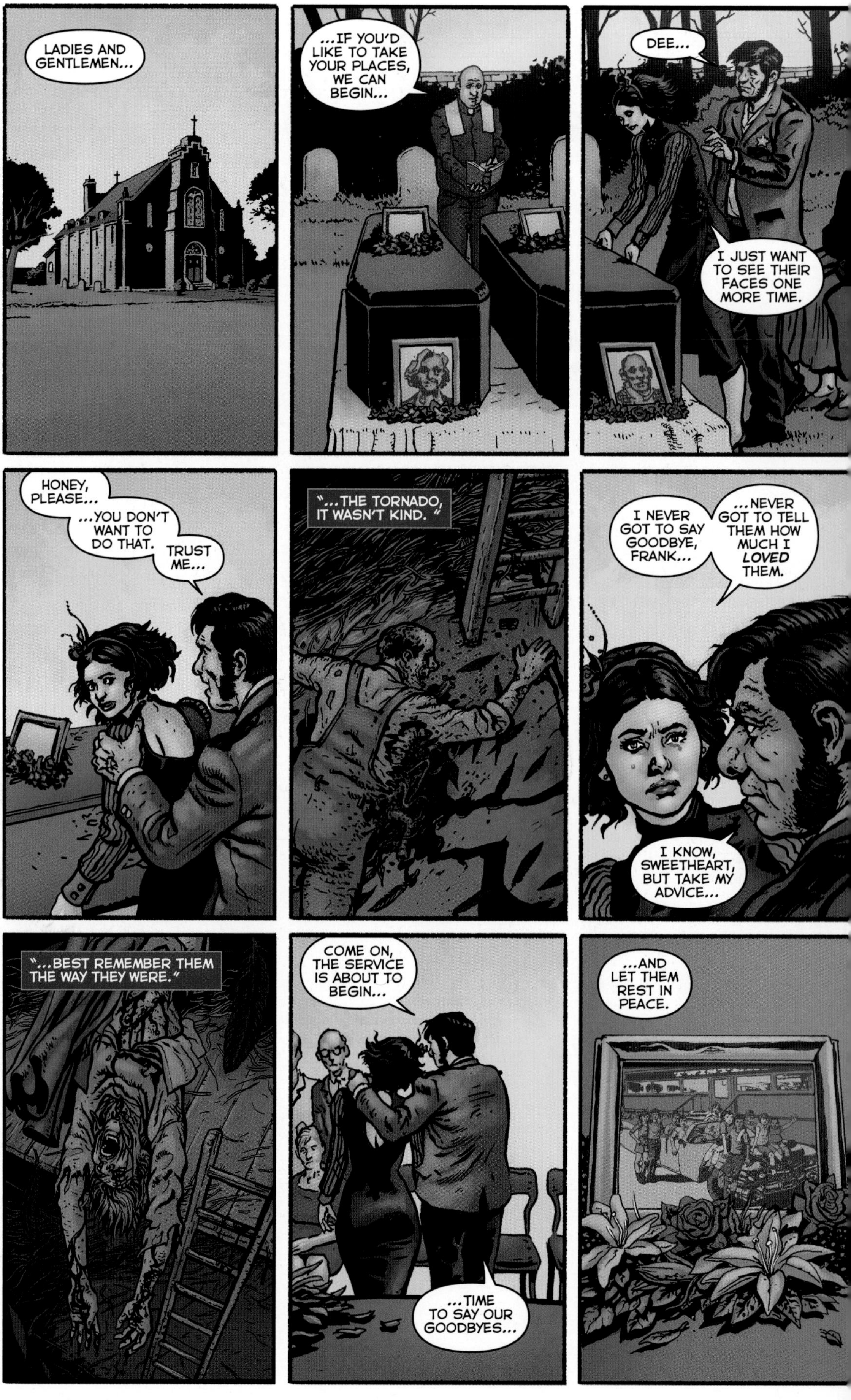
LADIES AND GENTLEMEN...
...IF YOU'D LIKE TO TAKE YOUR PLACES, WE CAN BEGIN...
DEE...
I JUST WANT TO SEE THEIR FACES ONE MORE TIME.
HONEY, PLEASE...
...YOU DON'T WANT TO DO THAT.
TRUST ME...
"...THE TORNADO, IT WASN'T KIND."
I NEVER GOT TO SAY GOODBYE, FRANK...
...NEVER GOT TO TELL THEM HOW MUCH I *LOVED* THEM.
I KNOW, SWEETHEART, BUT TAKE MY ADVICE...
"...BEST REMEMBER THEM THE WAY THEY WERE."
COME ON, THE SERVICE IS ABOUT TO BEGIN...
...TIME TO SAY OUR GOODBYES...
...AND LET THEM REST IN PEACE.

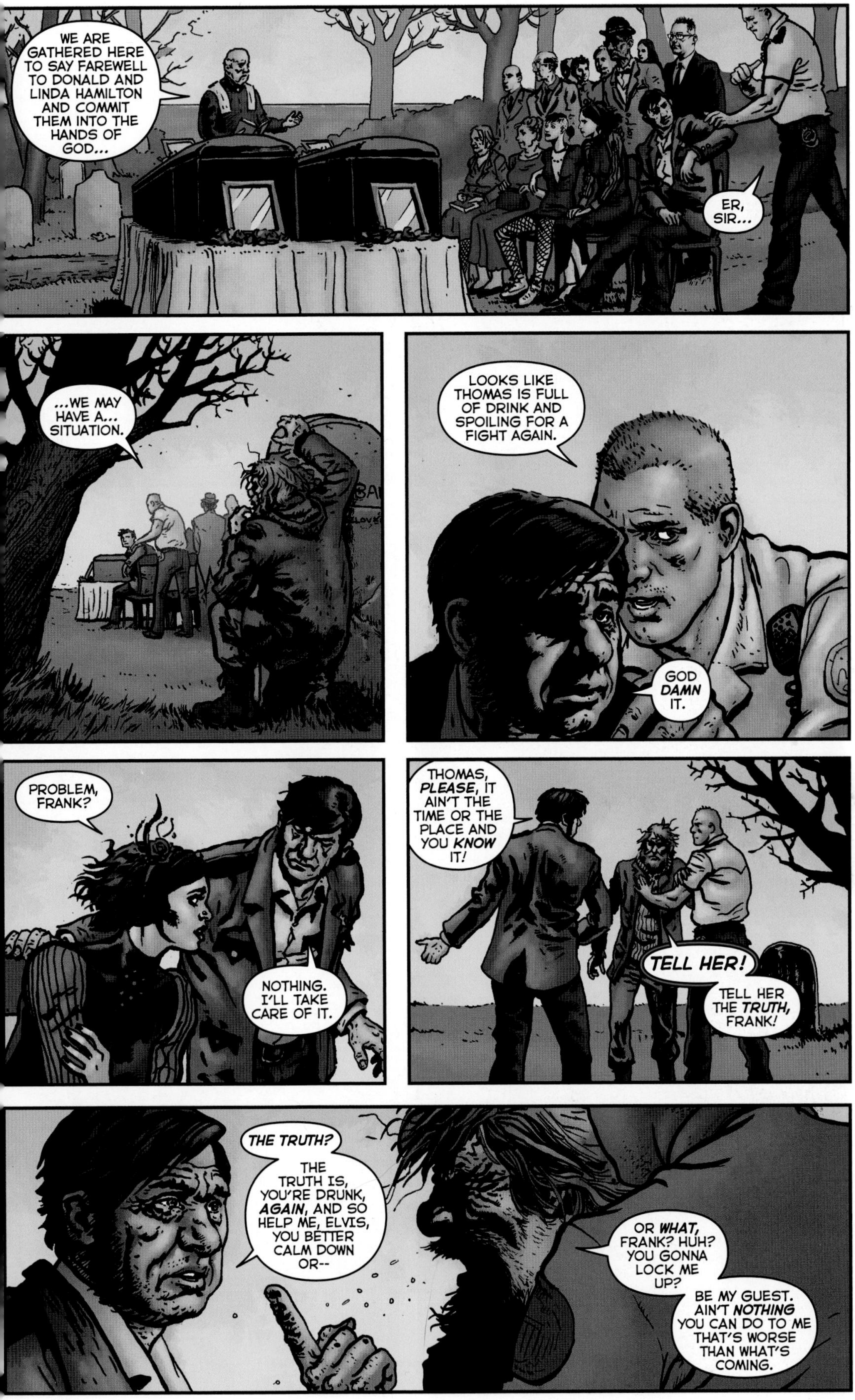

WE ARE GATHERED HERE TO SAY FAREWELL TO DONALD AND LINDA HAMILTON AND COMMIT THEM INTO THE HANDS OF GOD...
ER, SIR...
...WE MAY HAVE A... SITUATION.
LOOKS LIKE THOMAS IS FULL OF DRINK AND SPOILING FOR A FIGHT AGAIN.
GOD *DAMN* IT.
PROBLEM, FRANK?
NOTHING. I'LL TAKE CARE OF IT.
THOMAS, *PLEASE*, IT AIN'T THE TIME OR THE PLACE AND YOU *KNOW* IT!
TELL HER!
TELL HER THE *TRUTH*, FRANK!
THE TRUTH?
THE TRUTH IS, YOU'RE DRUNK, *AGAIN*, AND SO HELP ME, ELVIS, YOU BETTER CALM DOWN OR--
OR *WHAT*, FRANK? HUH? YOU GONNA LOCK ME UP?
BE MY GUEST. AIN'T *NOTHING* YOU CAN DO TO ME THAT'S WORSE THAN WHAT'S COMING.

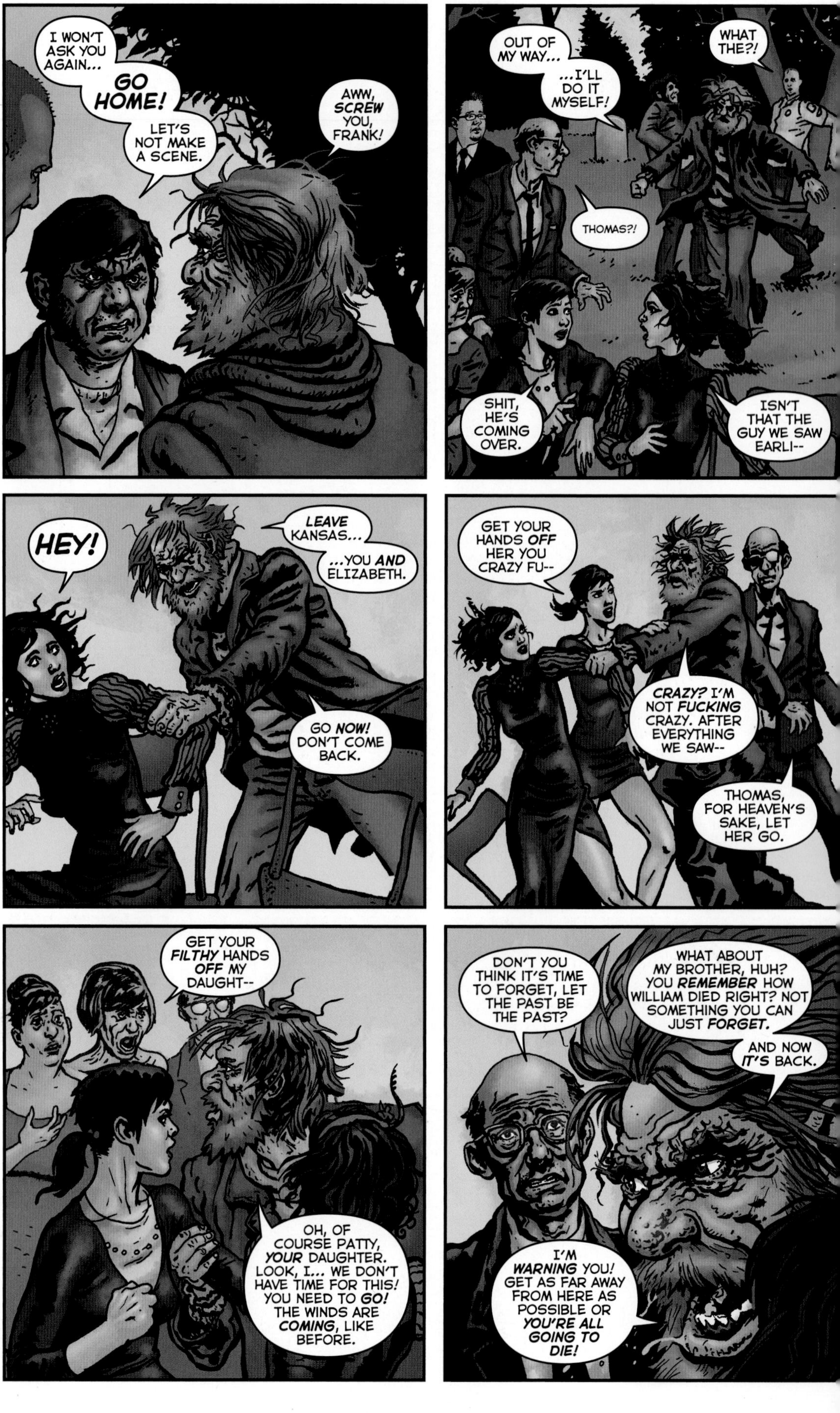
I WON'T ASK YOU AGAIN...
GO HOME!
LET'S NOT MAKE A SCENE.
AWW, SCREW YOU, FRANK!
OUT OF MY WAY...
...I'LL DO IT MYSELF!
WHAT THE?!
THOMAS?!
SHIT, HE'S COMING OVER.
ISN'T THAT THE GUY WE SAW EARLI--
HEY!
LEAVE KANSAS...
...YOU AND ELIZABETH.
GO NOW! DON'T COME BACK.
GET YOUR HANDS OFF HER YOU CRAZY FU--
CRAZY? I'M NOT FUCKING CRAZY. AFTER EVERYTHING WE SAW--
THOMAS, FOR HEAVEN'S SAKE, LET HER GO.
GET YOUR FILTHY HANDS OFF MY DAUGHT--
OH, OF COURSE PATTY, YOUR DAUGHTER. LOOK, I... WE DON'T HAVE TIME FOR THIS! YOU NEED TO GO! THE WINDS ARE COMING, LIKE BEFORE.
DON'T YOU THINK IT'S TIME TO FORGET, LET THE PAST BE THE PAST?
WHAT ABOUT MY BROTHER, HUH? YOU REMEMBER HOW WILLIAM DIED RIGHT? NOT SOMETHING YOU CAN JUST FORGET.
AND NOW IT'S BACK.
I'M WARNING YOU! GET AS FAR AWAY FROM HERE AS POSSIBLE OR YOU'RE ALL GOING TO DIE!

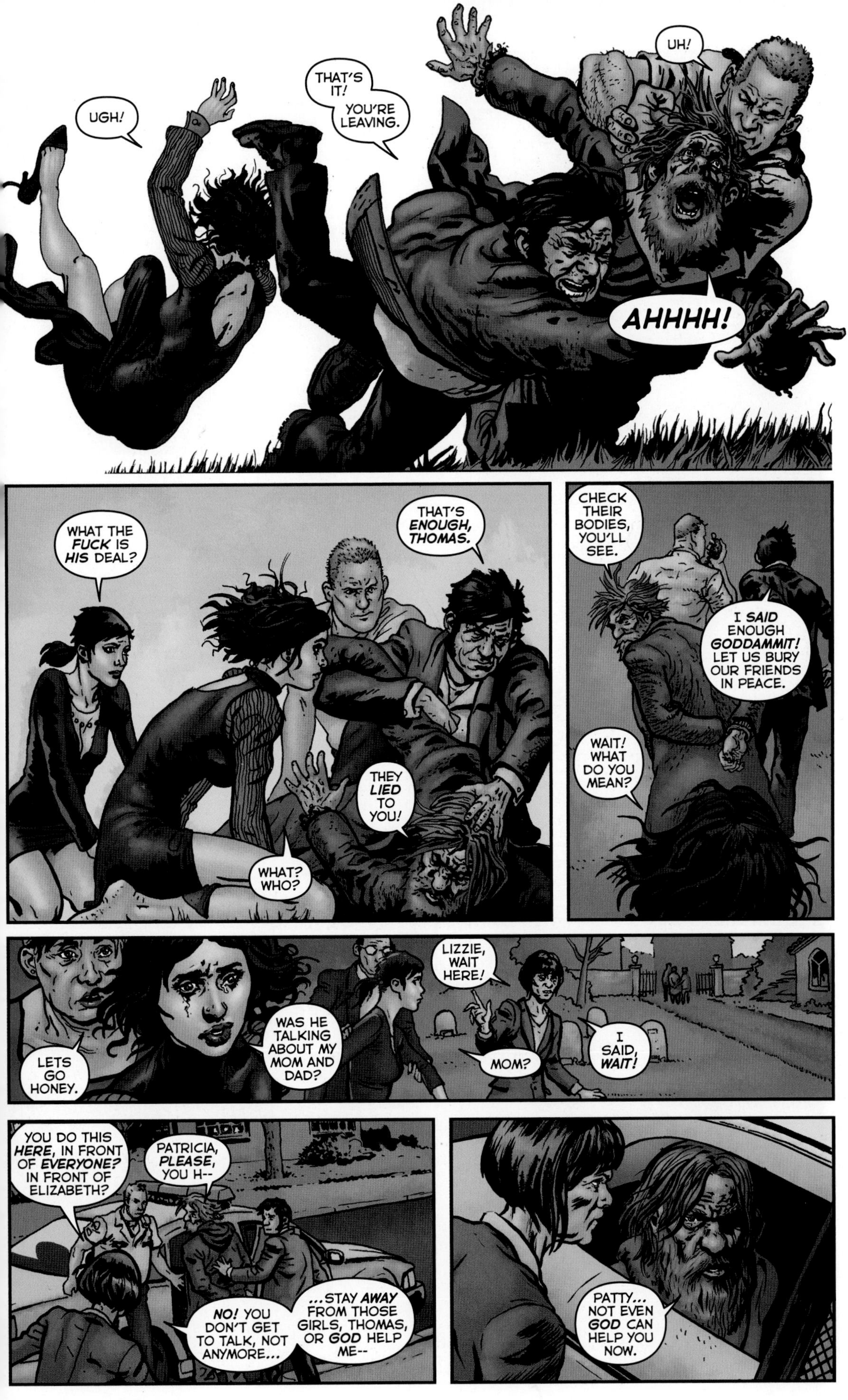
UGH!
THAT'S IT! YOU'RE LEAVING.
UH!
AHHHH!
WHAT THE FUCK IS HIS DEAL?
THAT'S ENOUGH, THOMAS.
THEY LIED TO YOU!
WHAT? WHO?
CHECK THEIR BODIES, YOU'LL SEE.
I SAID ENOUGH GODDAMMIT! LET US BURY OUR FRIENDS IN PEACE.
WAIT! WHAT DO YOU MEAN?
LETS GO HONEY.
WAS HE TALKING ABOUT MY MOM AND DAD?
LIZZIE, WAIT HERE!
MOM?
I SAID, WAIT!
YOU DO THIS HERE, IN FRONT OF EVERYONE? IN FRONT OF ELIZABETH?
PATRICIA, PLEASE, YOU H--
NO! YOU DON'T GET TO TALK, NOT ANYMORE...
...STAY AWAY FROM THOSE GIRLS, THOMAS, OR GOD HELP ME--
PATTY... NOT EVEN GOD CAN HELP YOU NOW.

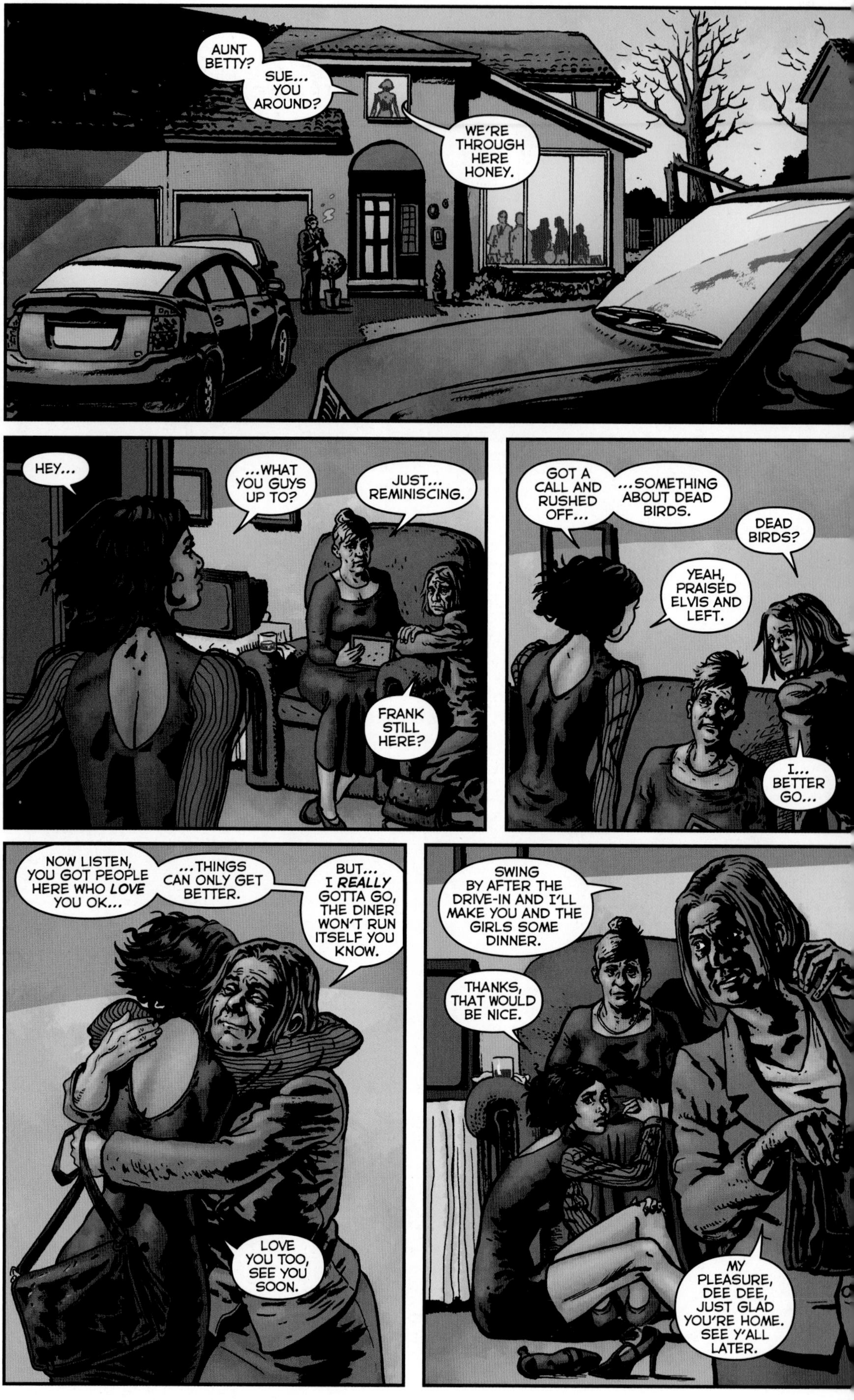
AUNT BETTY?
SUE... YOU AROUND?
WE'RE THROUGH HERE HONEY.
HEY...
...WHAT YOU GUYS UP TO?
JUST... REMINISCING.
FRANK STILL HERE?
GOT A CALL AND RUSHED OFF...
...SOMETHING ABOUT DEAD BIRDS.
DEAD BIRDS?
YEAH, PRAISED ELVIS AND LEFT.
I... BETTER GO...
NOW LISTEN, YOU GOT PEOPLE HERE WHO LOVE YOU OK...
...THINGS CAN ONLY GET BETTER.
BUT... I REALLY GOTTA GO, THE DINER WON'T RUN ITSELF YOU KNOW.
LOVE YOU TOO, SEE YOU SOON.
SWING BY AFTER THE DRIVE-IN AND I'LL MAKE YOU AND THE GIRLS SOME DINNER.
THANKS, THAT WOULD BE NICE.
MY PLEASURE, DEE DEE, JUST GLAD YOU'RE HOME. SEE Y'ALL LATER.

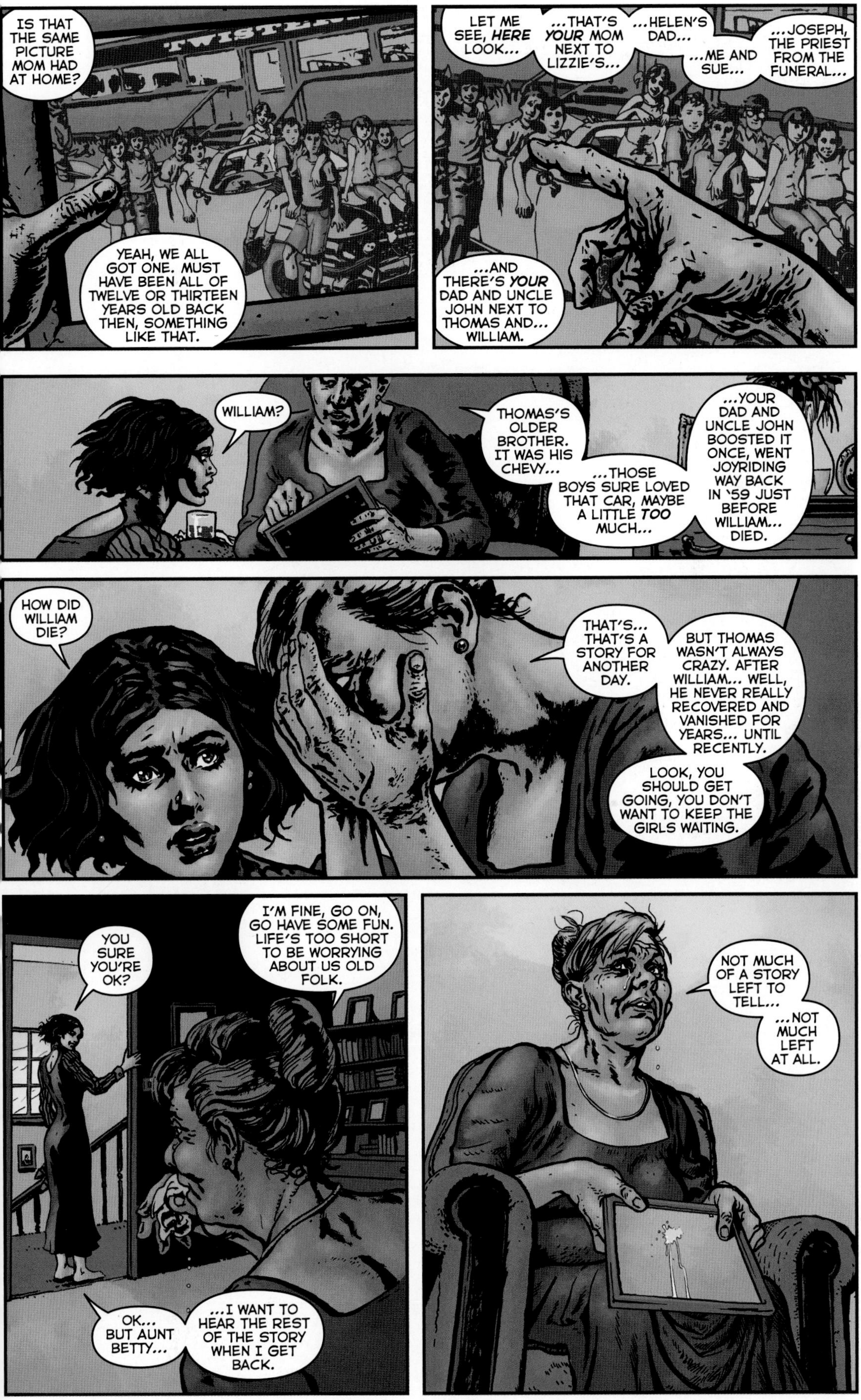
IS THAT THE SAME PICTURE MOM HAD AT HOME?
YEAH, WE ALL GOT ONE. MUST HAVE BEEN ALL OF TWELVE OR THIRTEEN YEARS OLD BACK THEN, SOMETHING LIKE THAT.
LET ME SEE, *HERE* LOOK...
...THAT'S *YOUR* MOM NEXT TO LIZZIE'S...
...HELEN'S DAD...
...ME AND SUE...
...JOSEPH, THE PRIEST FROM THE FUNERAL...
...AND THERE'S *YOUR* DAD AND UNCLE JOHN NEXT TO THOMAS AND... WILLIAM.
WILLIAM?
THOMAS'S OLDER BROTHER. IT WAS HIS CHEVY...
...THOSE BOYS SURE LOVED THAT CAR, MAYBE A LITTLE *TOO* MUCH...
...YOUR DAD AND UNCLE JOHN BOOSTED IT ONCE, WENT JOYRIDING WAY BACK IN '59 JUST BEFORE WILLIAM... DIED.
HOW DID WILLIAM DIE?
THAT'S... THAT'S A STORY FOR ANOTHER DAY.
BUT THOMAS WASN'T ALWAYS CRAZY. AFTER WILLIAM... WELL, HE NEVER REALLY RECOVERED AND VANISHED FOR YEARS... UNTIL RECENTLY.
LOOK, YOU SHOULD GET GOING, YOU DON'T WANT TO KEEP THE GIRLS WAITING.
YOU SURE YOU'RE OK?
I'M FINE, GO ON, GO HAVE SOME FUN. LIFE'S TOO SHORT TO BE WORRYING ABOUT US OLD FOLK.
OK... BUT AUNT BETTY...
...I WANT TO HEAR THE REST OF THE STORY WHEN I GET BACK.
NOT MUCH OF A STORY LEFT TO TELL...
...NOT MUCH LEFT AT ALL.

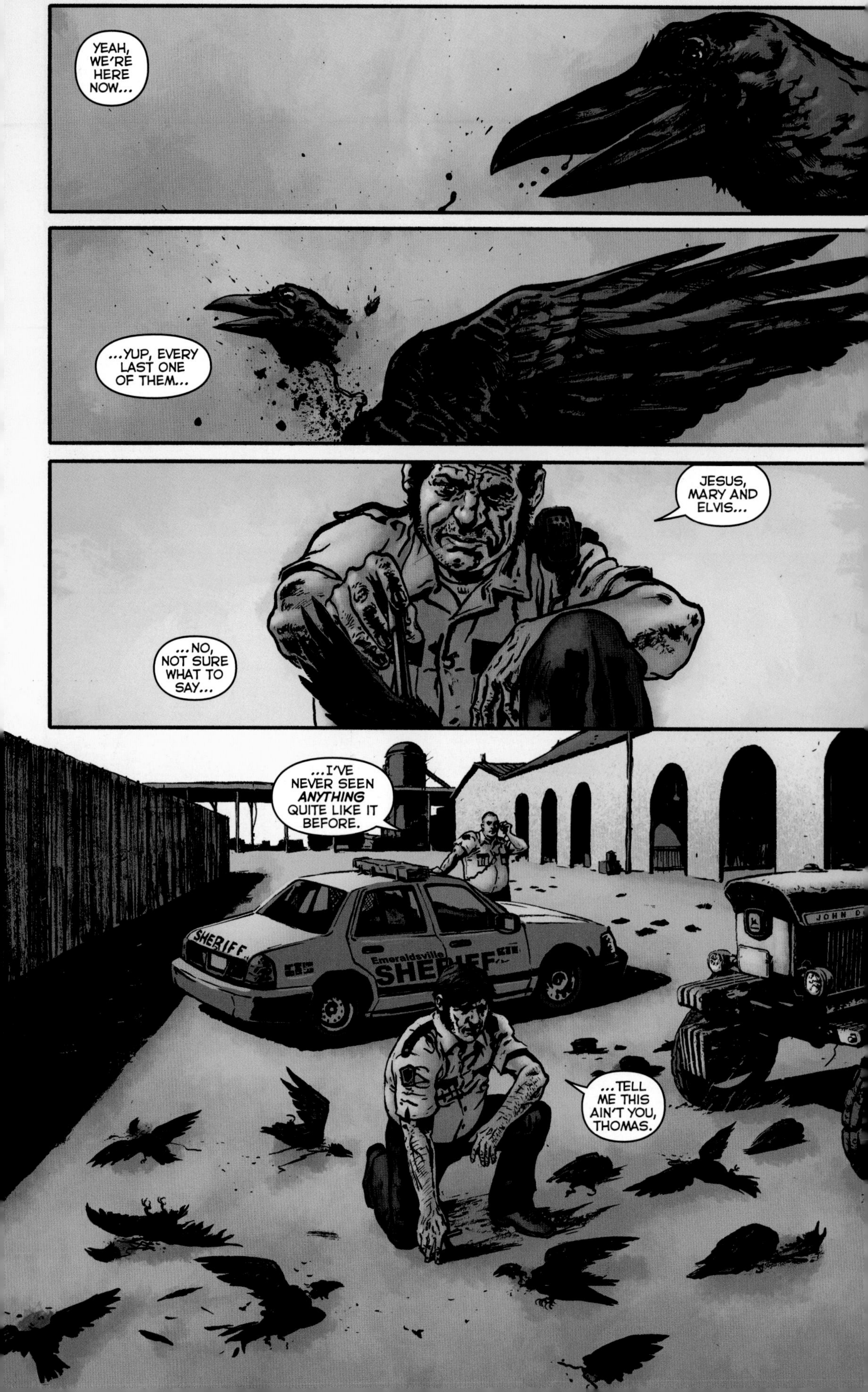
YEAH, WE'RE HERE NOW...
...YUP, EVERY LAST ONE OF THEM...
JESUS, MARY AND ELVIS...
...NO, NOT SURE WHAT TO SAY...
...I'VE NEVER SEEN ANYTHING QUITE LIKE IT BEFORE.
SHERIFF
Emeraldsville SHERIFF
JOHN D
...TELL ME THIS AIN'T YOU, THOMAS.

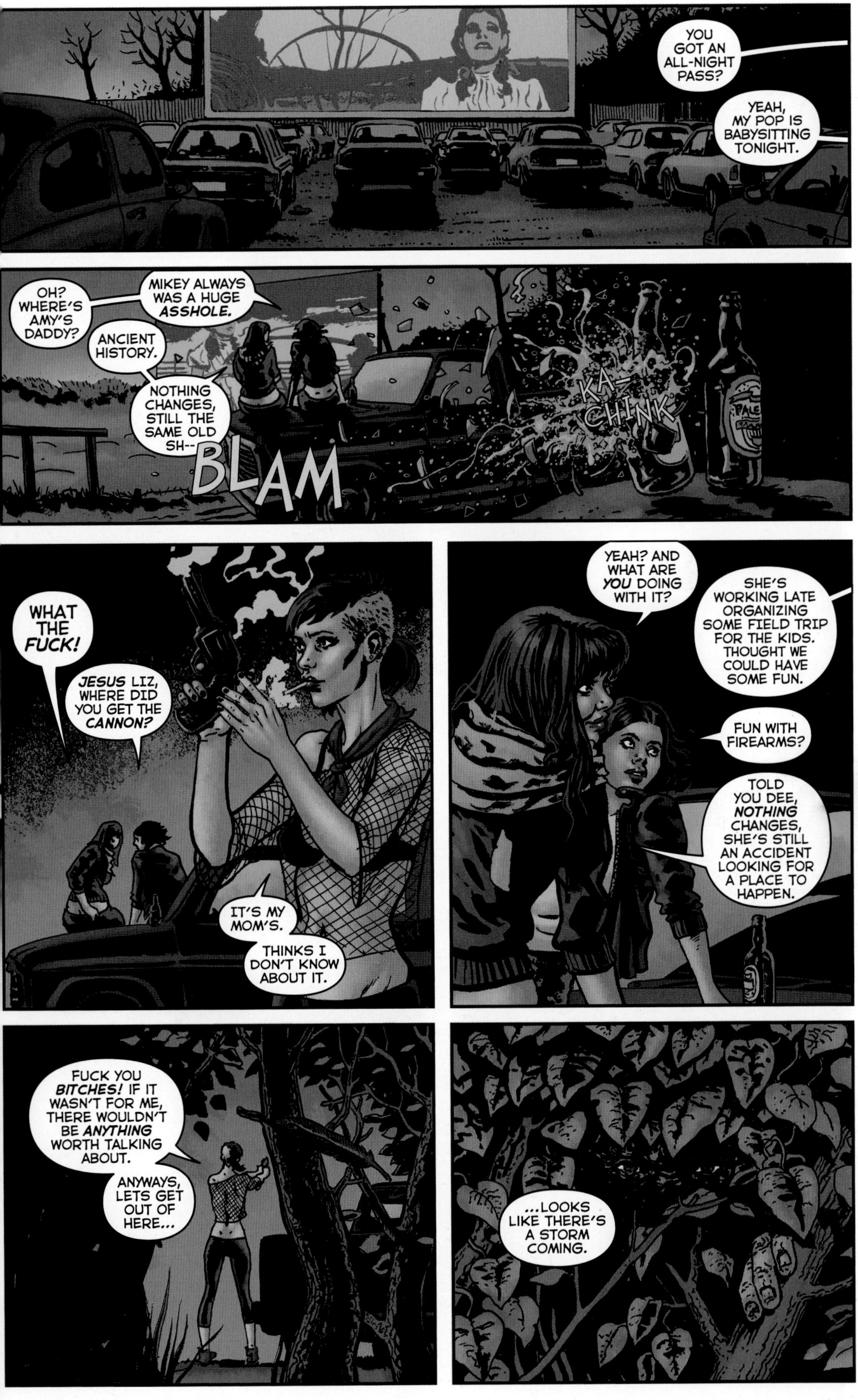
YOU GOT AN ALL-NIGHT PASS?
YEAH, MY POP IS BABYSITTING TONIGHT.
OH? WHERE'S AMY'S DADDY?
MIKEY ALWAYS WAS A HUGE ASSHOLE.
ANCIENT HISTORY.
NOTHING CHANGES, STILL THE SAME OLD SH--
BLAM
KA-CHINK
WHAT THE FUCK!
JESUS LIZ, WHERE DID YOU GET THE CANNON?
IT'S MY MOM'S.
THINKS I DON'T KNOW ABOUT IT.
YEAH? AND WHAT ARE YOU DOING WITH IT?
SHE'S WORKING LATE ORGANIZING SOME FIELD TRIP FOR THE KIDS. THOUGHT WE COULD HAVE SOME FUN.
FUN WITH FIREARMS?
TOLD YOU DEE, NOTHING CHANGES, SHE'S STILL AN ACCIDENT LOOKING FOR A PLACE TO HAPPEN.
FUCK YOU BITCHES! IF IT WASN'T FOR ME, THERE WOULDN'T BE ANYTHING WORTH TALKING ABOUT.
ANYWAYS, LETS GET OUT OF HERE...
...LOOKS LIKE THERE'S A STORM COMING.

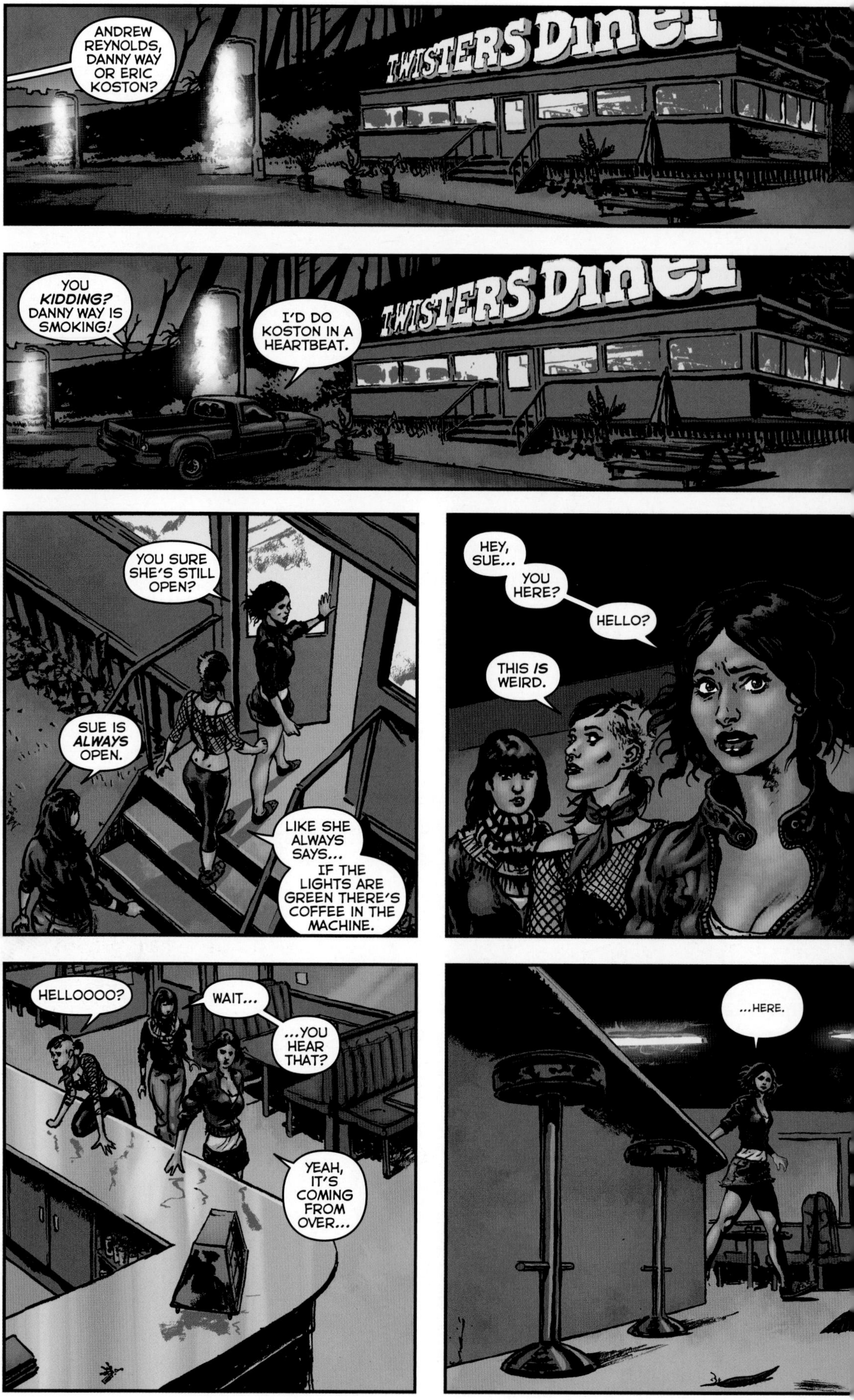
ANDREW REYNOLDS, DANNY WAY OR ERIC KOSTON?
TWISTERS Diner
TWISTERS Diner
YOU *KIDDING?* DANNY WAY IS SMOKING!
I'D DO KOSTON IN A HEARTBEAT.
YOU SURE SHE'S STILL OPEN?
SUE IS *ALWAYS* OPEN.
LIKE SHE ALWAYS SAYS... IF THE LIGHTS ARE GREEN THERE'S COFFEE IN THE MACHINE.
HEY, SUE...
YOU HERE?
HELLO?
THIS *IS* WEIRD.
HELLOOOO?
WAIT...
...YOU HEAR THAT?
YEAH, IT'S COMING FROM OVER...
...HERE.

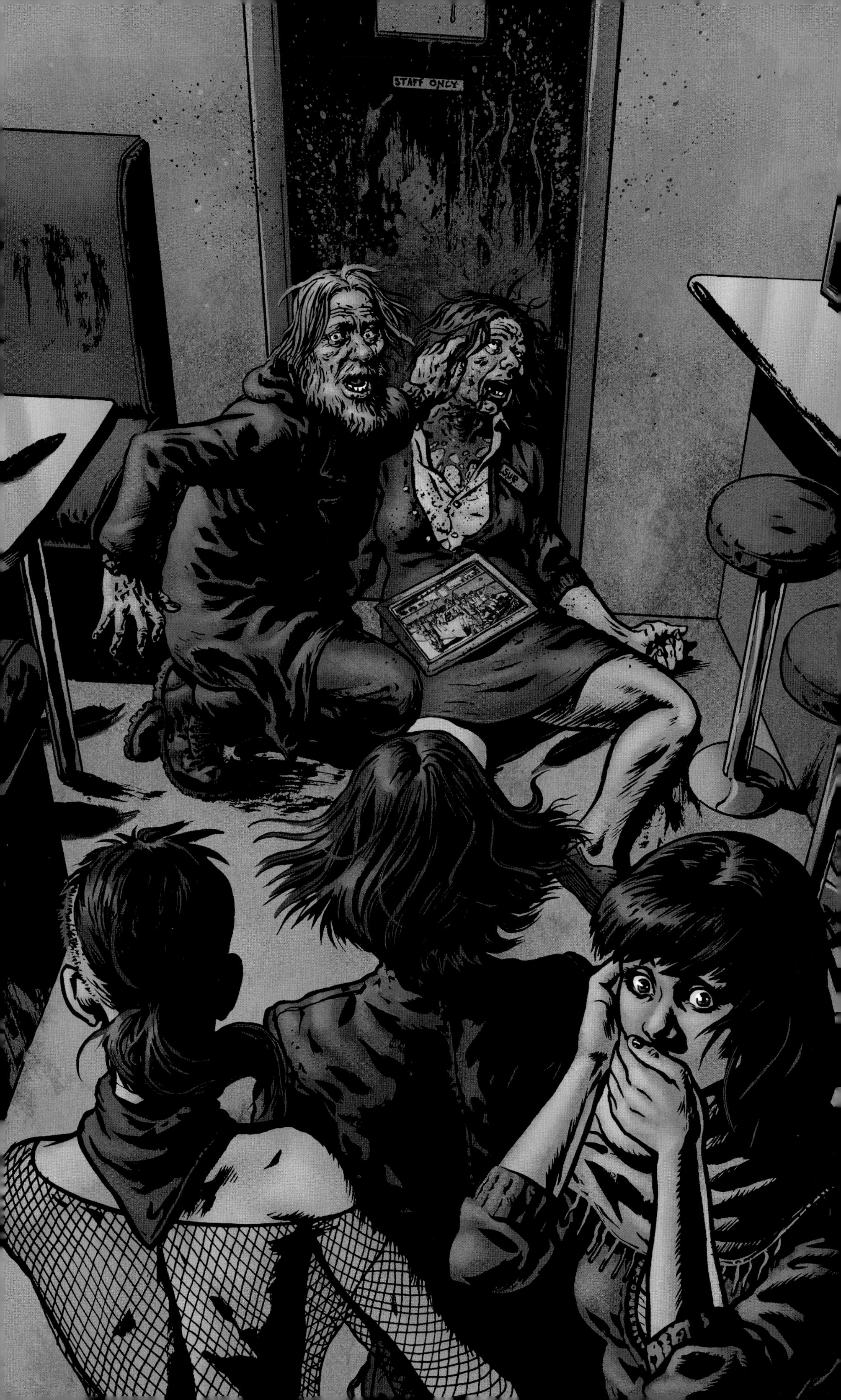
STAFF ONLY

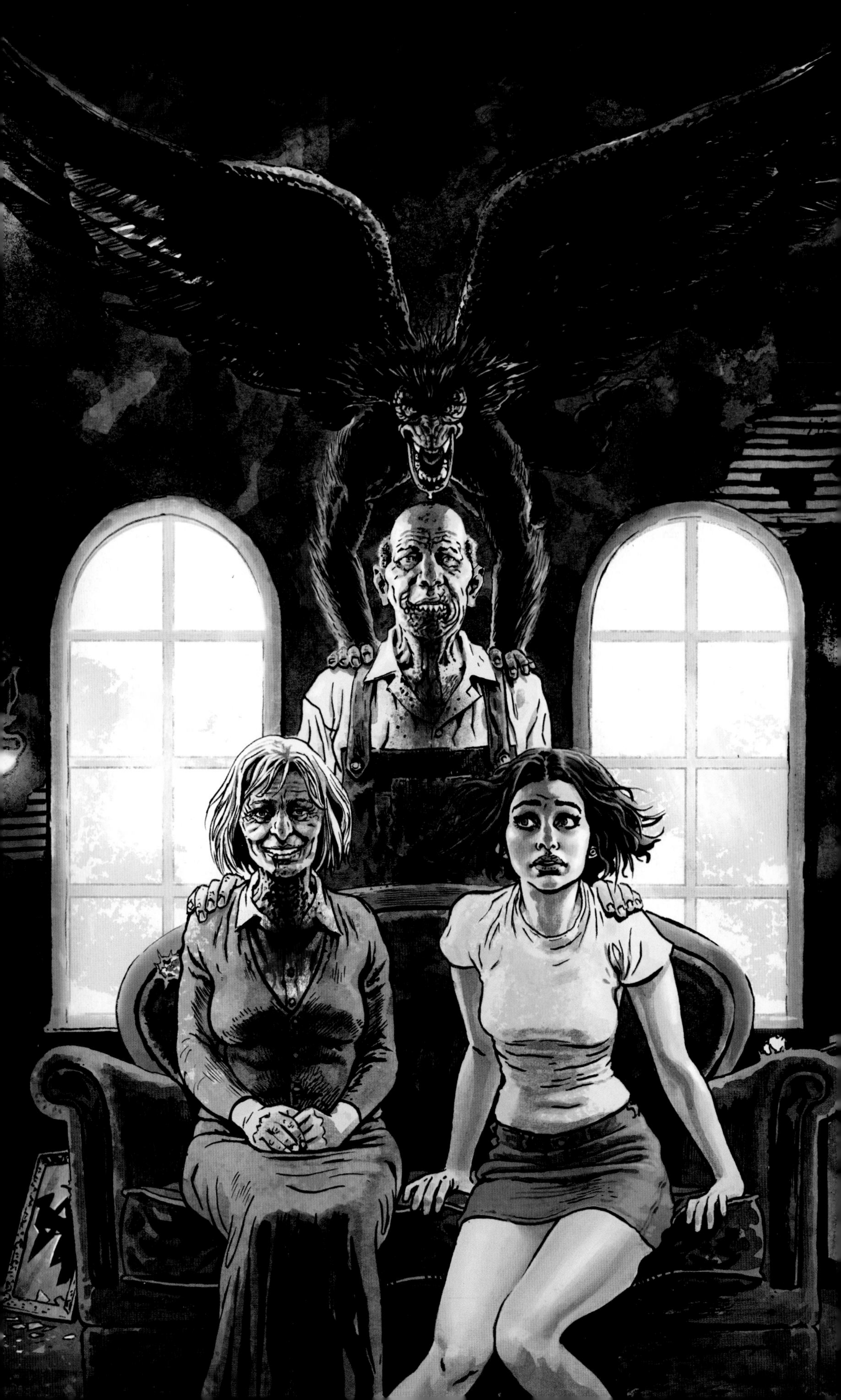

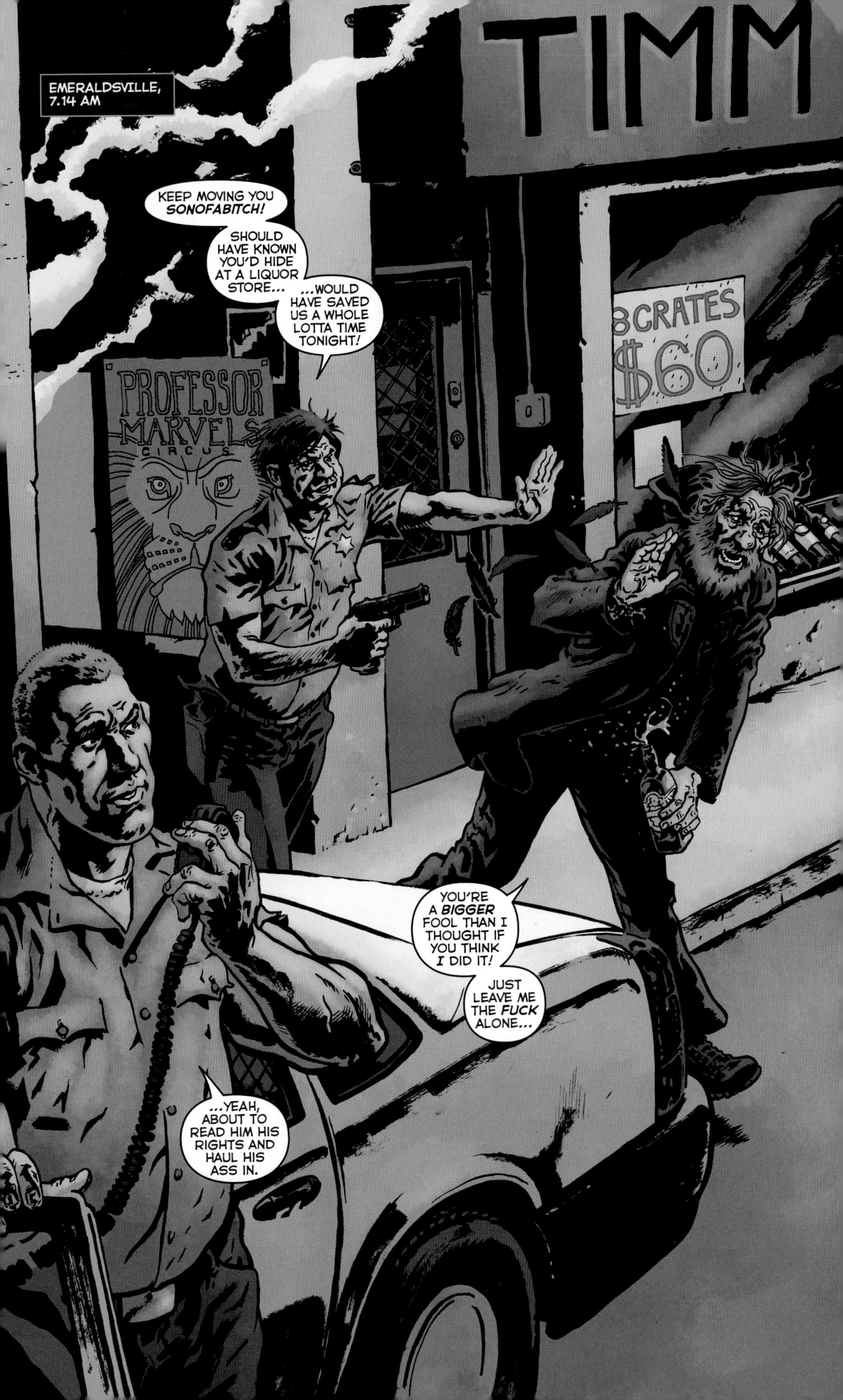
EMERALDSVILLE, 7.14 AM
TIMM
KEEP MOVING YOU SONOFABITCH!
SHOULD HAVE KNOWN YOU'D HIDE AT A LIQUOR STORE...
...WOULD HAVE SAVED US A WHOLE LOTTA TIME TONIGHT!
8 CRATES $60
PROFESSOR MARVELS CIRCUS
YOU'RE A BIGGER FOOL THAN I THOUGHT IF YOU THINK I DID IT!
JUST LEAVE ME THE FUCK ALONE...
...YEAH, ABOUT TO READ HIM HIS RIGHTS AND HAUL HIS ASS IN.

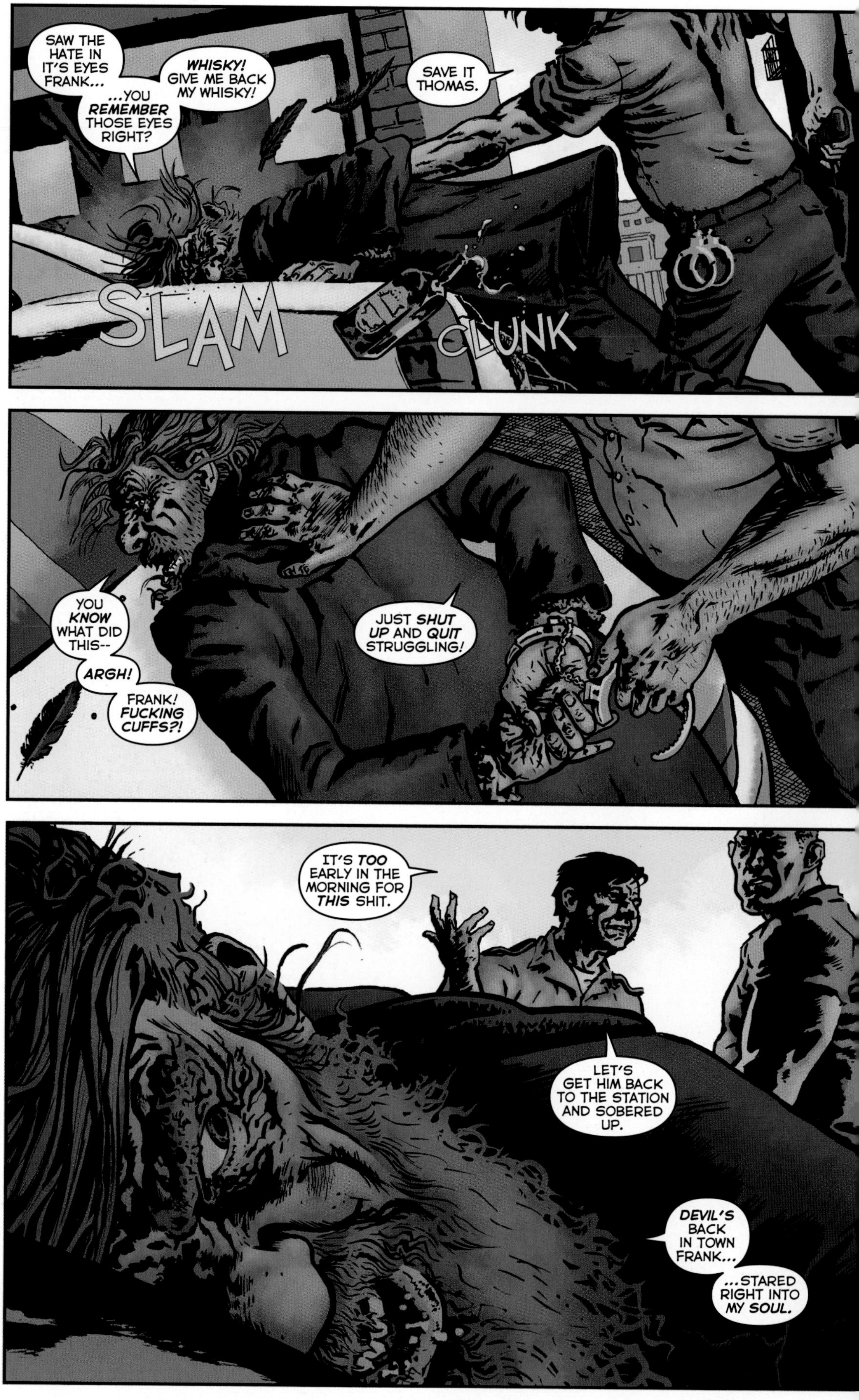
SAW THE HATE IN IT'S EYES FRANK...
...YOU *REMEMBER* THOSE EYES RIGHT?
WHISKY! GIVE ME BACK MY WHISKY!
SAVE IT THOMAS.
SLAM
CLUNK
YOU *KNOW* WHAT DID THIS--
ARGH!
JUST *SHUT UP* AND *QUIT* STRUGGLING!
FRANK! *FUCKING CUFFS?!*
IT'S *TOO* EARLY IN THE MORNING FOR *THIS* SHIT.
LET'S GET HIM BACK TO THE STATION AND SOBERED UP.
DEVIL'S BACK IN TOWN FRANK...
...STARED RIGHT INTO MY *SOUL.*

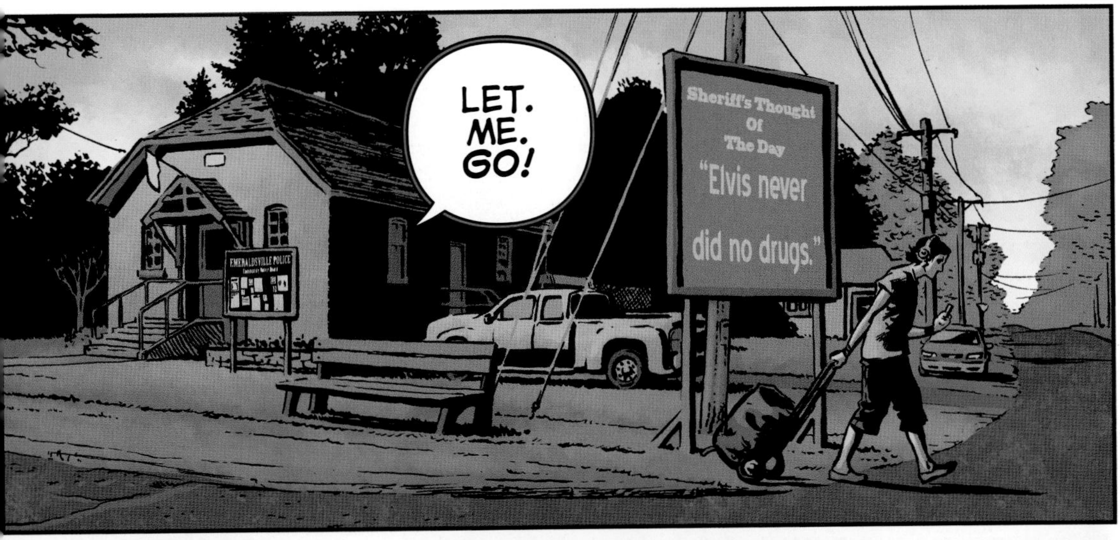
LET. ME. GO!
EMERALDSVILLE POLICE
Sheriff's Thought Of The Day
"Elvis never did no drugs."

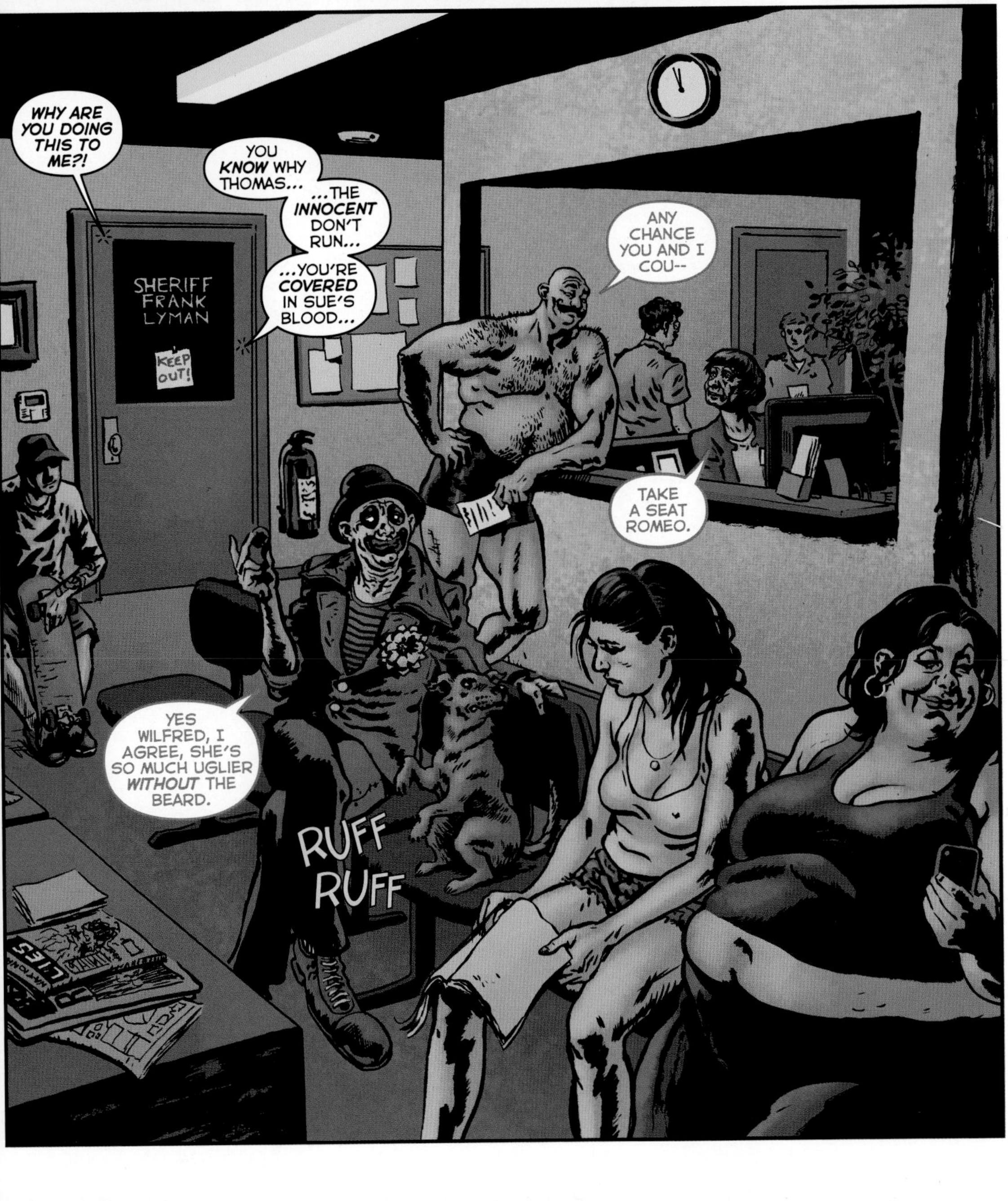
WHY ARE YOU DOING THIS TO ME?!
YOU KNOW WHY THOMAS...
...THE INNOCENT DON'T RUN...
...YOU'RE COVERED IN SUE'S BLOOD...
SHERIFF FRANK LYMAN
KEEP OUT!
ANY CHANCE YOU AND I COU--
TAKE A SEAT ROMEO.
YES WILFRED, I AGREE, SHE'S SO MUCH UGLIER WITHOUT THE BEARD.
RUFF RUFF

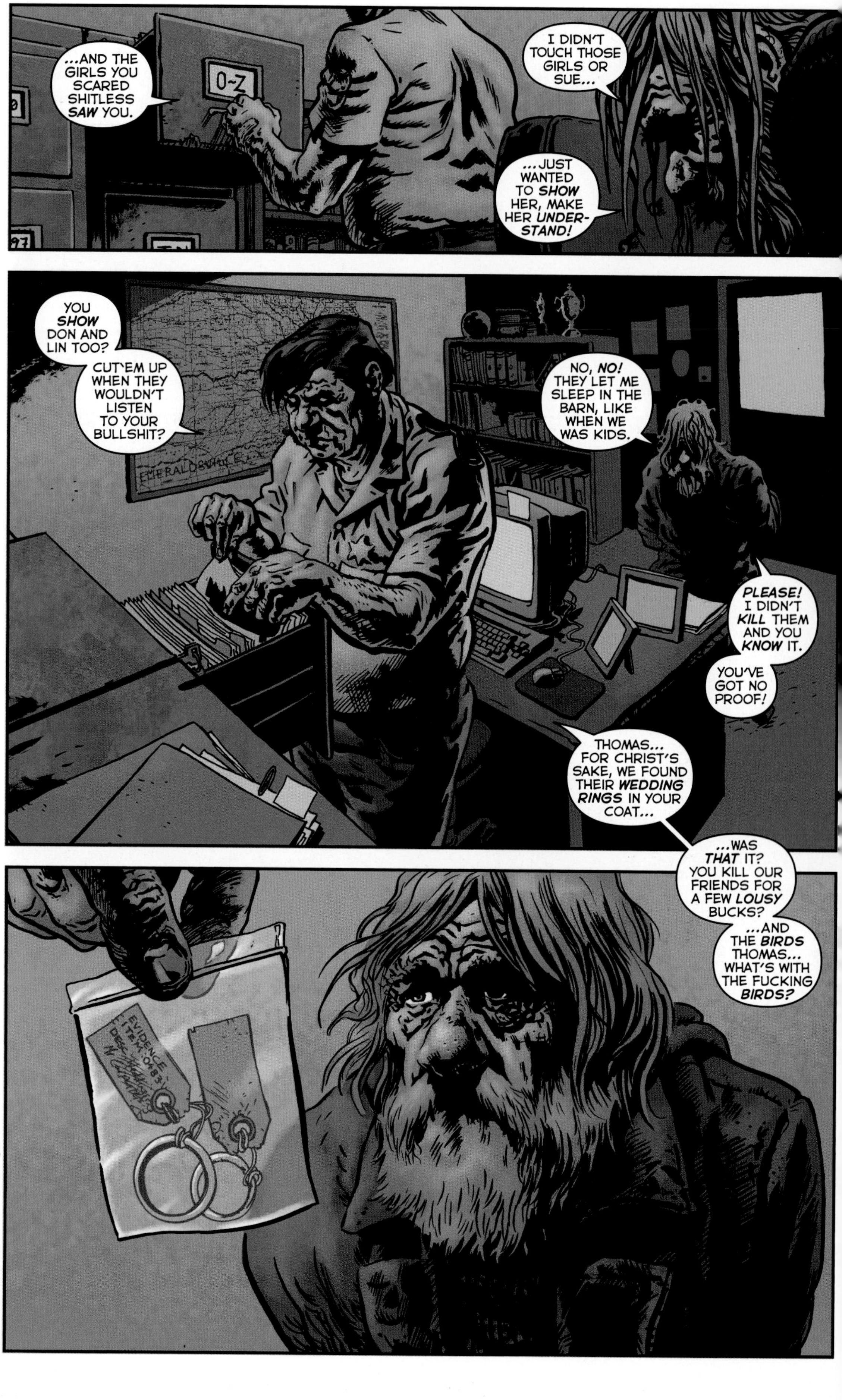
...AND THE GIRLS YOU SCARED SHITLESS SAW YOU.
O-Z
I DIDN'T TOUCH THOSE GIRLS OR SUE...
...JUST WANTED TO SHOW HER, MAKE HER UNDER-STAND!
YOU SHOW DON AND LIN TOO?
CUT'EM UP WHEN THEY WOULDN'T LISTEN TO YOUR BULLSHIT?
NO, NO! THEY LET ME SLEEP IN THE BARN, LIKE WHEN WE WAS KIDS.
PLEASE! I DIDN'T KILL THEM AND YOU KNOW IT.
YOU'VE GOT NO PROOF!
THOMAS... FOR CHRIST'S SAKE, WE FOUND THEIR WEDDING RINGS IN YOUR COAT...
...WAS THAT IT? YOU KILL OUR FRIENDS FOR A FEW LOUSY BUCKS?
...AND THE BIRDS THOMAS... WHAT'S WITH THE FUCKING BIRDS?

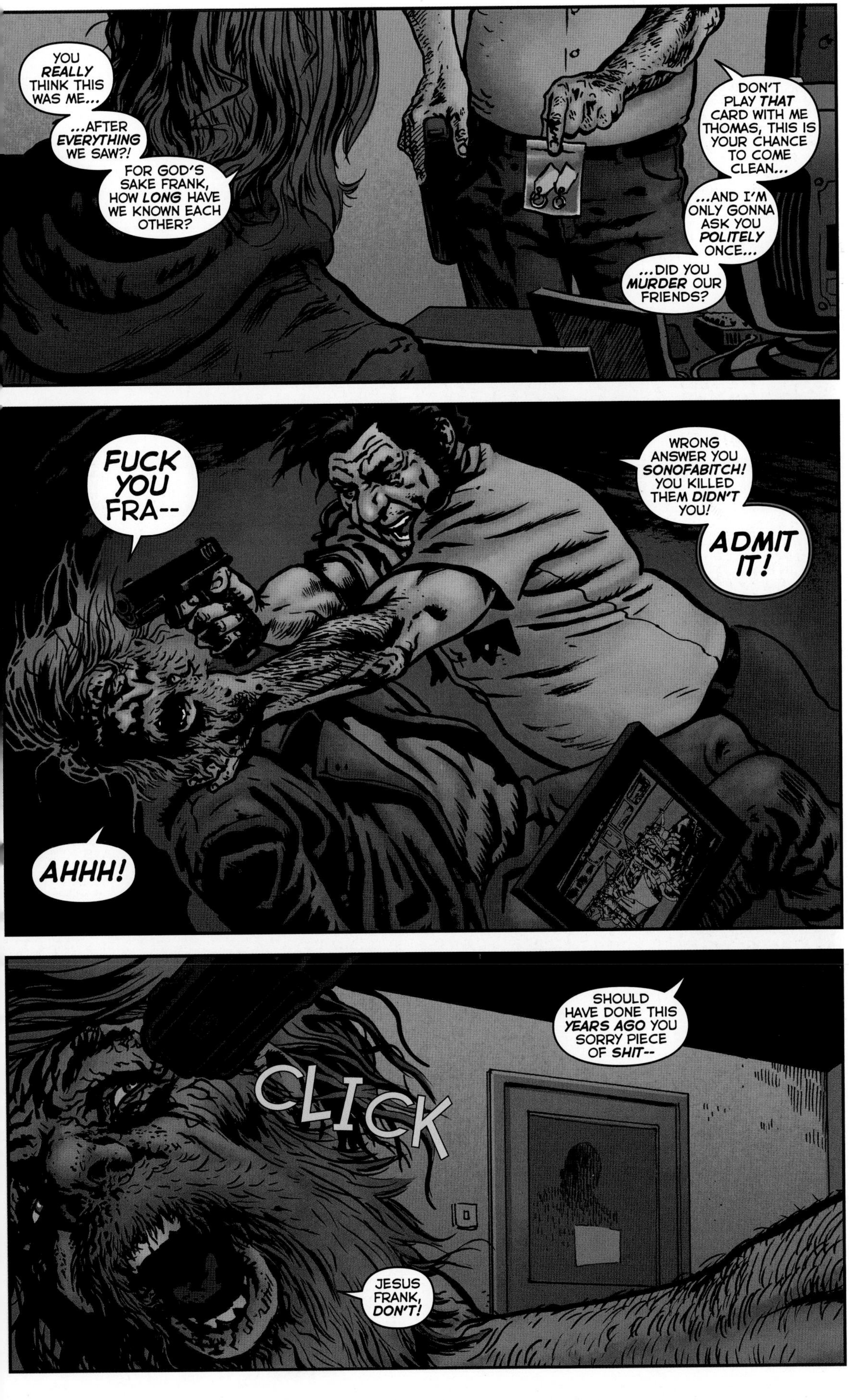

YOU REALLY THINK THIS WAS ME...
...AFTER EVERYTHING WE SAW?!
FOR GOD'S SAKE FRANK, HOW LONG HAVE WE KNOWN EACH OTHER?
DON'T PLAY THAT CARD WITH ME THOMAS, THIS IS YOUR CHANCE TO COME CLEAN...
...AND I'M ONLY GONNA ASK YOU POLITELY ONCE...
...DID YOU MURDER OUR FRIENDS?
FUCK YOU FRA--
WRONG ANSWER YOU SONOFABITCH! YOU KILLED THEM DIDN'T YOU!
ADMIT IT!
AHHH!
SHOULD HAVE DONE THIS YEARS AGO YOU SORRY PIECE OF SHIT--
CLICK
JESUS FRANK, DON'T!

FRANK!
DON'T DO IT...
...IT AIN'T WORTH IT!
TELL ME THE TRUTH DAMN IT!
CAN'T... BREATHE.
SHERIFF FRANK LYMAN
EASY NOW FRANK, LET GO OF THE GUN... YOU DON'T WANT TO DO THIS...
GET THE HELL OFFA ME!
-COUGH- JESUS. -SPLUTTER- FUCK.
FRANK, I--
GET HIM OUT OF MY SIGHT.
GET HIM THE FUCK OUTTA HERE.
THEY SHOULD HAVE LISTENED TO ME...
...STILL BE ALIVE IF THEY HAD...
...DO SOMETHING FRANK...
...IT'S COMING FOR US ALL!

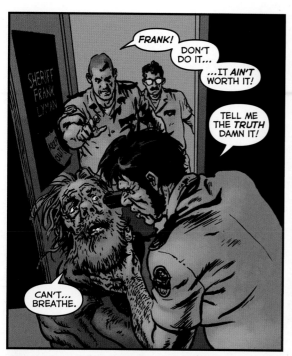

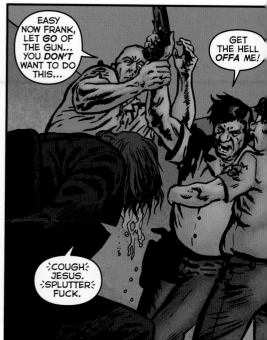

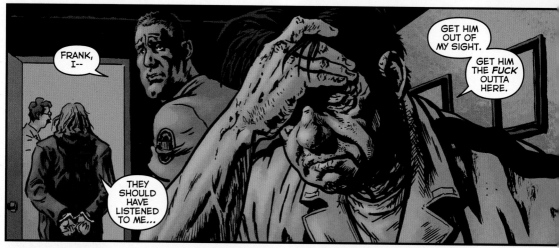

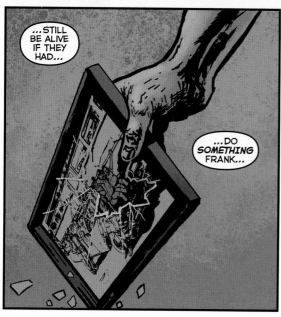

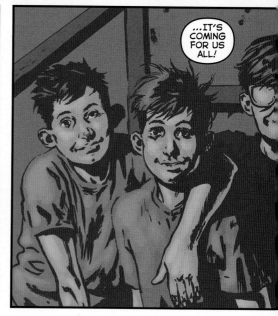

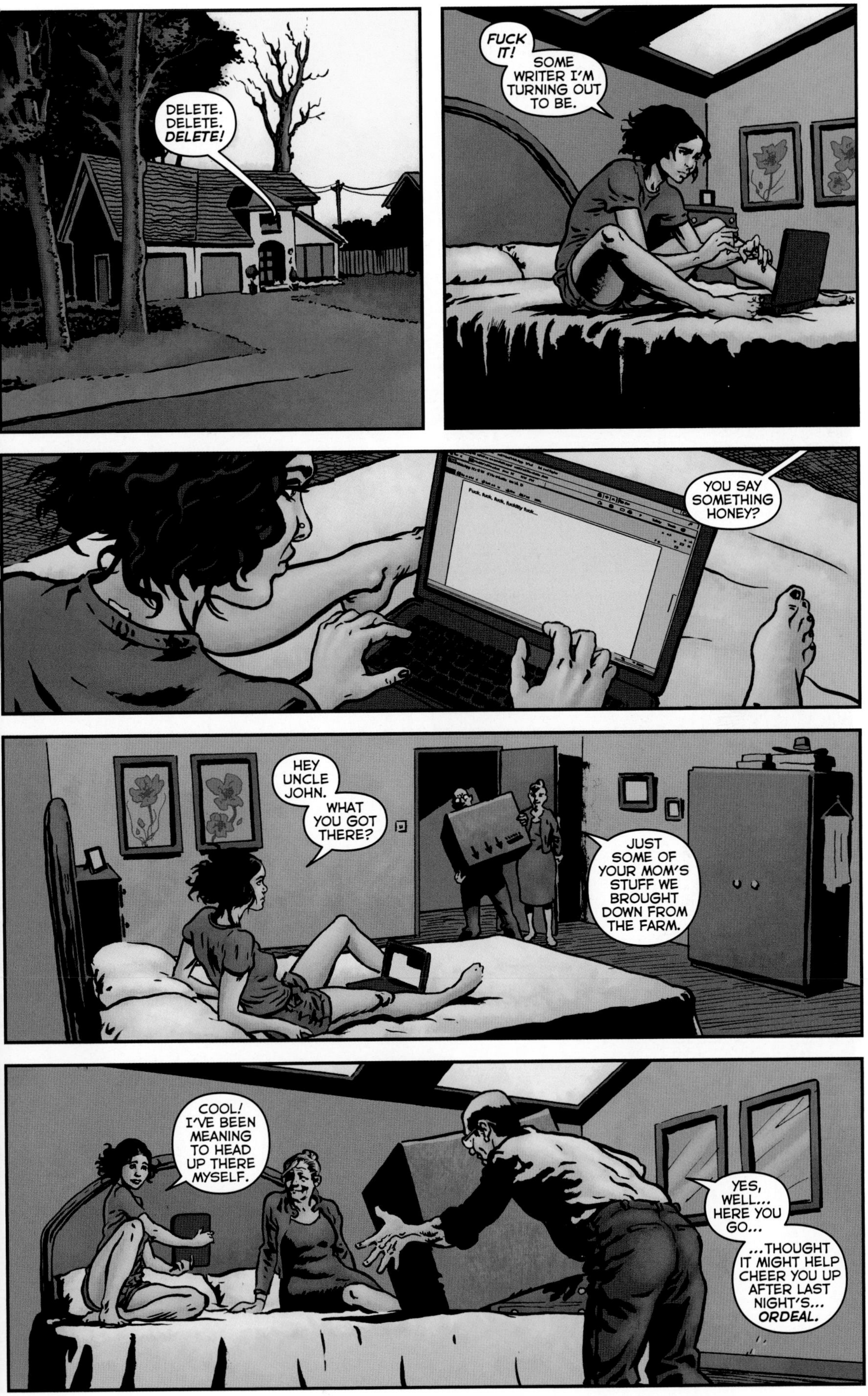
DELETE. DELETE. *DELETE!*
FUCK IT!
SOME WRITER I'M TURNING OUT TO BE.
Fuck, fuck, fuck, fuckity fuck...
YOU SAY SOMETHING HONEY?
HEY UNCLE JOHN.
WHAT YOU GOT THERE?
JUST SOME OF YOUR MOM'S STUFF WE BROUGHT DOWN FROM THE FARM.
COOL! I'VE BEEN MEANING TO HEAD UP THERE MYSELF.
YES, WELL... HERE YOU GO...
...THOUGHT IT MIGHT HELP CHEER YOU UP AFTER LAST NIGHT'S... *ORDEAL.*

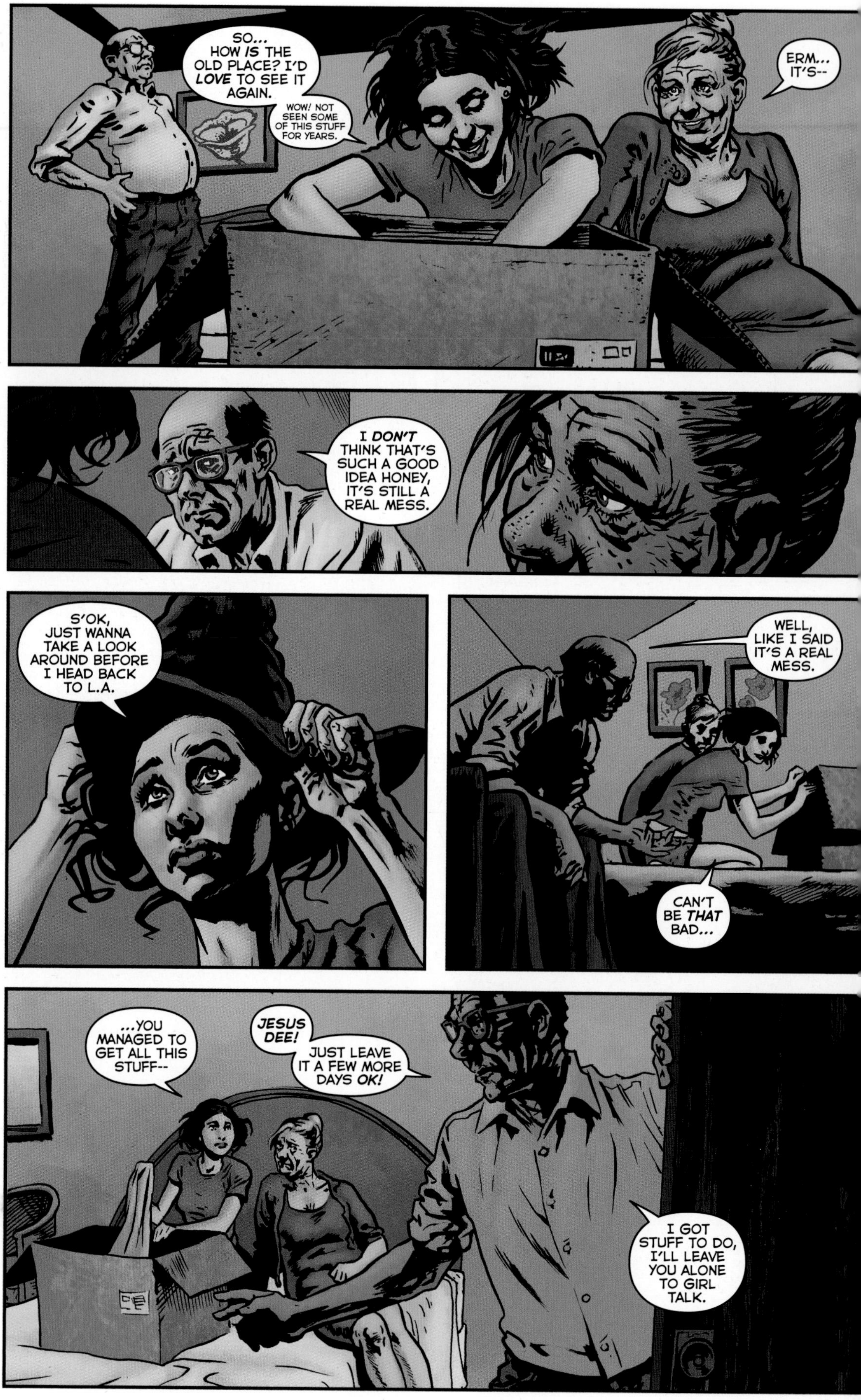
SO... HOW IS THE OLD PLACE? I'D LOVE TO SEE IT AGAIN.
WOW! NOT SEEN SOME OF THIS STUFF FOR YEARS.
ERM... IT'S--
I DON'T THINK THAT'S SUCH A GOOD IDEA HONEY, IT'S STILL A REAL MESS.
S'OK, JUST WANNA TAKE A LOOK AROUND BEFORE I HEAD BACK TO L.A.
WELL, LIKE I SAID IT'S A REAL MESS.
CAN'T BE THAT BAD...
...YOU MANAGED TO GET ALL THIS STUFF--
JESUS DEE!
JUST LEAVE IT A FEW MORE DAYS OK!
I GOT STUFF TO DO, I'LL LEAVE YOU ALONE TO GIRL TALK.

WHAT'S EATING HIM?

NOTHING DEAR, IT'S JUST BEEN *STRESSFUL* FOR HIM TOO.

OK... BUT WHEN DO *YOU* THINK I *CAN* GO UP THERE?

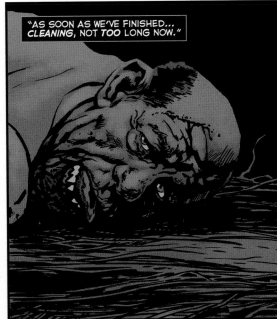

"AS SOON AS WE'VE FINISHED... *CLEANING*, NOT *TOO* LONG NOW."

WELL, AS LONG AS I GET TO VISIT BEFORE I GO...

YOU WILL DEE DEE, I PROMISE. ANYWAY... TIME FOR LUNCH. YOU'RE HUNGRY RIGHT?

"YOU KNOW ME, I'M *ALWAYS* HUNGRY."

MOM *REALLY* WORE THESE?

THEY'D LOOK BETTER IN RED.

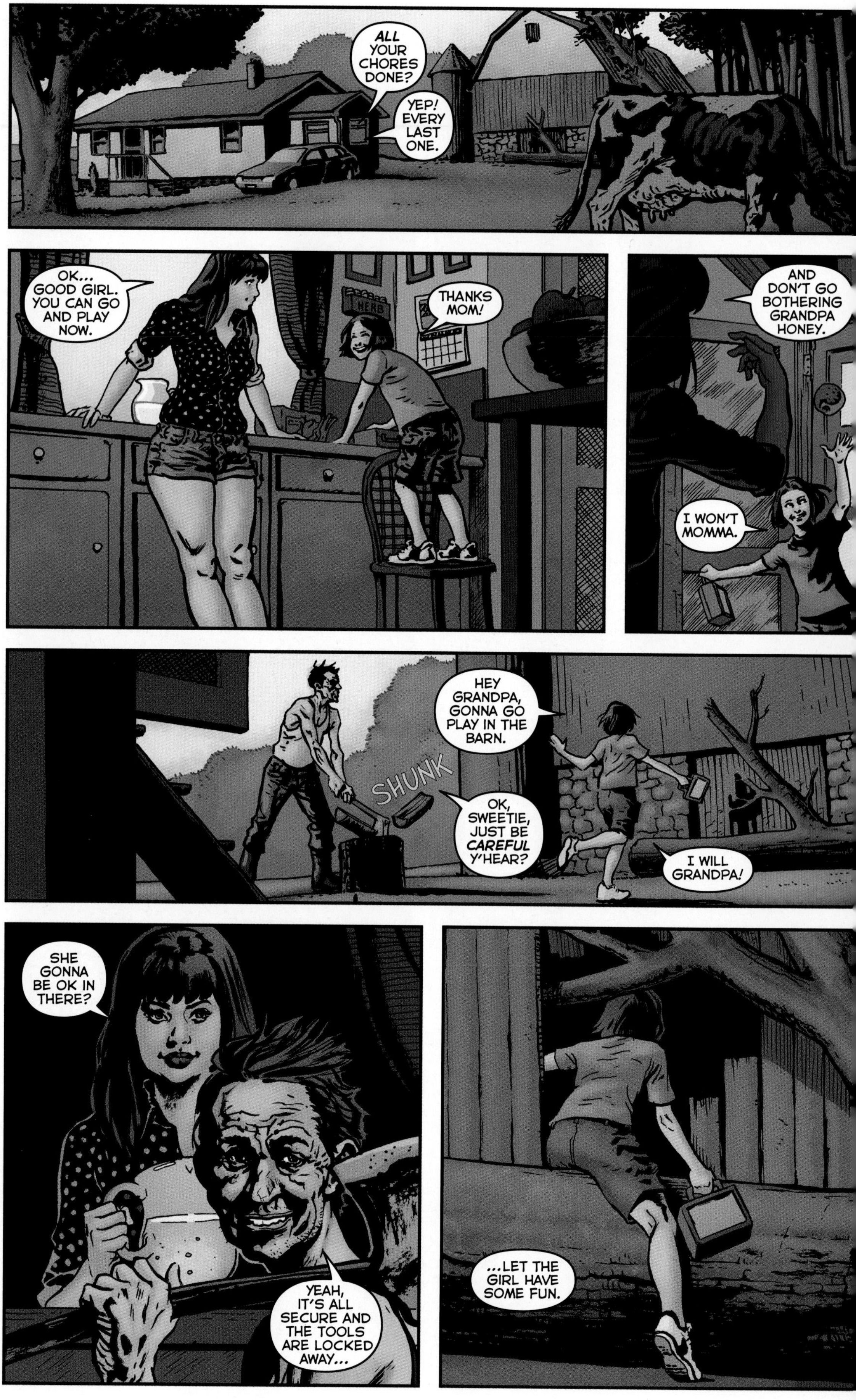
ALL YOUR CHORES DONE?
YEP! EVERY LAST ONE.
OK... GOOD GIRL. YOU CAN GO AND PLAY NOW.
THANKS MOM!
AND DON'T GO BOTHERING GRANDPA HONEY.
I WON'T MOMMA.
HEY GRANDPA, GONNA GO PLAY IN THE BARN.
SHUNK
OK, SWEETIE, JUST BE CAREFUL Y'HEAR?
I WILL GRANDPA!
SHE GONNA BE OK IN THERE?
YEAH, IT'S ALL SECURE AND THE TOOLS ARE LOCKED AWAY...
...LET THE GIRL HAVE SOME FUN.

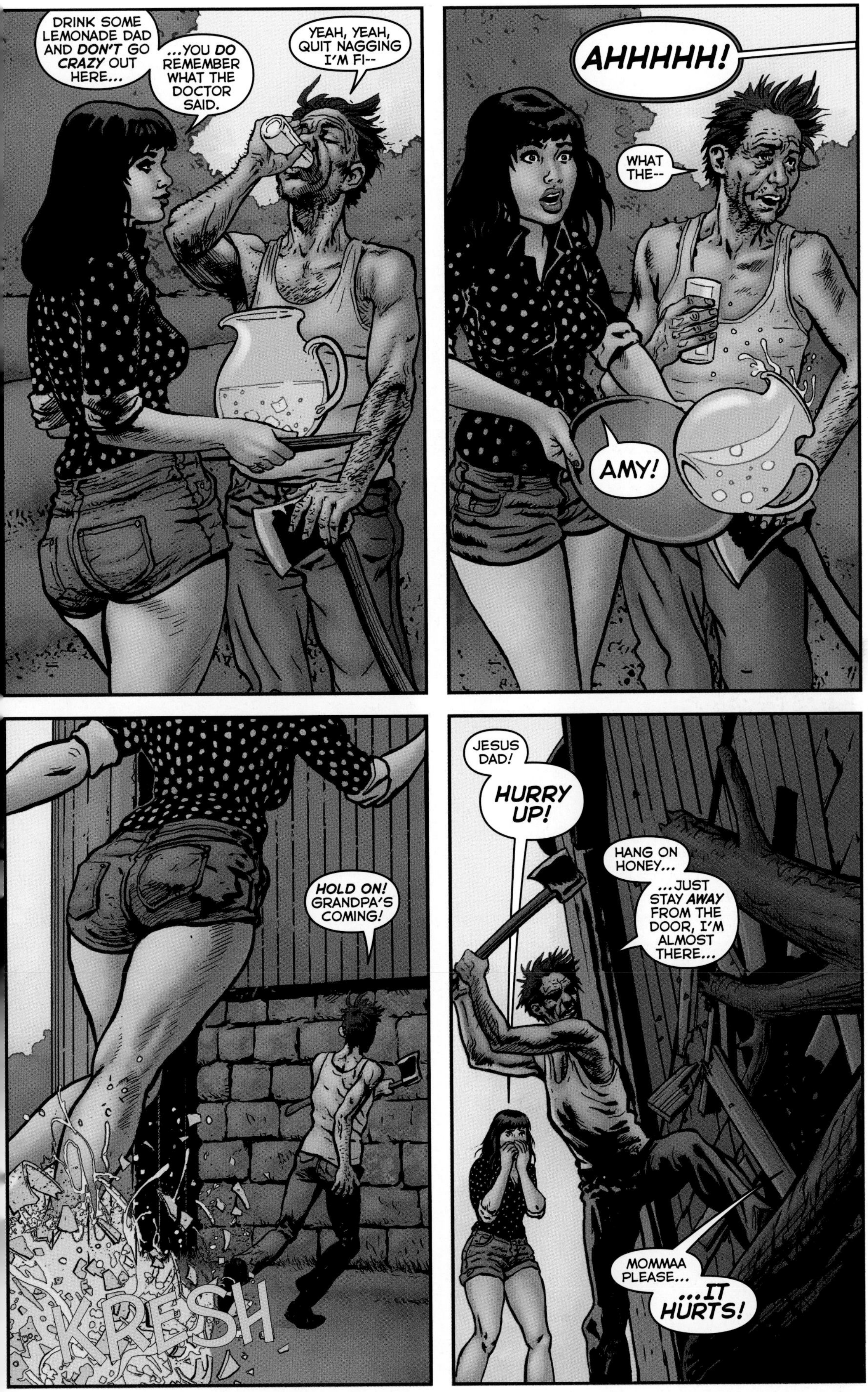
DRINK SOME LEMONADE DAD AND DON'T GO CRAZY OUT HERE...
...YOU DO REMEMBER WHAT THE DOCTOR SAID.
YEAH, YEAH, QUIT NAGGING I'M FI--
AHHHHH!
WHAT THE--
AMY!
HOLD ON! GRANDPA'S COMING!
KRESH
JESUS DAD!
HURRY UP!
HANG ON HONEY...
...JUST STAY AWAY FROM THE DOOR, I'M ALMOST THERE...
MOMMAA PLEASE...
...IT HURTS!

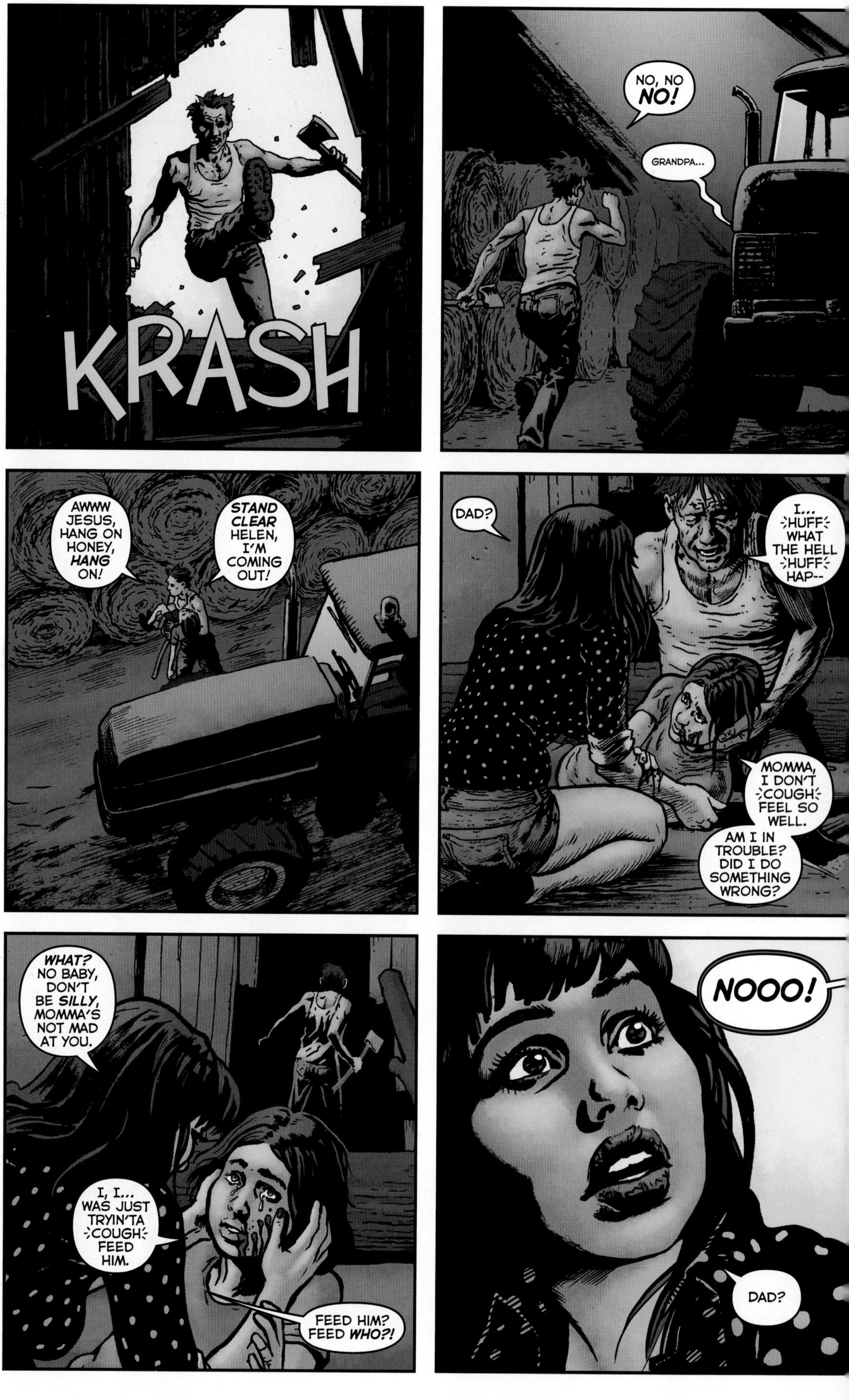
KRASH
NO, NO NO!
GRANDPA...
AWWW JESUS, HANG ON HONEY, HANG ON!
STAND CLEAR HELEN, I'M COMING OUT!
DAD?
I... HUFF WHAT THE HELL HUFF HAP--
MOMMA, I DON'T COUGH FEEL SO WELL.
AM I IN TROUBLE? DID I DO SOMETHING WRONG?
WHAT? NO BABY, DON'T BE SILLY, MOMMA'S NOT MAD AT YOU.
I, I... WAS JUST TRYIN'TA COUGH FEED HIM.
FEED HIM? FEED WHO?!
NOOO!
DAD?

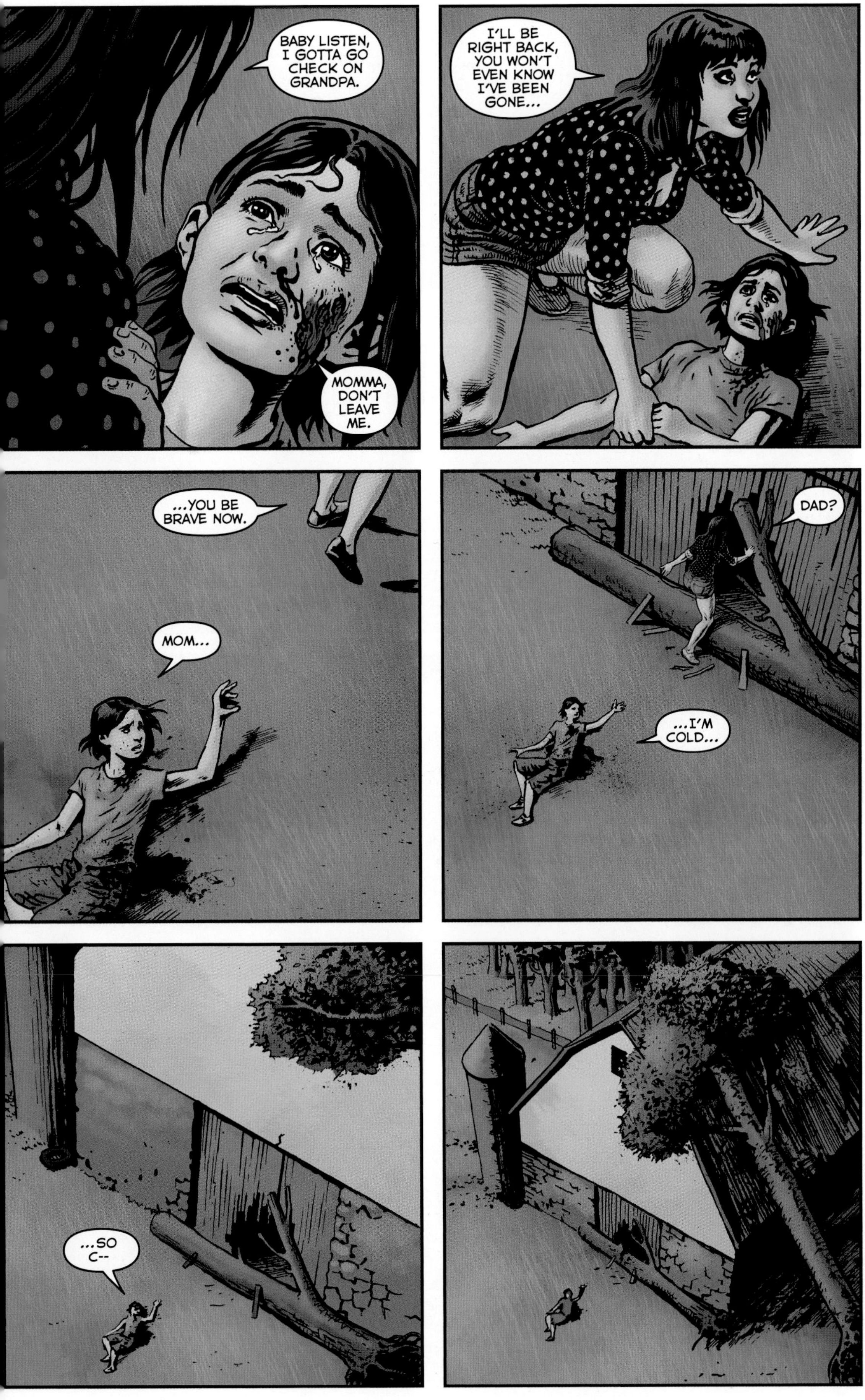
BABY LISTEN, I GOTTA GO CHECK ON GRANDPA.
MOMMA, DON'T LEAVE ME.
I'LL BE RIGHT BACK, YOU WON'T EVEN KNOW I'VE BEEN GONE...
...YOU BE BRAVE NOW.
MOM...
DAD?
...I'M COLD...
...SO C--

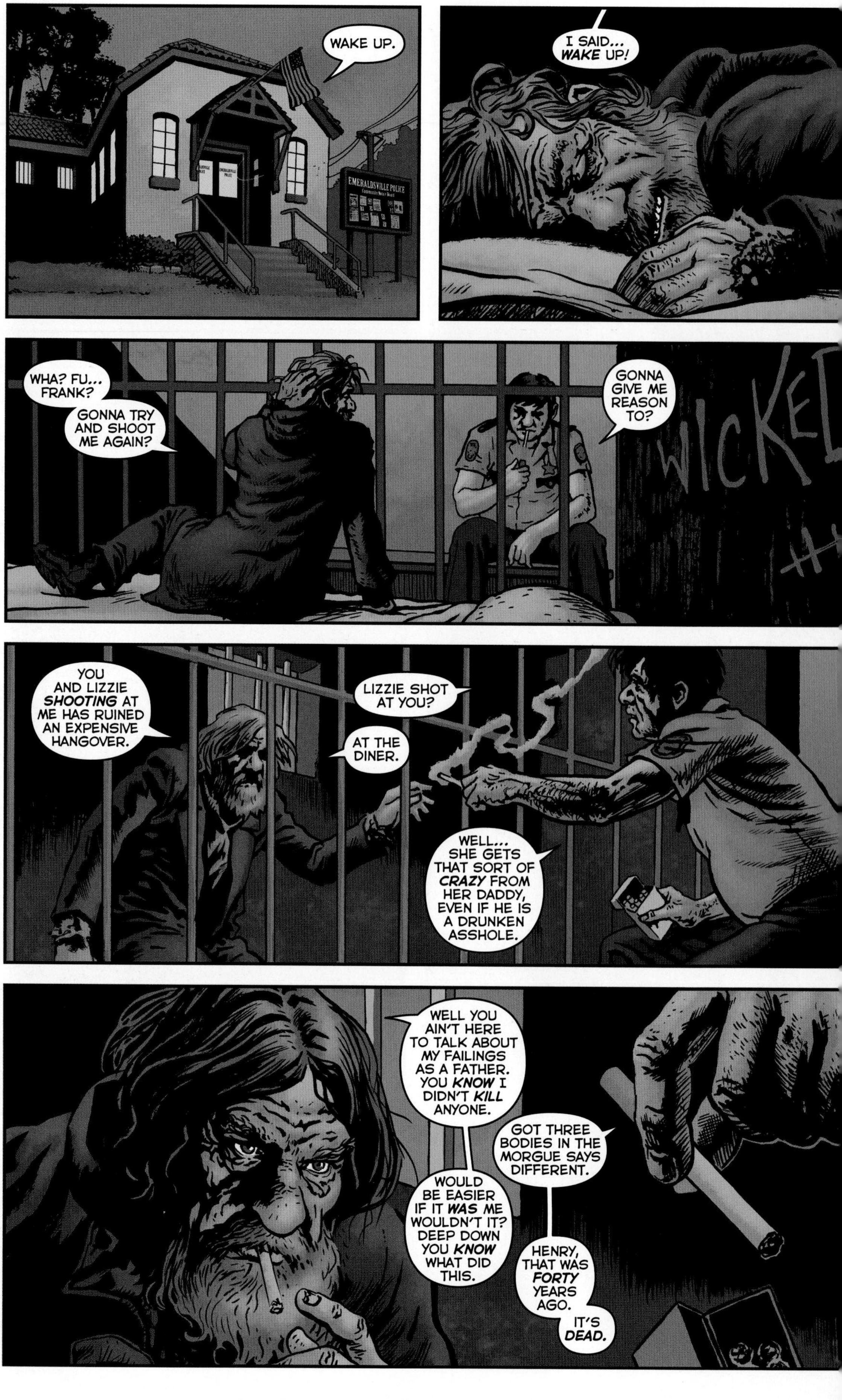

WAKE UP.
EMERALDSVILLE POLICE
I SAID... *WAKE* UP!
WHA? FU... FRANK?
GONNA TRY AND SHOOT ME AGAIN?
GONNA GIVE ME REASON TO?
WICKED
YOU AND LIZZIE *SHOOTING* AT ME HAS RUINED AN EXPENSIVE HANGOVER.
LIZZIE SHOT AT YOU?
AT THE DINER.
WELL... SHE GETS THAT SORT OF *CRAZY* FROM HER DADDY, EVEN IF HE IS A DRUNKEN ASSHOLE.
WELL YOU AIN'T HERE TO TALK ABOUT *MY* FAILINGS AS A FATHER. YOU *KNOW* I DIDN'T *KILL* ANYONE.
GOT THREE BODIES IN THE MORGUE SAYS DIFFERENT.
WOULD BE EASIER IF IT *WAS* ME WOULDN'T IT? DEEP DOWN YOU *KNOW* WHAT DID THIS.
HENRY, THAT WAS *FORTY* YEARS AGO.
IT'S *DEAD.*

EVEN IF IT *WAS* ALIVE, IT WOULD BE JUST LIKE US, OLD AND TIRED...

...COULDN'T PISS IN A POT UNLESS YOU HELD IT'S DICK AND POINTED IT.

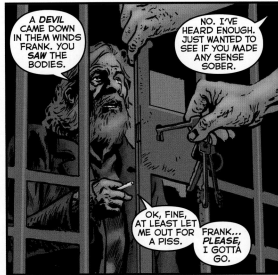

A *DEVIL* CAME DOWN IN THEM WINDS FRANK. YOU *SAW* THE BODIES.

NO. I'VE HEARD ENOUGH. JUST WANTED TO SEE IF YOU MADE ANY SENSE SOBER.

OK, FINE, AT LEAST LET ME OUT FOR A PISS.

FRANK... *PLEASE*, I GOTTA GO.

YOU KNOW, IN ALL THESE YEARS, THE ONE THING ABOUT YOU THAT'S *NEVER* CHANGED?

DO TELL...

OWW!

MOTHERFU--

FLIK

YOU ALWAYS *WERE* TOO TRUSTING FRANK.

GOD *DAMN* IT!

WHAT THE *HELL* YOU PLAYIN' AT?!

ARGH!

MY LEG!

KRACK

YOU THINK I'M JUST GONNA *LET* YOU WALK ON OUTTA HERE?

WAY I SEE IT, YOU *DON'T* HAVE A CHOICE.

THIS AIN'T OVER, YOU HEAR ME?! *THIS AIN'T OVER!*

YOU'RE RIGHT. I GOTTA FIND THEM GIRLS AND *FINISH* THIS...

...LOOK AFTER THAT LEG NOW Y'HEAR.

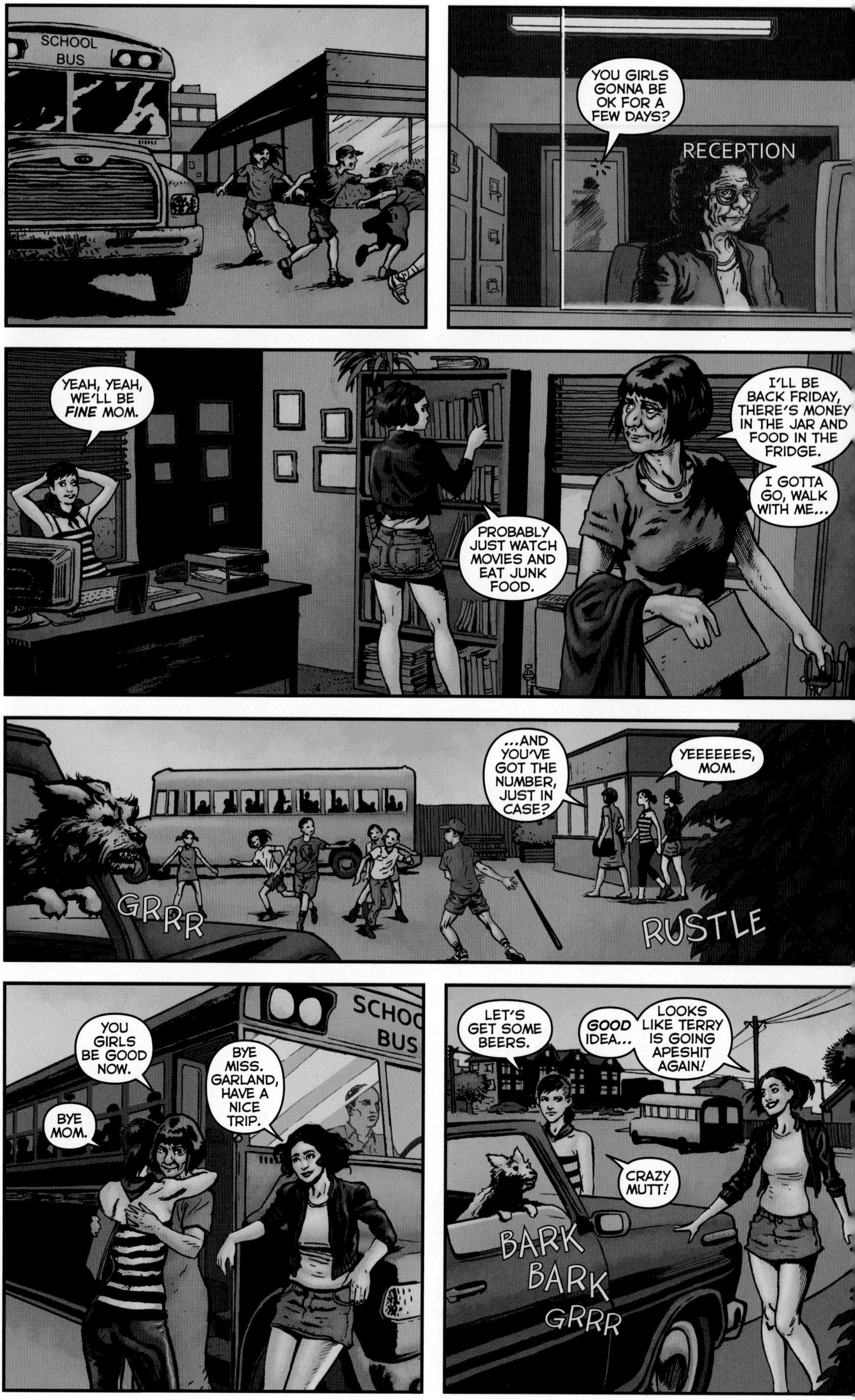
SCHOOL BUS
YOU GIRLS GONNA BE OK FOR A FEW DAYS?
RECEPTION
PRINCIPAL
YEAH, YEAH, WE'LL BE *FINE* MOM.
PROBABLY JUST WATCH MOVIES AND EAT JUNK FOOD.
I'LL BE BACK FRIDAY, THERE'S MONEY IN THE JAR AND FOOD IN THE FRIDGE.
I GOTTA GO, WALK WITH ME...
GRRR
...AND YOU'VE GOT THE NUMBER, JUST IN CASE?
YEEEEEES, MOM.
RUSTLE
SCHOO BUS
YOU GIRLS BE GOOD NOW.
BYE MOM.
BYE MISS. GARLAND, HAVE A NICE TRIP.
LET'S GET SOME BEERS.
GOOD IDEA...
LOOKS LIKE TERRY IS GOING APESHIT AGAIN!
CRAZY MUTT!
BARK
BARK
GRRR

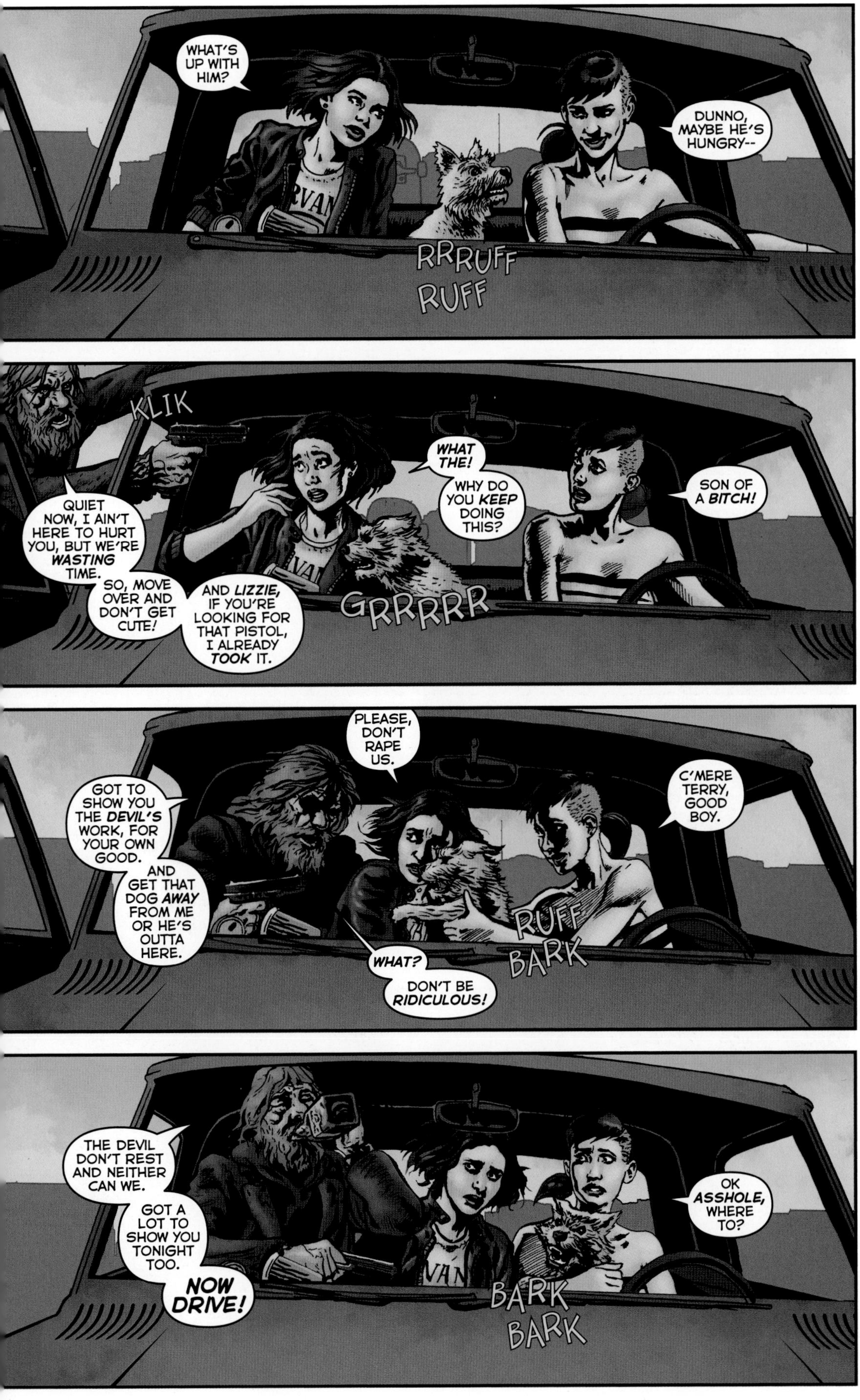
WHAT'S UP WITH HIM?
DUNNO, MAYBE HE'S HUNGRY--
RRRUFF RUFF
KLIK
QUIET NOW, I AIN'T HERE TO HURT YOU, BUT WE'RE *WASTING* TIME.
SO, MOVE OVER AND DON'T GET CUTE!
AND *LIZZIE,* IF YOU'RE LOOKING FOR THAT PISTOL, I ALREADY *TOOK* IT.
WHAT THE!
WHY DO YOU *KEEP* DOING THIS?
SON OF A *BITCH!*
GRRRRRR
PLEASE, DON'T RAPE US.
GOT TO SHOW YOU THE *DEVIL'S* WORK, FOR YOUR OWN GOOD.
AND GET THAT DOG *AWAY* FROM ME OR HE'S OUTTA HERE.
C'MERE TERRY, GOOD BOY.
RUFF BARK
WHAT?
DON'T BE *RIDICULOUS!*
THE DEVIL DON'T REST AND NEITHER CAN WE.
GOT A LOT TO SHOW YOU TONIGHT TOO.
NOW DRIVE!
OK *ASSHOLE,* WHERE TO?
BARK BARK

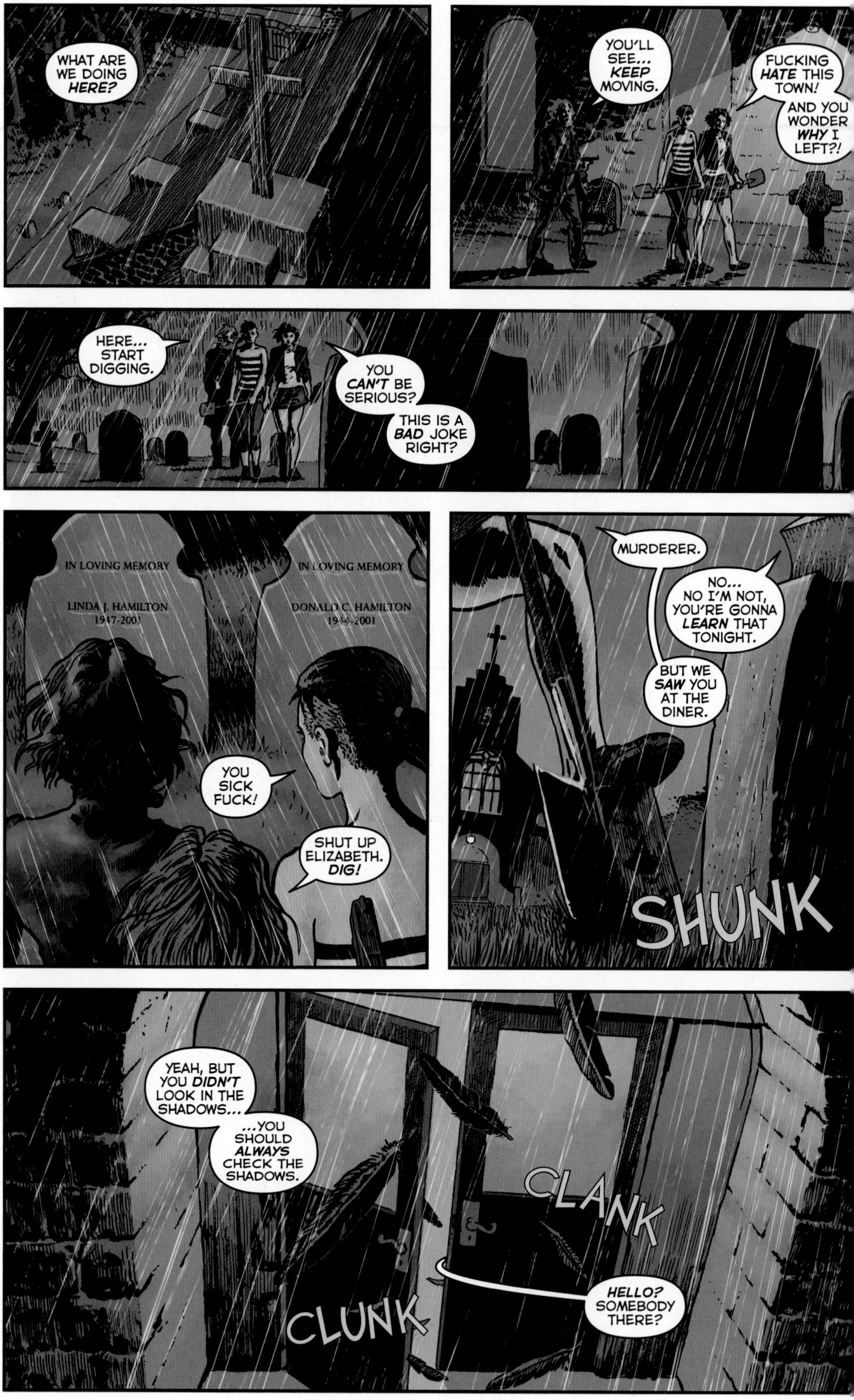
WHAT ARE WE DOING HERE?
YOU'LL SEE... KEEP MOVING.
FUCKING HATE THIS TOWN!
AND YOU WONDER WHY I LEFT?!
HERE... START DIGGING.
YOU CAN'T BE SERIOUS?
THIS IS A BAD JOKE RIGHT?
IN LOVING MEMORY
LINDA J. HAMILTON
1947-2001
IN LOVING MEMORY
DONALD C. HAMILTON
2001
YOU SICK FUCK!
SHUT UP ELIZABETH. DIG!
MURDERER.
NO... NO I'M NOT, YOU'RE GONNA LEARN THAT TONIGHT.
BUT WE SAW YOU AT THE DINER.
SHUNK
YEAH, BUT YOU DIDN'T LOOK IN THE SHADOWS...
...YOU SHOULD ALWAYS CHECK THE SHADOWS.
CLANK
HELLO? SOMEBODY THERE?
CLUNK

-SIGH- KIDS!

YOU'D THINK THEY'D HAVE BETTER THINGS TO DO THAN BANG CHURCH DOORS...

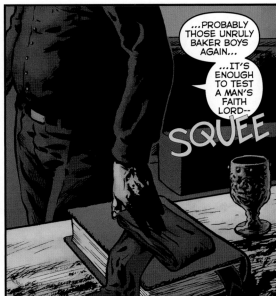

...PROBABLY THOSE UNRULY BAKER BOYS AGAIN...

...IT'S ENOUGH TO TEST A MAN'S FAITH LORD--

SQUEE

WHAT ON EARTH?

WHO'S THERE?

I'M WARNING YOU! COME OUT NOW OR I'LL CALL THE...

KLUNK

...SHERIFF.

GOOD LORD!

HELLO, SHERIFF'S OFFICE.

HEY MILLIE, IT'S FATHER JOE HERE.

HEY JOE, WHAT CAN WE DO FOR YOU TONIGHT?

WELL, REMEMBER FRANK HAD THAT HEADLESS BIRD PROBLEM? WELL, I JUST FOUN--

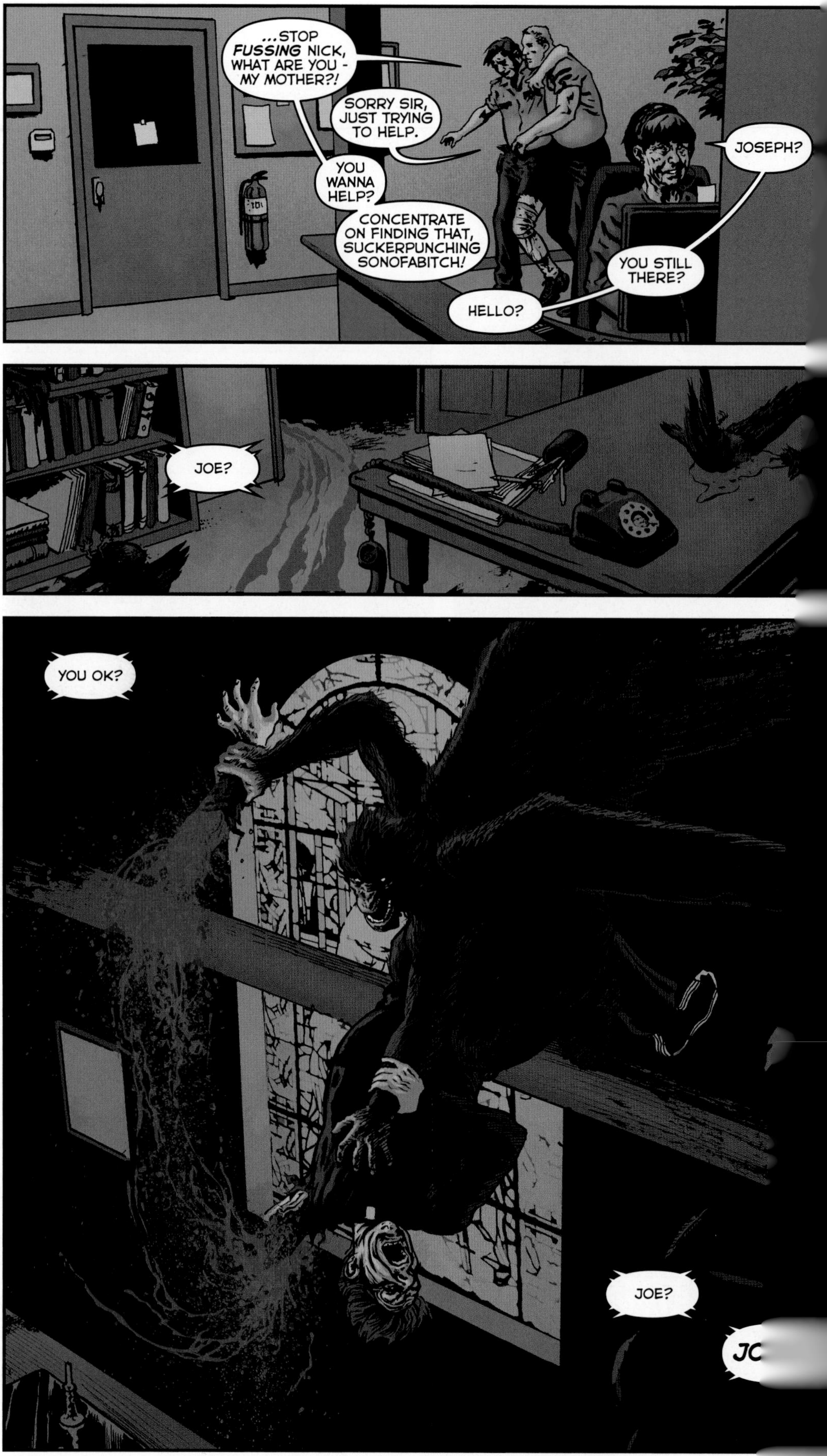
...STOP FUSSING NICK, WHAT ARE YOU - MY MOTHER?!
SORRY SIR, JUST TRYING TO HELP.
YOU WANNA HELP?
CONCENTRATE ON FINDING THAT, SUCKERPUNCHING SONOFABITCH!
JOSEPH?
YOU STILL THERE?
HELLO?
JOE?
YOU OK?
JOE?

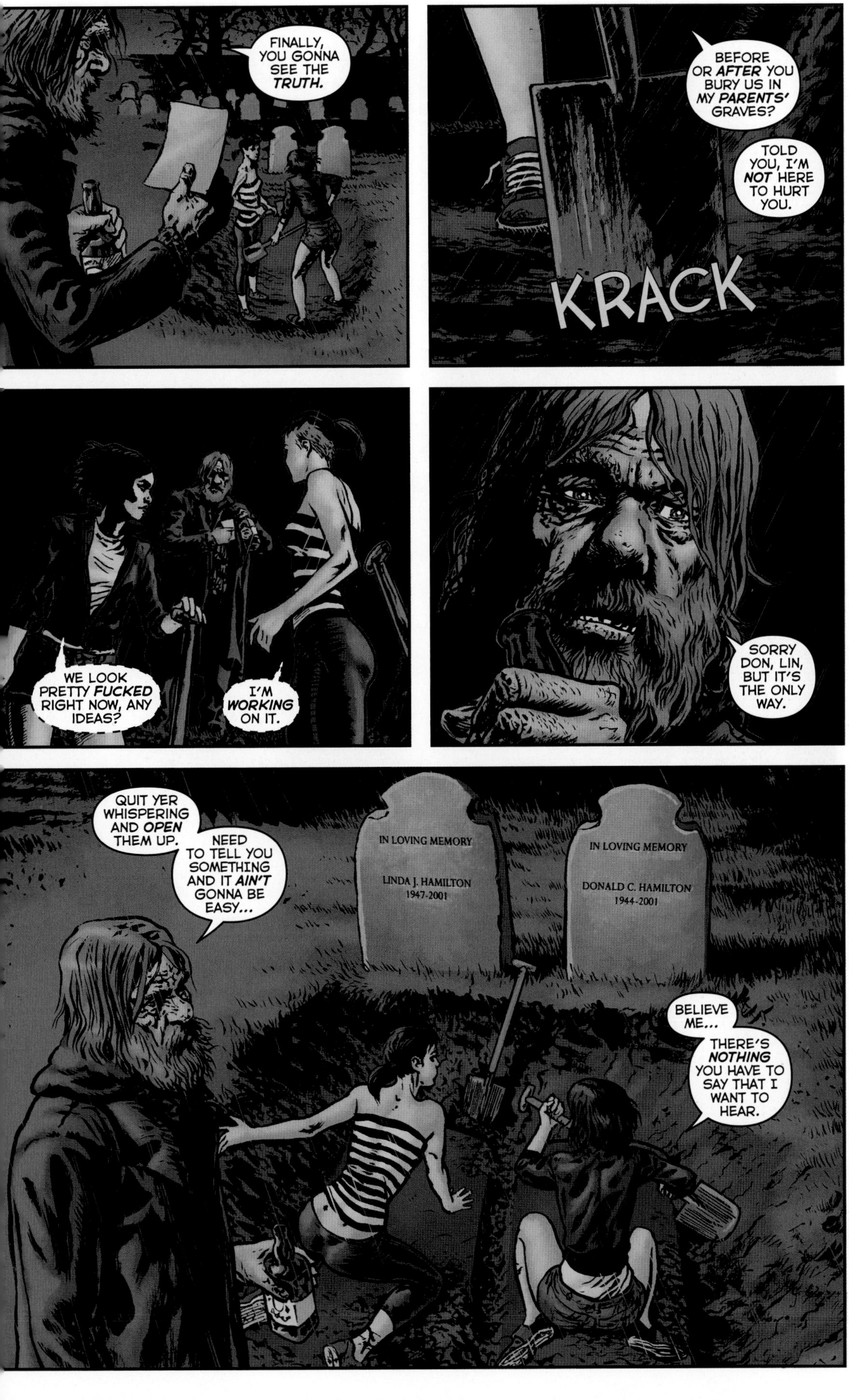
FINALLY, YOU GONNA SEE THE TRUTH.
BEFORE OR AFTER YOU BURY US IN MY PARENTS' GRAVES?
TOLD YOU, I'M NOT HERE TO HURT YOU.
KRACK
WE LOOK PRETTY FUCKED RIGHT NOW, ANY IDEAS?
I'M WORKING ON IT.
SORRY DON, LIN, BUT IT'S THE ONLY WAY.
QUIT YER WHISPERING AND OPEN THEM UP.
NEED TO TELL YOU SOMETHING AND IT AIN'T GONNA BE EASY...
IN LOVING MEMORY
LINDA J. HAMILTON
1947-2001
IN LOVING MEMORY
DONALD C. HAMILTON
1944-2001
BELIEVE ME...
THERE'S NOTHING YOU HAVE TO SAY THAT I WANT TO HEAR.

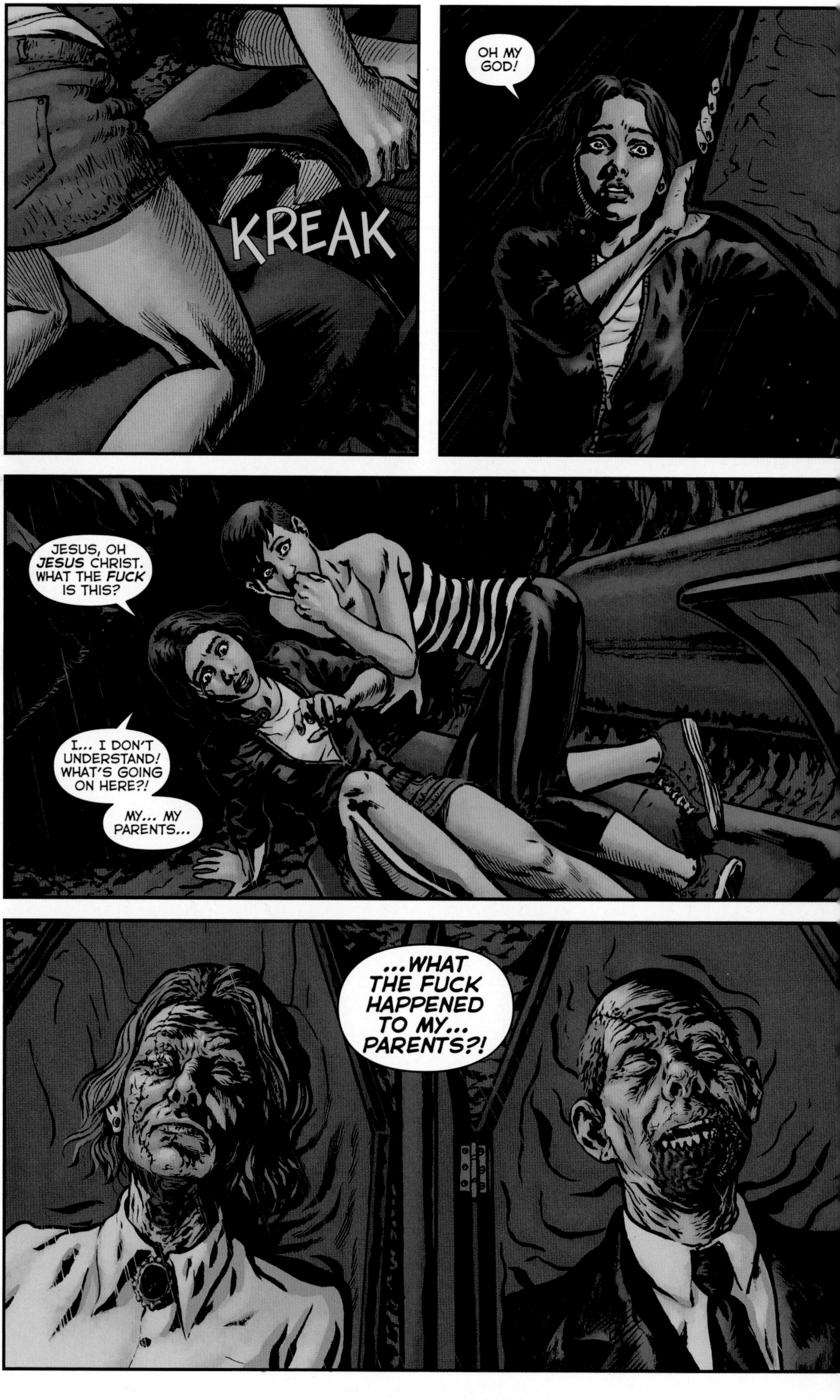
KREAK
OH MY GOD!
JESUS, OH JESUS CHRIST. WHAT THE FUCK IS THIS?
I... I DON'T UNDERSTAND! WHAT'S GOING ON HERE?!
MY... MY PARENTS...
...WHAT THE FUCK HAPPENED TO MY... PARENTS?!

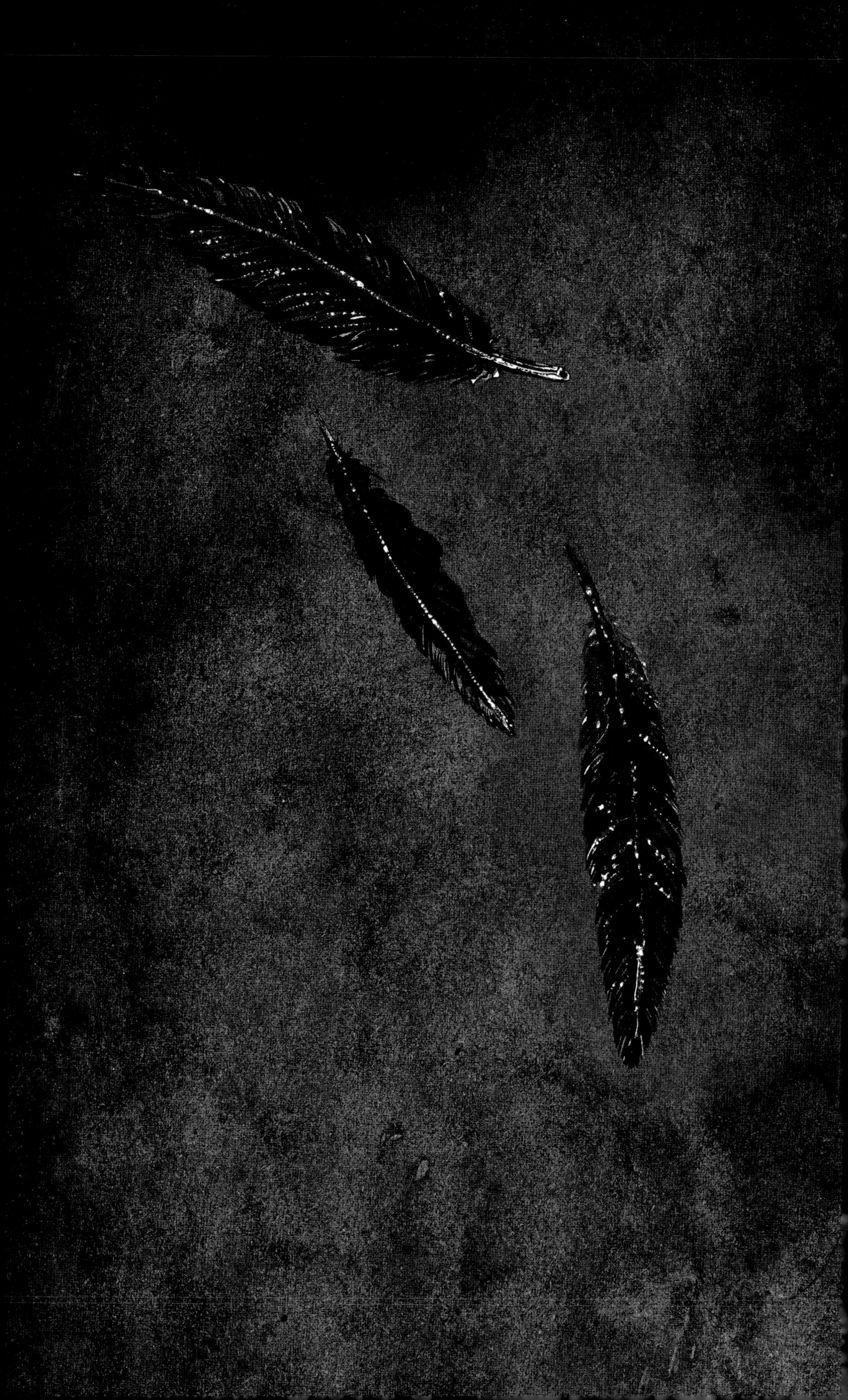

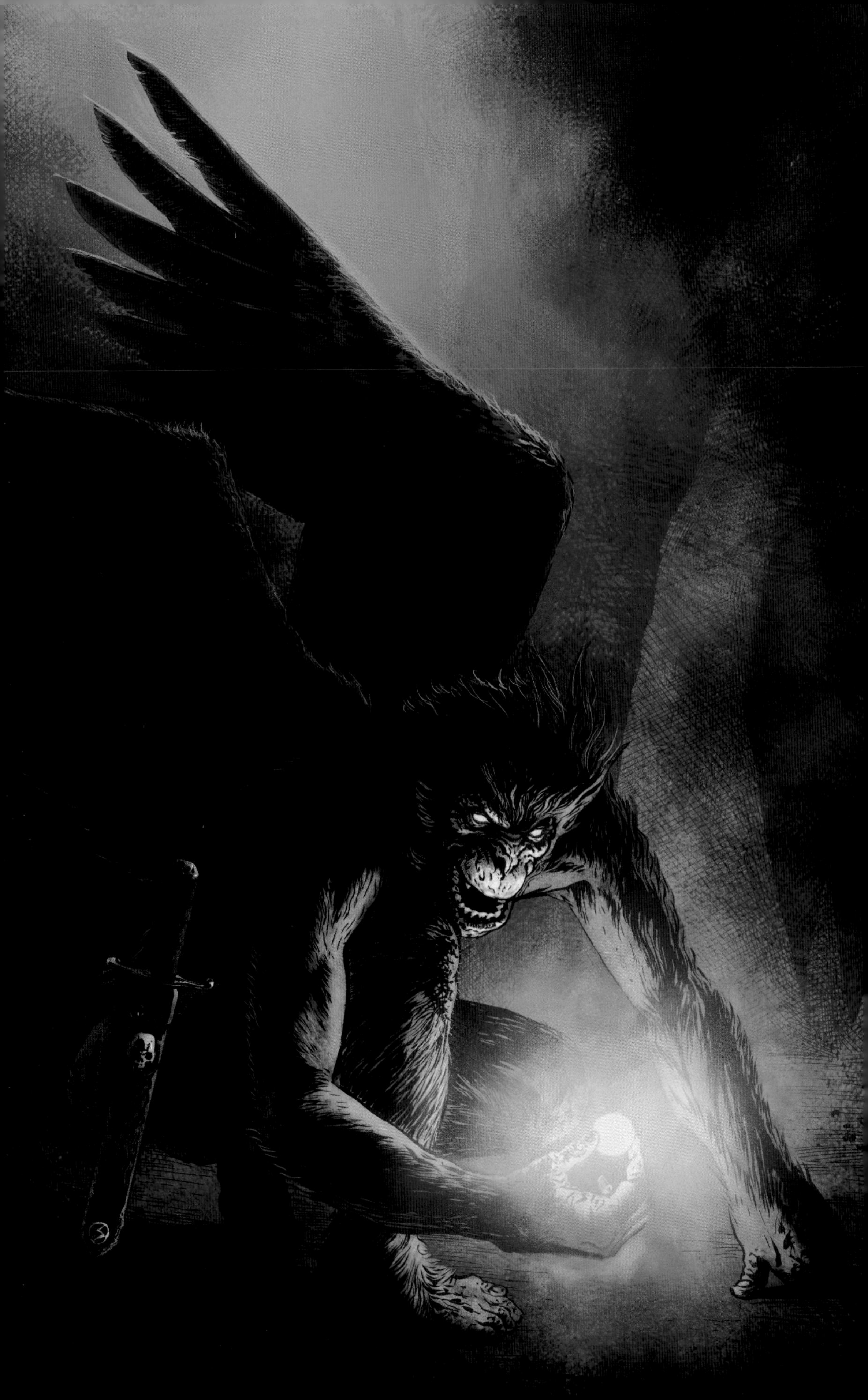

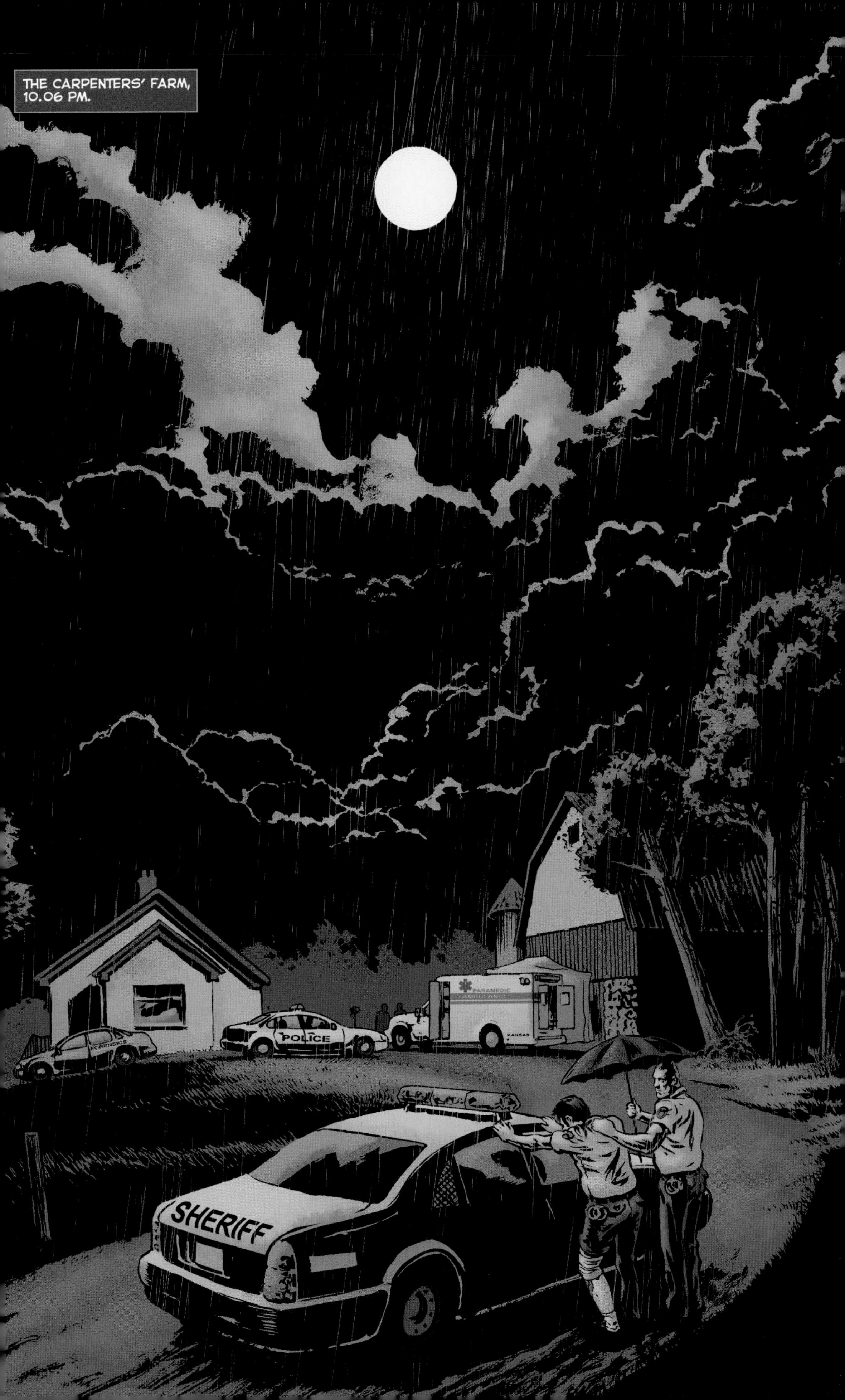
THE CARPENTERS' FARM, 10.06 PM.
PARAMEDIC
POLICE
FORENSICS
SHERIFF

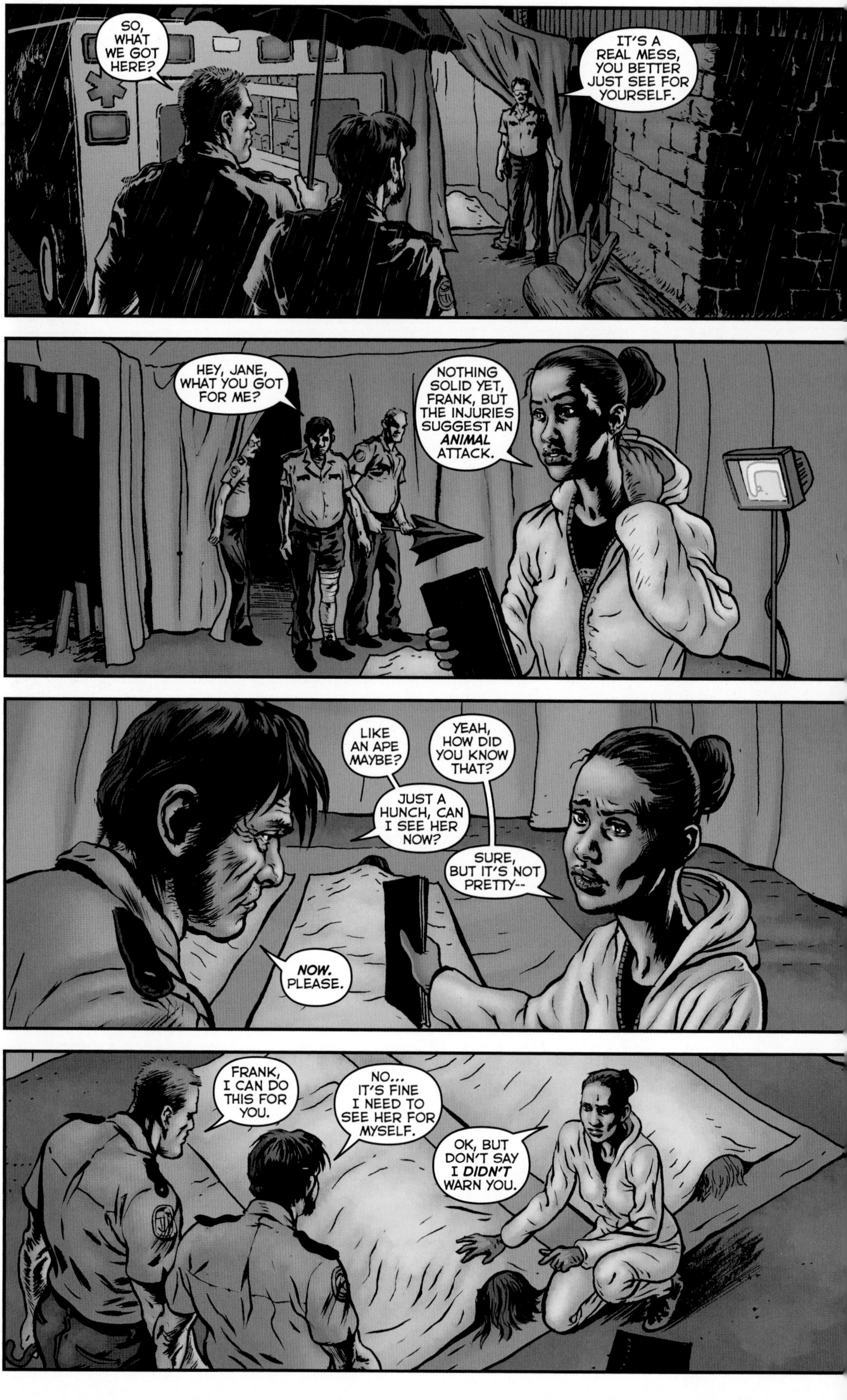
SO, WHAT WE GOT HERE?
IT'S A REAL MESS, YOU BETTER JUST SEE FOR YOURSELF.
HEY, JANE, WHAT YOU GOT FOR ME?
NOTHING SOLID YET, FRANK, BUT THE INJURIES SUGGEST AN *ANIMAL* ATTACK.
LIKE AN APE MAYBE?
YEAH, HOW DID YOU KNOW THAT?
JUST A HUNCH, CAN I SEE HER NOW?
SURE, BUT IT'S NOT PRETTY--
NOW. PLEASE.
FRANK, I CAN DO THIS FOR YOU.
NO... IT'S FINE I NEED TO SEE HER FOR MYSELF.
OK, BUT DON'T SAY I *DIDN'T* WARN YOU.

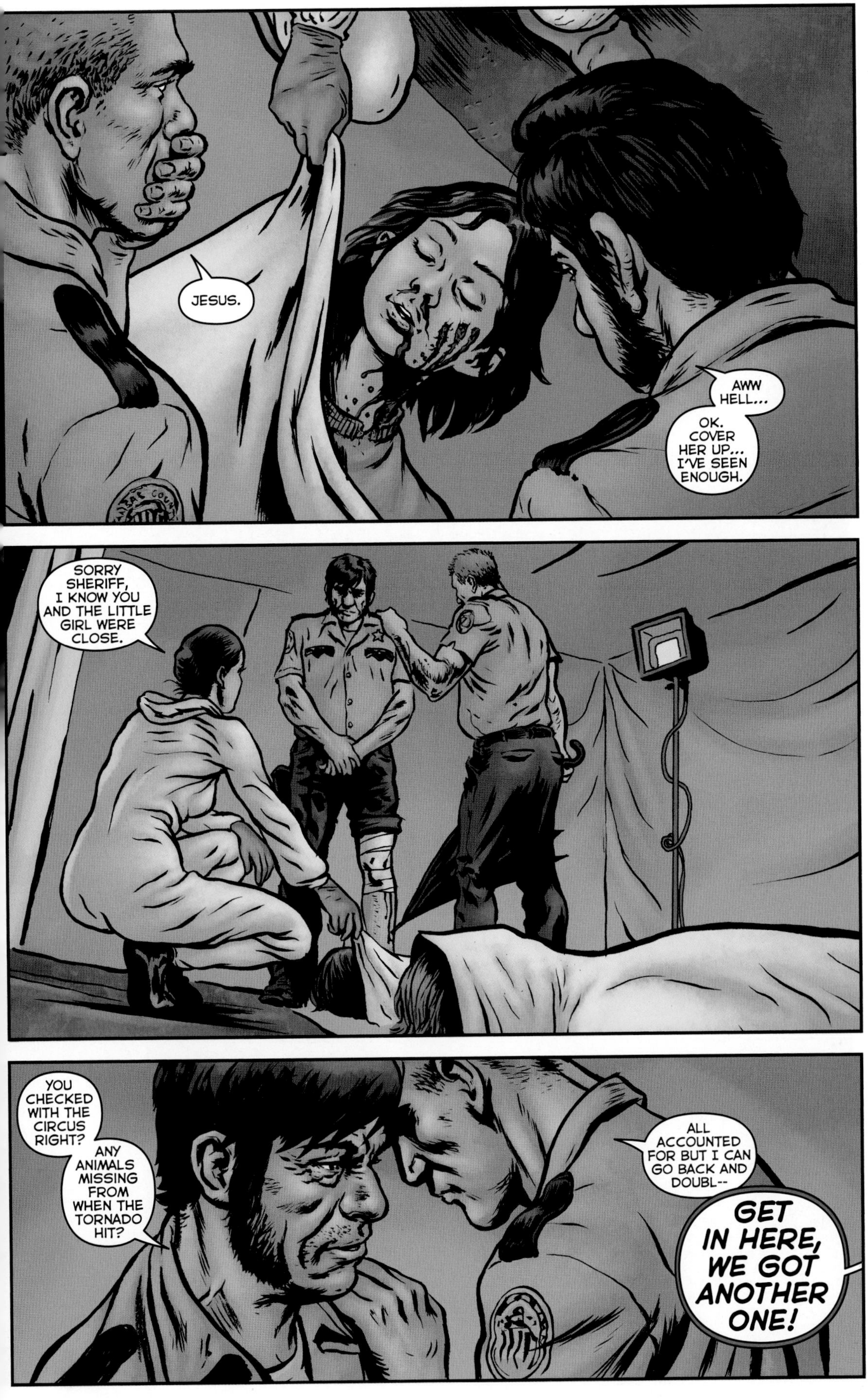
JESUS.
AWW HELL...
OK. COVER HER UP... I'VE SEEN ENOUGH.
SORRY SHERIFF, I KNOW YOU AND THE LITTLE GIRL WERE CLOSE.
YOU CHECKED WITH THE CIRCUS RIGHT?
ANY ANIMALS MISSING FROM WHEN THE TORNADO HIT?
ALL ACCOUNTED FOR BUT I CAN GO BACK AND DOUBL--
GET IN HERE, WE GOT ANOTHER ONE!

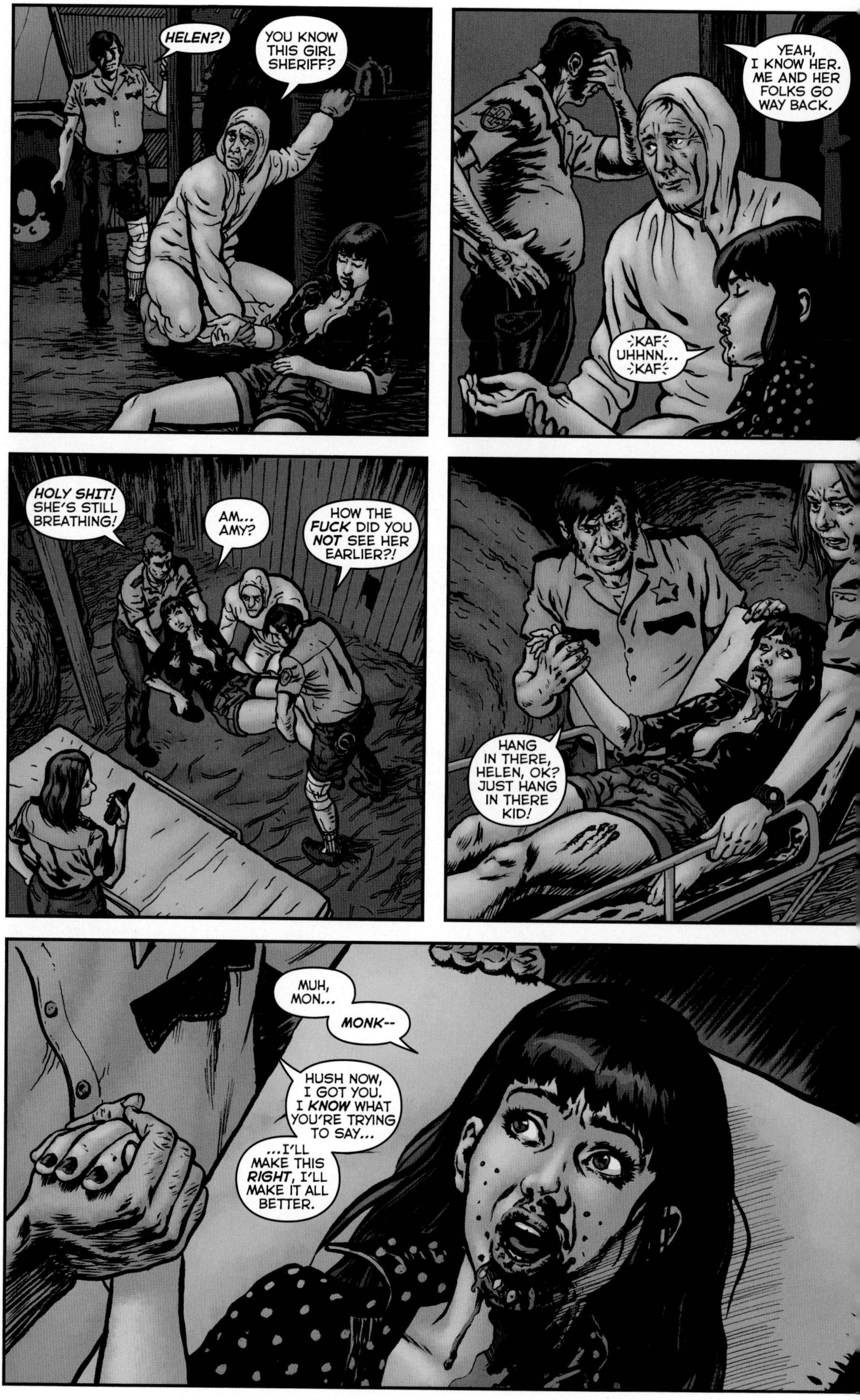
HELEN?!
YOU KNOW THIS GIRL SHERIFF?
YEAH, I KNOW HER. ME AND HER FOLKS GO WAY BACK.
KAF UHHNN... KAF
HOLY SHIT! SHE'S STILL BREATHING!
AM... AMY?
HOW THE FUCK DID YOU NOT SEE HER EARLIER?!
HANG IN THERE, HELEN, OK? JUST HANG IN THERE KID!
MUH, MON...
MONK--
HUSH NOW, I GOT YOU. I KNOW WHAT YOU'RE TRYING TO SAY...
...I'LL MAKE THIS RIGHT, I'LL MAKE IT ALL BETTER.

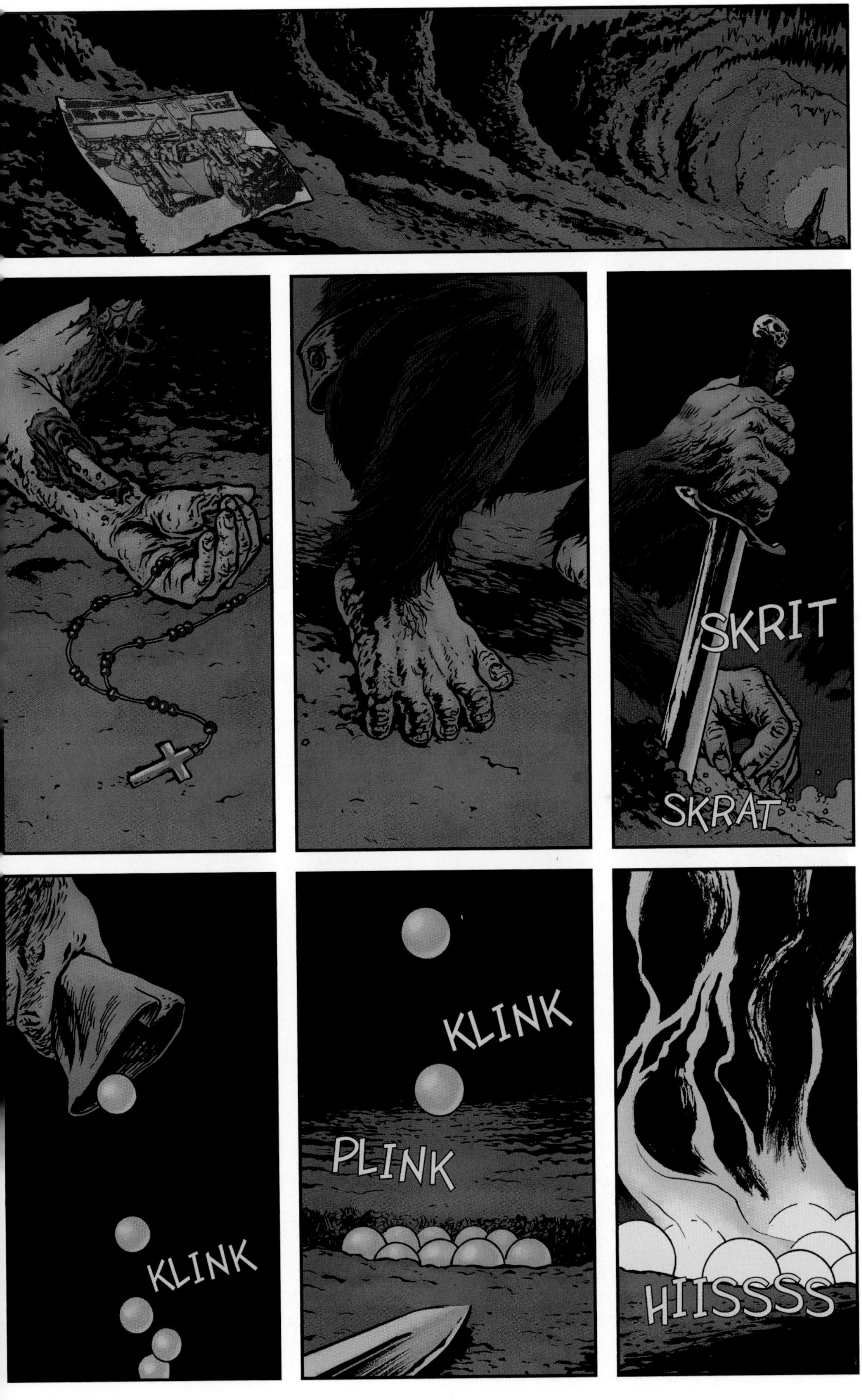
SKRIT
SKRAT
KLINK
KLINK
PLINK
HIISSSS

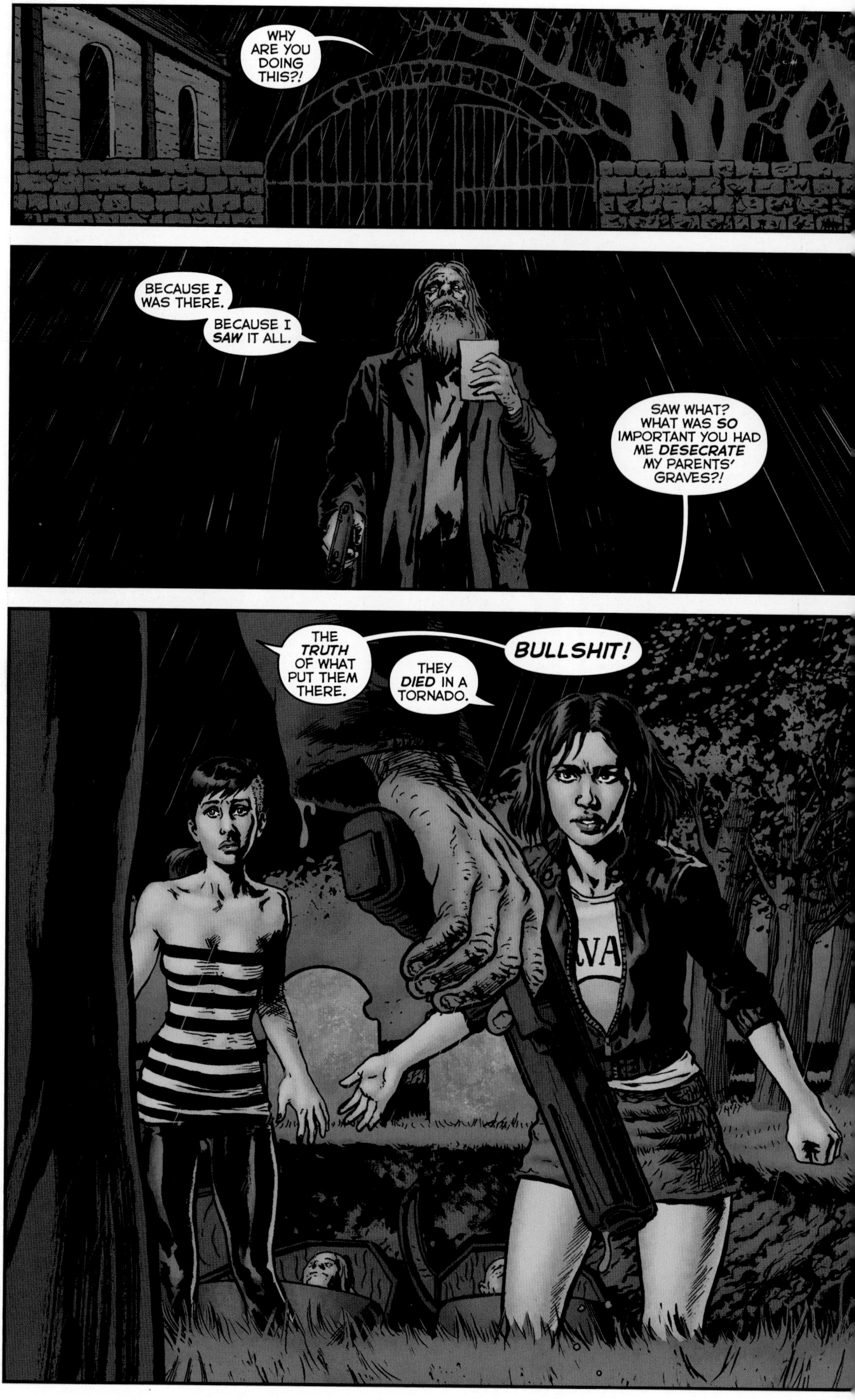
WHY ARE YOU DOING THIS?!
CEMETERY
BECAUSE *I* WAS THERE.
BECAUSE I *SAW* IT ALL.
SAW WHAT? WHAT WAS **SO** IMPORTANT YOU HAD ME ***DESECRATE*** MY PARENTS' GRAVES?!
THE *TRUTH* OF WHAT PUT THEM THERE.
BULLSHIT!
THEY *DIED* IN A TORNADO.

I WAS SLEEPING IN THE BARN WHEN THE WINDS CAME.

YOU MEAN *DRINKING*.

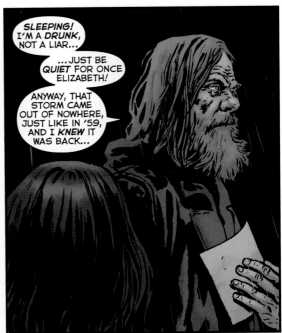

SLEEPING! I'M A *DRUNK*, NOT A *LIAR*...

...JUST BE *QUIET* FOR ONCE ELIZABETH!

ANYWAY, THAT STORM CAME OUT OF NOWHERE, JUST LIKE IN '59, AND I *KNEW* IT WAS BACK...

...IT'S THE SULPHUR IN THE AIR, GETS IN YOUR NOSE, Y'CAN TASTE IT.

AND WHAT'S THIS GOT TO DO WITH MY MOM AND DAD?

ONCE I SAW IT STEP OUTTA THE WINDS I FROZE....

...I, I COULDN'T DO *ANYTHING* TO STOP IT, NOT A THING!

STOP WHAT?!

DON'T YOU SEE? DON'T YOU GET IT?

THE *DEVIL* CAME TO KANSAS!

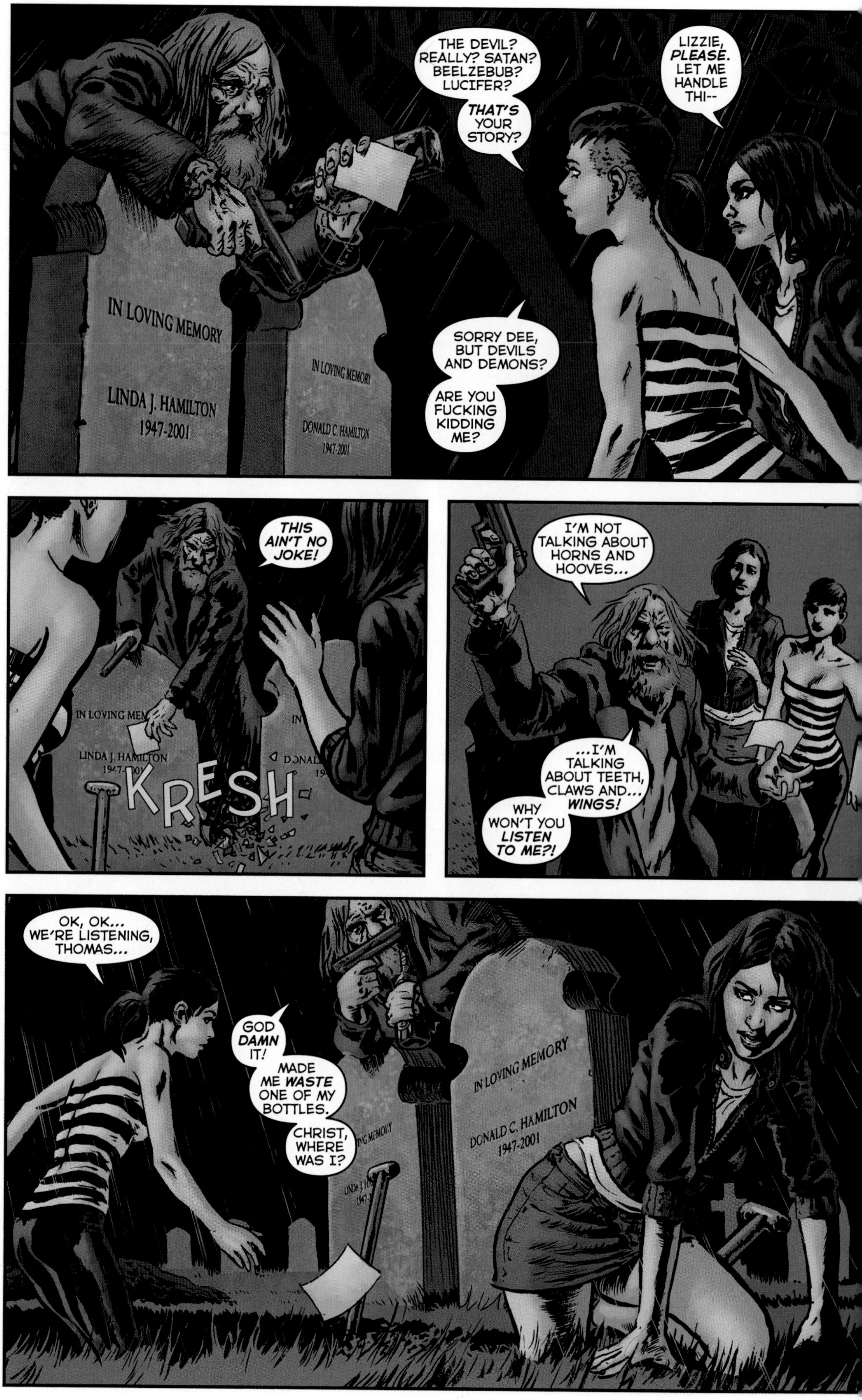
IN LOVING MEMORY
LINDA J. HAMILTON
1947-2001
IN LOVING MEMORY
DONALD C. HAMILTON
1947-2001
THE DEVIL? REALLY? SATAN? BEELZEBUB? LUCIFER?
THAT'S YOUR STORY?
LIZZIE, PLEASE. LET ME HANDLE THI--
SORRY DEE, BUT DEVILS AND DEMONS?
ARE YOU FUCKING KIDDING ME?
THIS AIN'T NO JOKE!
KRESH
I'M NOT TALKING ABOUT HORNS AND HOOVES...
...I'M TALKING ABOUT TEETH, CLAWS AND... WINGS!
WHY WON'T YOU LISTEN TO ME?!
OK, OK... WE'RE LISTENING, THOMAS...
GOD DAMN IT!
MADE ME WASTE ONE OF MY BOTTLES.
CHRIST, WHERE WAS I?
IN LOVING MEMORY
DONALD C. HAMILTON
1947-2001

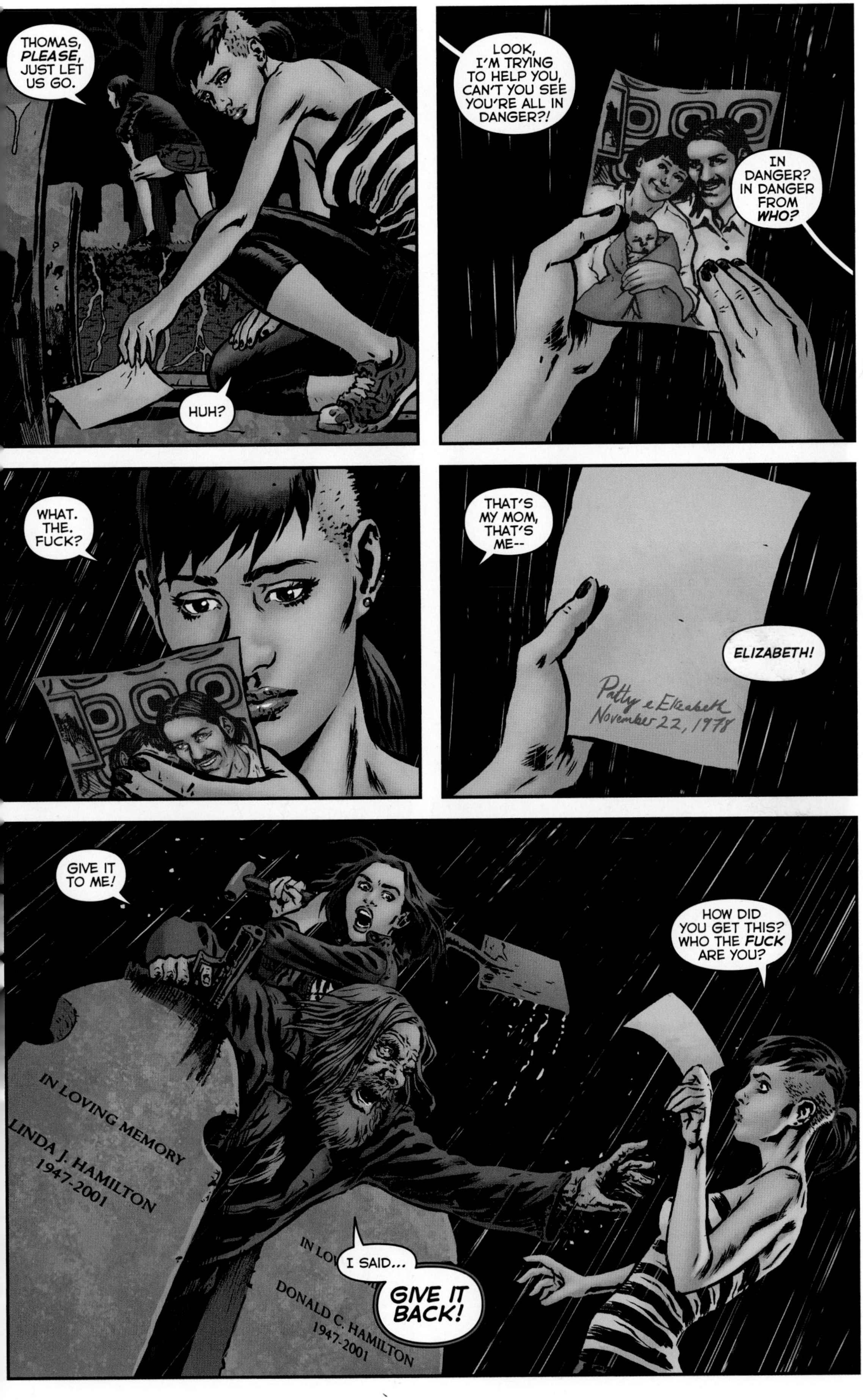
THOMAS, PLEASE, JUST LET US GO.
HUH?
LOOK, I'M TRYING TO HELP YOU, CAN'T YOU SEE YOU'RE ALL IN DANGER?!
IN DANGER? IN DANGER FROM WHO?
WHAT. THE. FUCK?
THAT'S MY MOM, THAT'S ME--
ELIZABETH!
Patty e Elizabeth November 22, 1978
GIVE IT TO ME!
HOW DID YOU GET THIS? WHO THE FUCK ARE YOU?
IN LOVING MEMORY
LINDA J. HAMILTON
1947-2001
I SAID...
GIVE IT BACK!
DONALD C. HAMILTON
1947-2001

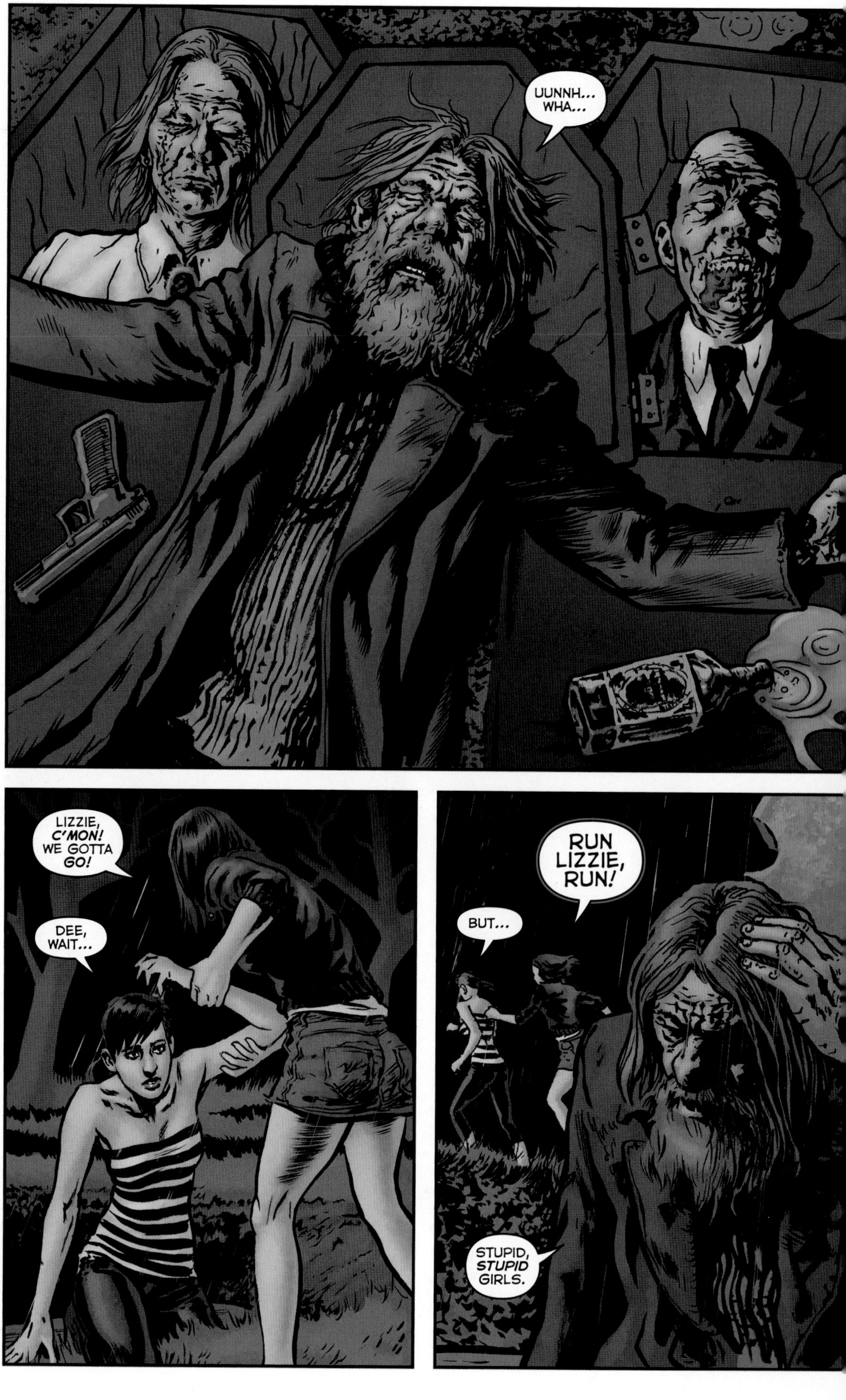
UUNNH... WHA...
LIZZIE, C'MON! WE GOTTA GO!
DEE, WAIT...
RUN LIZZIE, RUN!
BUT...
STUPID, STUPID GIRLS.

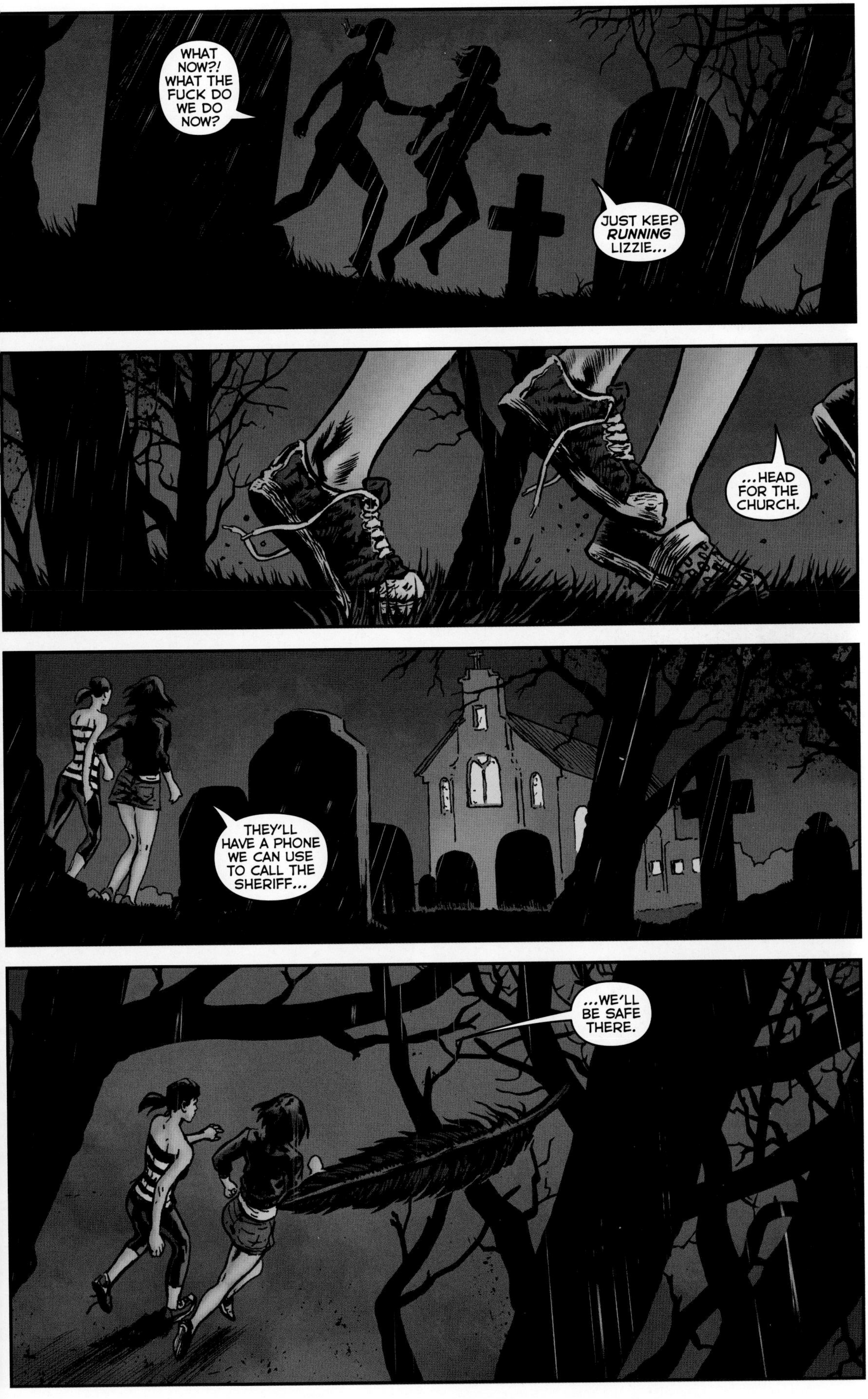
WHAT NOW?! WHAT THE FUCK DO WE DO NOW?
JUST KEEP RUNNING LIZZIE...
...HEAD FOR THE CHURCH.
THEY'LL HAVE A PHONE WE CAN USE TO CALL THE SHERIFF...
...WE'LL BE SAFE THERE.

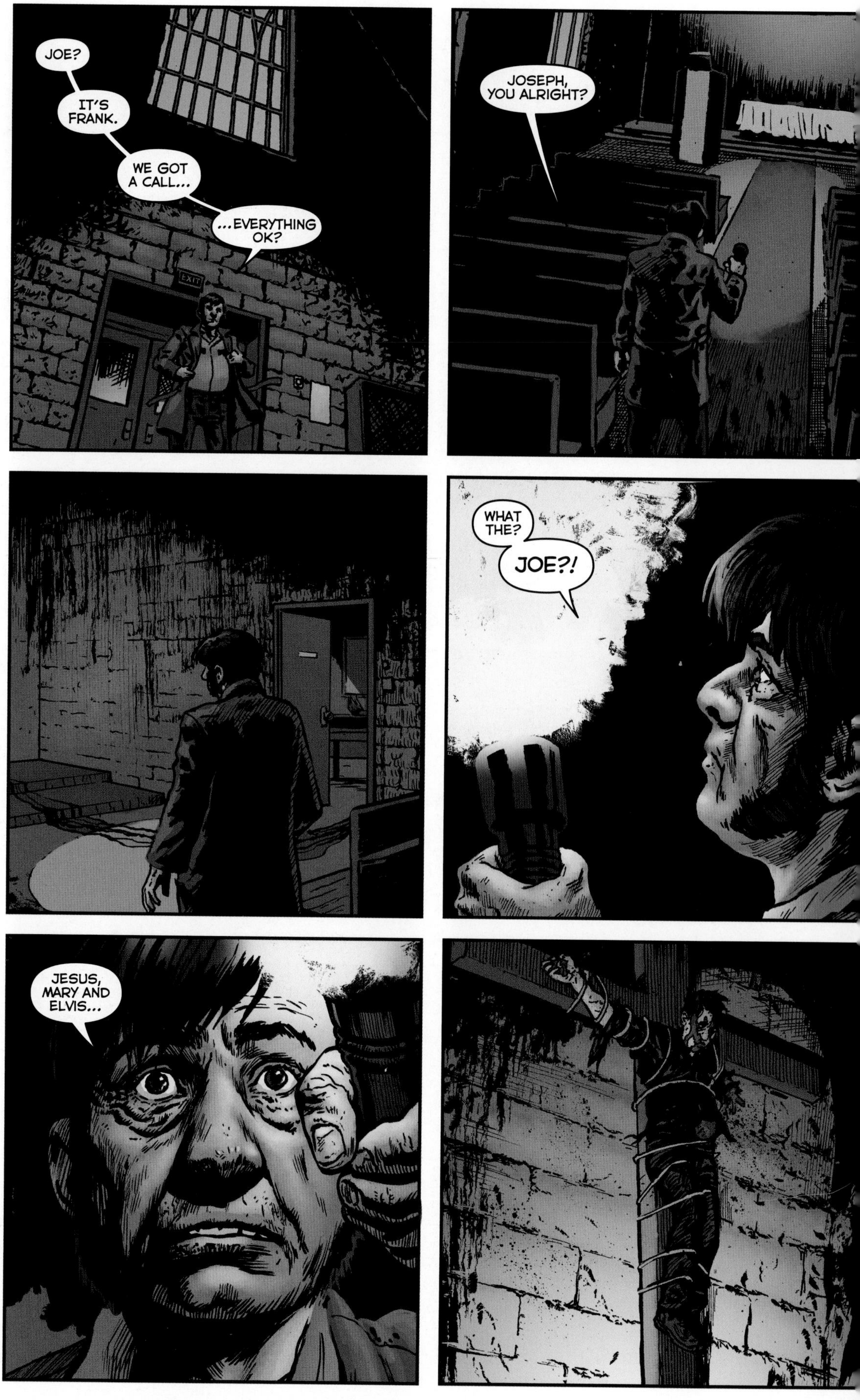
JOE?
IT'S FRANK.
WE GOT A CALL...
...EVERYTHING OK?
JOSEPH, YOU ALRIGHT?
WHAT THE?
JOE?!
JESUS, MARY AND ELVIS...

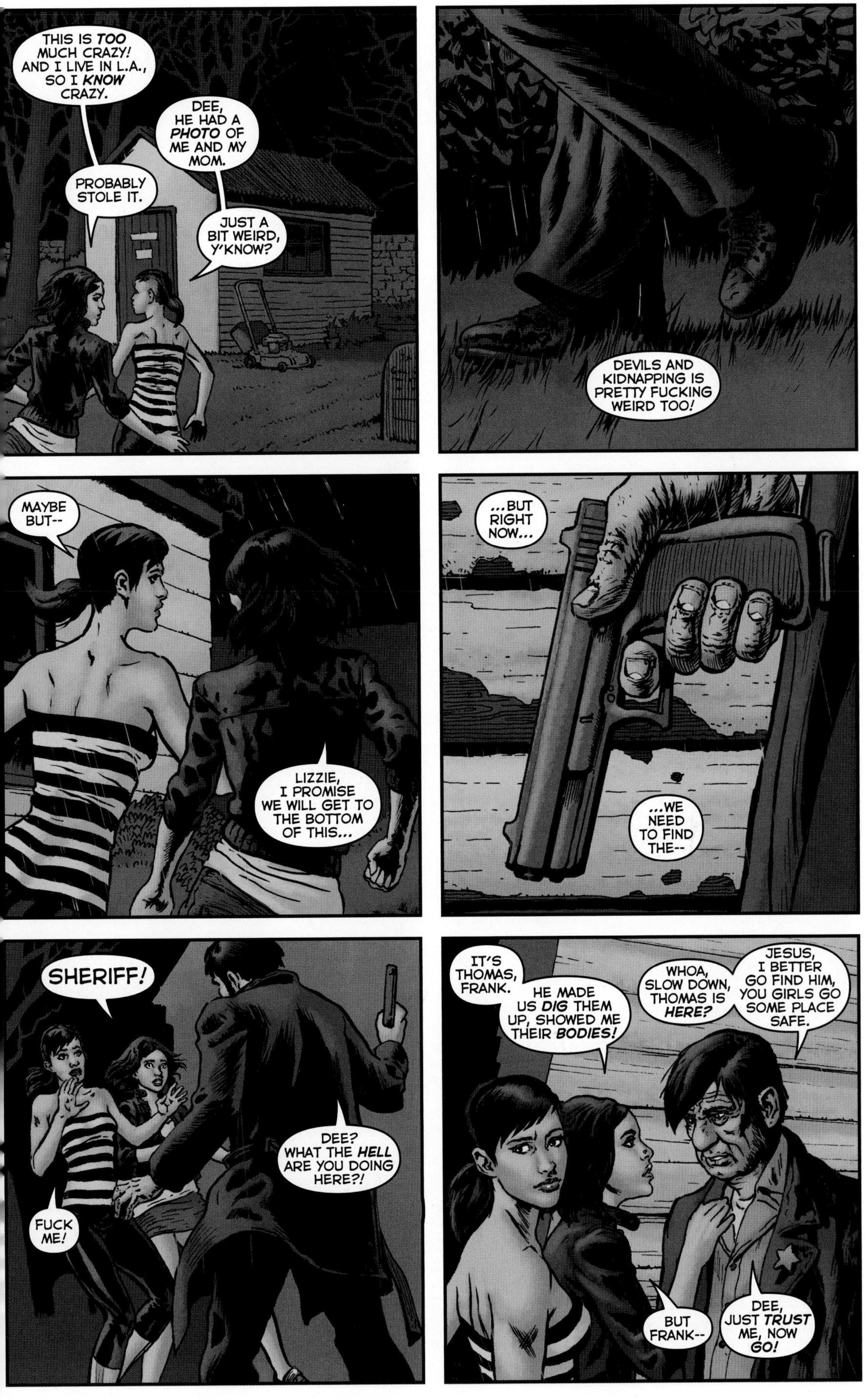

THIS IS TOO MUCH CRAZY! AND I LIVE IN L.A., SO I KNOW CRAZY.
DEE, HE HAD A PHOTO OF ME AND MY MOM.
PROBABLY STOLE IT.
JUST A BIT WEIRD, Y'KNOW?
DEVILS AND KIDNAPPING IS PRETTY FUCKING WEIRD TOO!
MAYBE BUT--
LIZZIE, I PROMISE WE WILL GET TO THE BOTTOM OF THIS...
...BUT RIGHT NOW...
...WE NEED TO FIND THE--
SHERIFF!
DEE? WHAT THE HELL ARE YOU DOING HERE?!
FUCK ME!
IT'S THOMAS, FRANK.
HE MADE US DIG THEM UP, SHOWED ME THEIR BODIES!
WHOA, SLOW DOWN, THOMAS IS HERE?
JESUS, I BETTER GO FIND HIM, YOU GIRLS GO SOME PLACE SAFE.
BUT FRANK--
DEE, JUST TRUST ME, NOW GO!

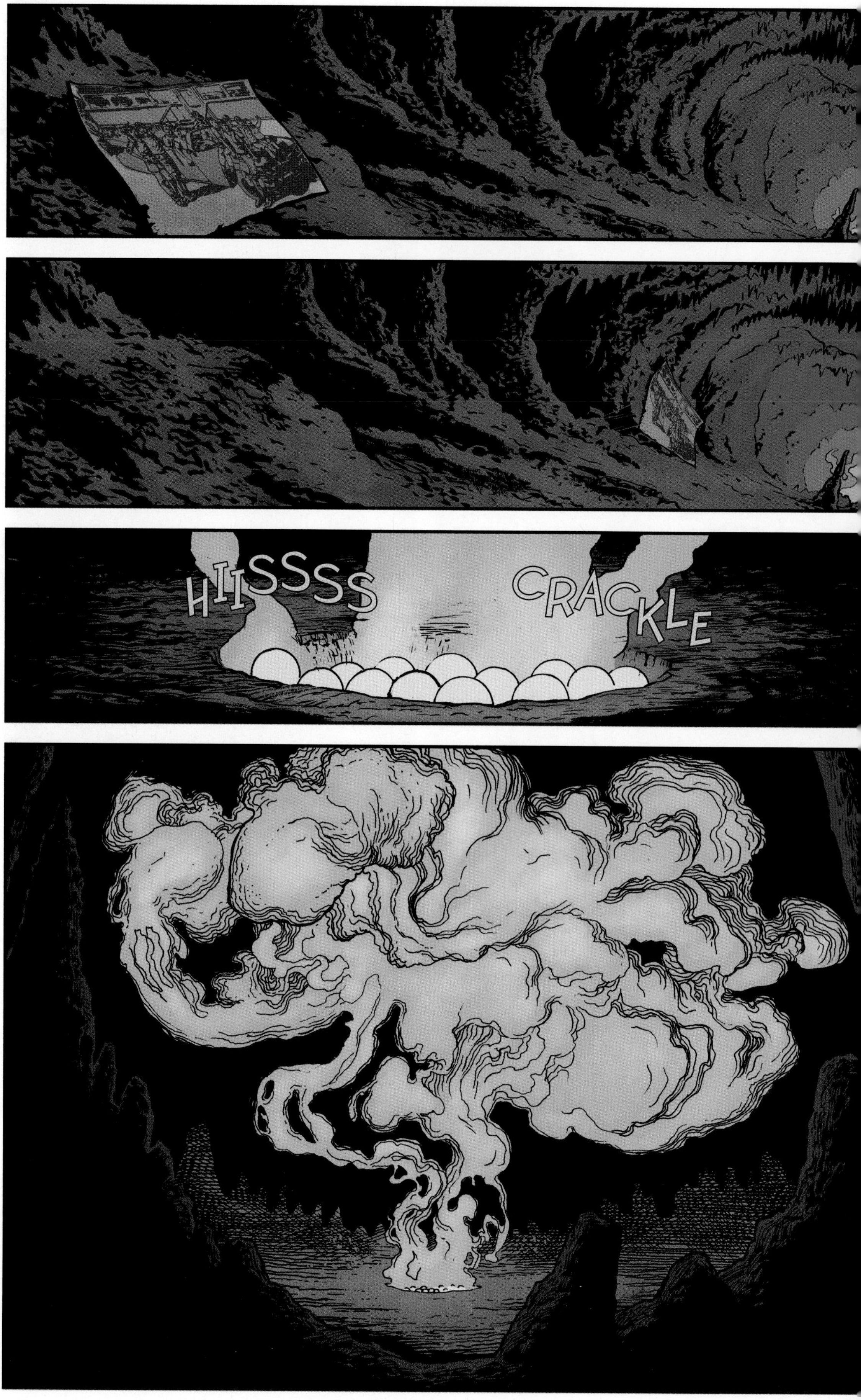
HIISSSS
CRACKLE

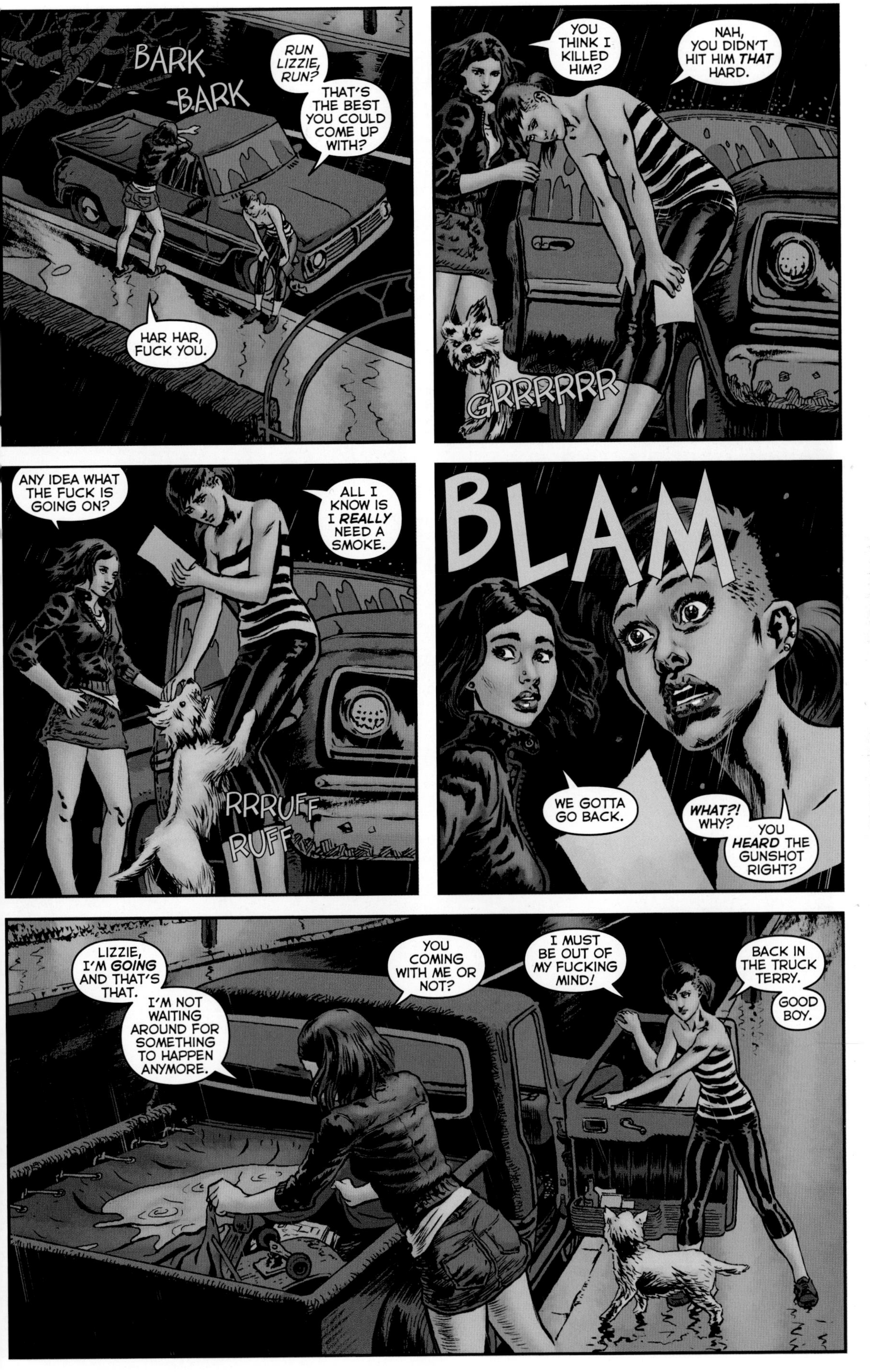
BARK
BARK
RUN LIZZIE, RUN?
THAT'S THE BEST YOU COULD COME UP WITH?
HAR HAR, FUCK YOU.
YOU THINK I KILLED HIM?
NAH, YOU DIDN'T HIT HIM THAT HARD.
GRRRRRR
ANY IDEA WHAT THE FUCK IS GOING ON?
ALL I KNOW IS I REALLY NEED A SMOKE.
RRRUFF
RUFF
BLAM
WE GOTTA GO BACK.
WHAT?! WHY?
YOU HEARD THE GUNSHOT RIGHT?
LIZZIE, I'M GOING AND THAT'S THAT.
I'M NOT WAITING AROUND FOR SOMETHING TO HAPPEN ANYMORE.
YOU COMING WITH ME OR NOT?
I MUST BE OUT OF MY FUCKING MIND!
BACK IN THE TRUCK TERRY.
GOOD BOY.

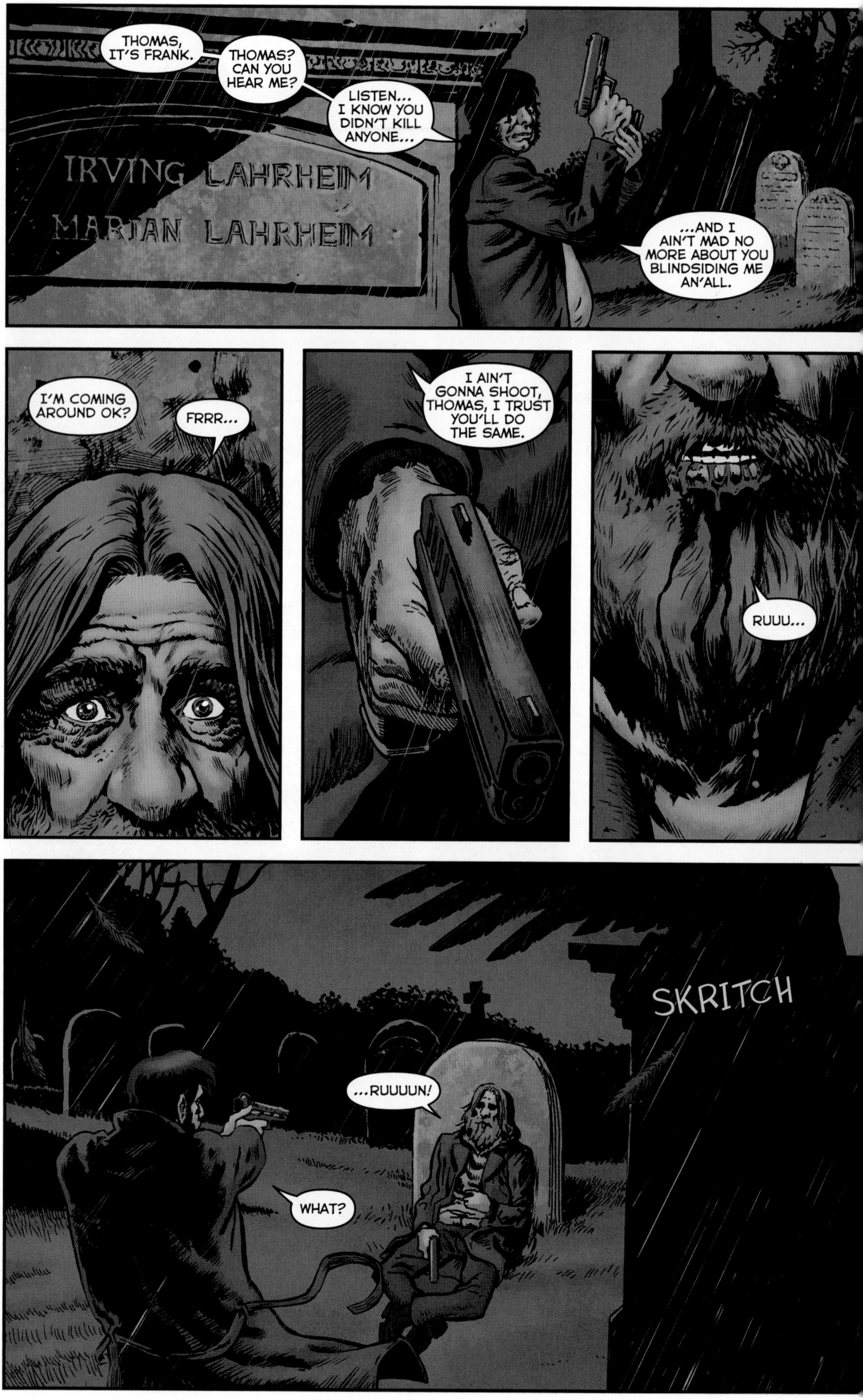
THOMAS, IT'S FRANK.
THOMAS? CAN YOU HEAR ME?
LISTEN... I KNOW YOU DIDN'T KILL ANYONE...
IRVING LAHRHEIM
MARJAN LAHRHEIM
...AND I AIN'T MAD NO MORE ABOUT YOU BLINDSIDING ME AN'ALL.
I'M COMING AROUND OK?
FRRR...
I AIN'T GONNA SHOOT, THOMAS, I TRUST YOU'LL DO THE SAME.
RUUU...
SKRITCH
...RUUUUN!
WHAT?

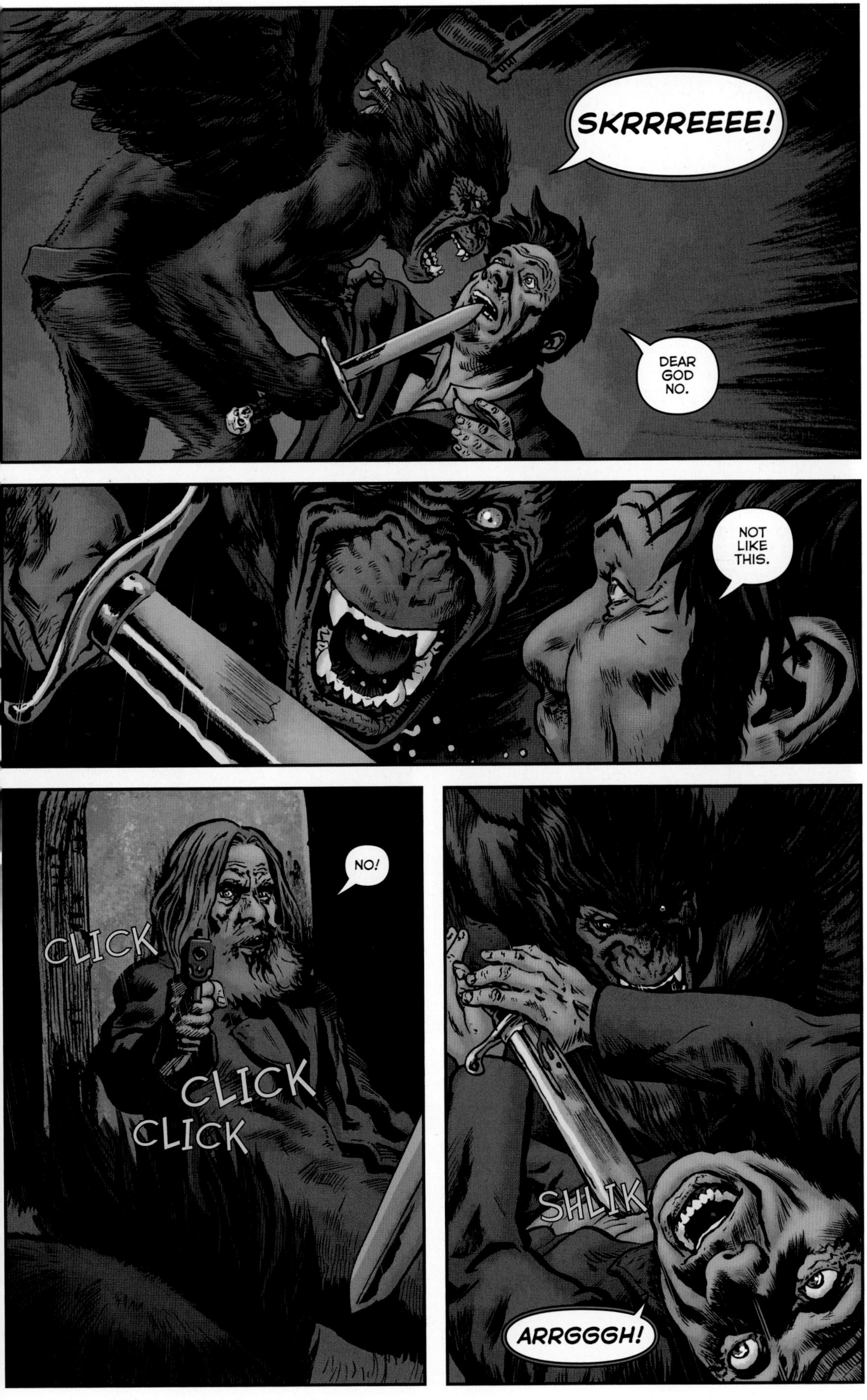
SKRRREEEE!
DEAR GOD NO.
NOT LIKE THIS.
NO!
CLICK
CLICK
CLICK
SHLIK
ARRGGGH!

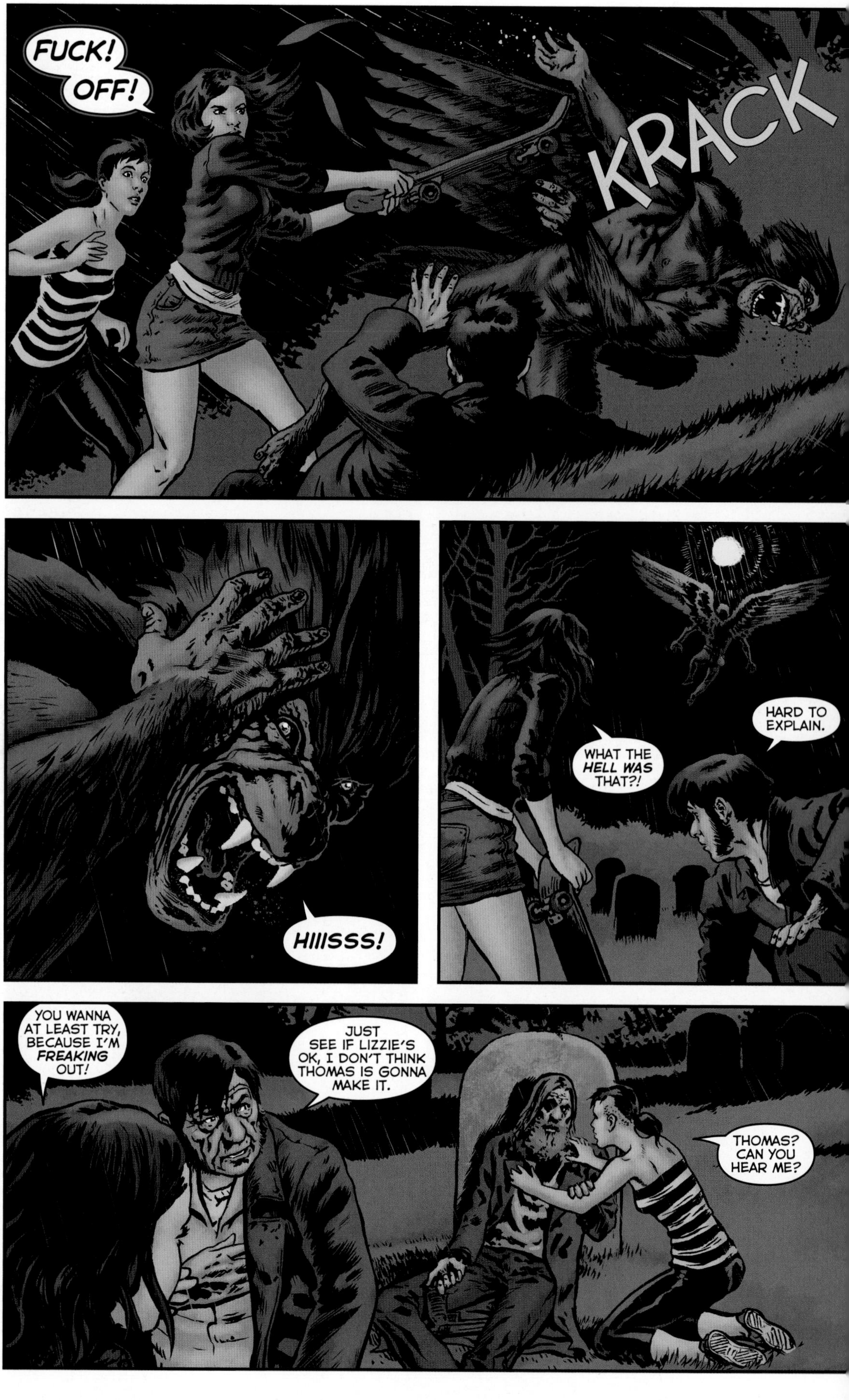
FUCK! OFF!
KRACK
HIIISSS!
WHAT THE HELL WAS THAT?!
HARD TO EXPLAIN.
YOU WANNA AT LEAST TRY, BECAUSE I'M FREAKING OUT!
JUST SEE IF LIZZIE'S OK, I DON'T THINK THOMAS IS GONNA MAKE IT.
THOMAS? CAN YOU HEAR ME?

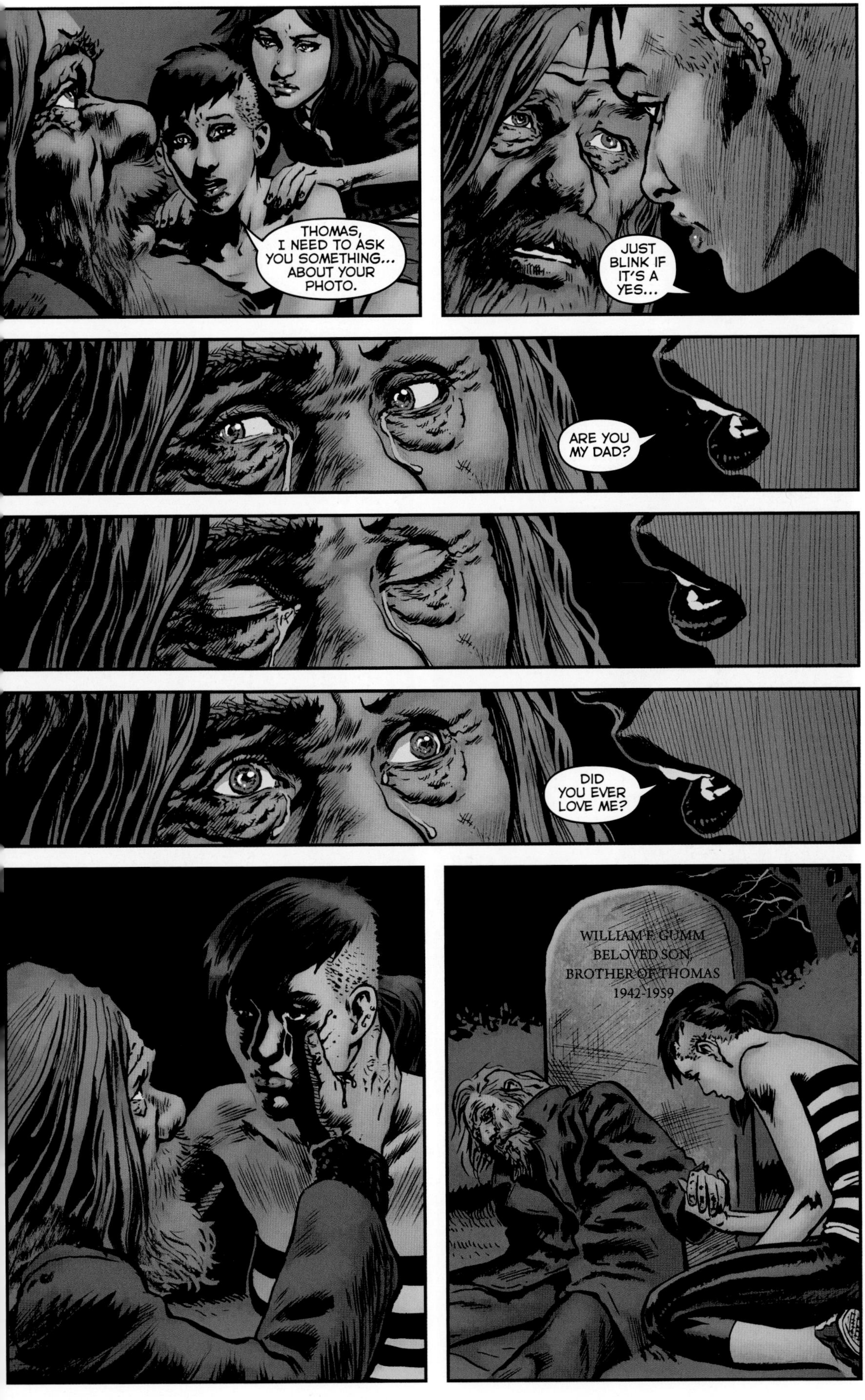
THOMAS, I NEED TO ASK YOU SOMETHING... ABOUT YOUR PHOTO.
JUST BLINK IF IT'S A YES...
ARE YOU MY DAD?
DID YOU EVER LOVE ME?
WILLIAM F. GUMM
BELOVED SON,
BROTHER OF THOMAS
1942-1959

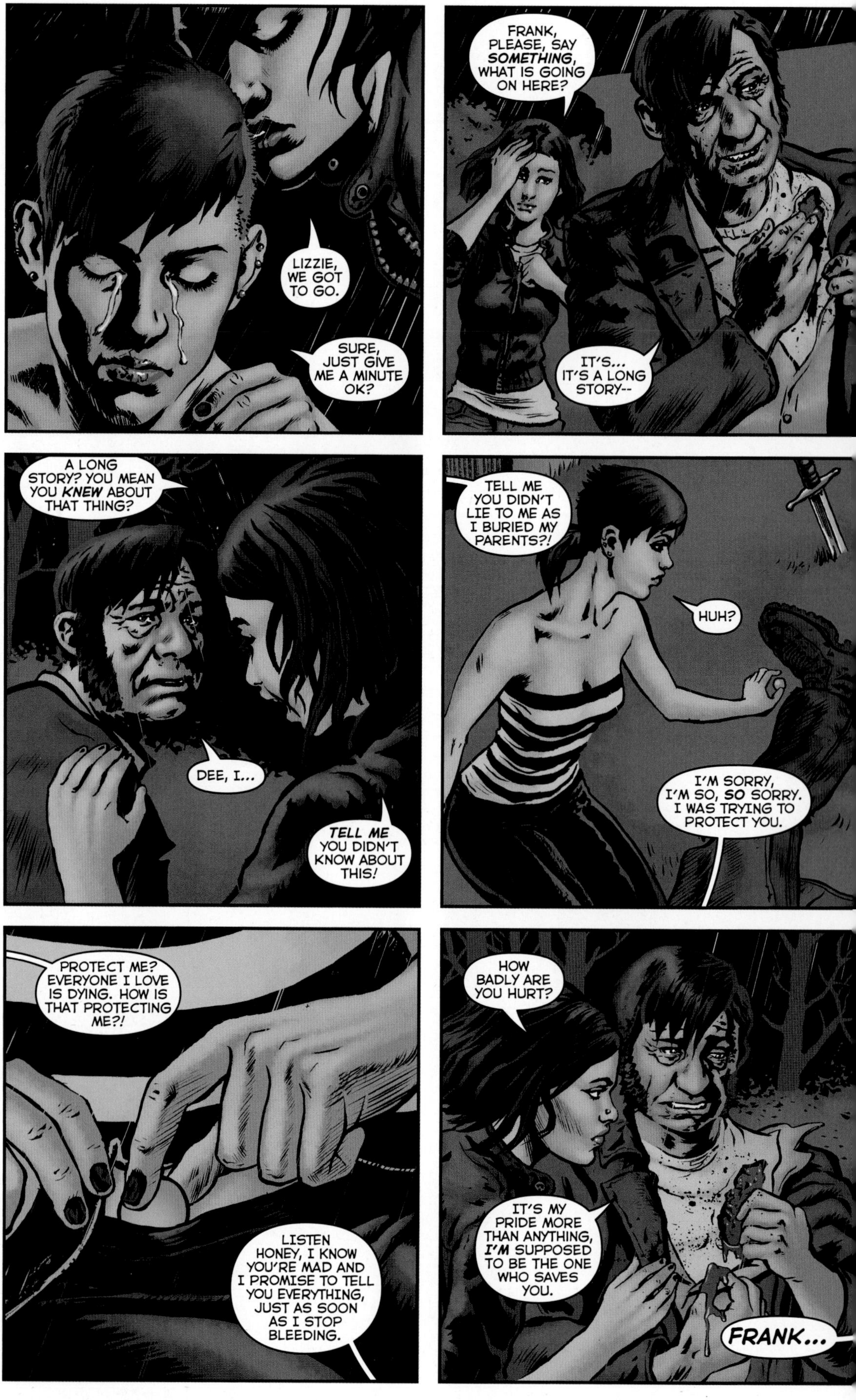
LIZZIE, WE GOT TO GO.
SURE, JUST GIVE ME A MINUTE OK?
FRANK, PLEASE, SAY *SOMETHING*, WHAT IS GOING ON HERE?
IT'S... IT'S A LONG STORY--
A LONG STORY? YOU MEAN YOU *KNEW* ABOUT THAT THING?
DEE, I...
TELL ME YOU DIDN'T KNOW ABOUT THIS!
TELL ME YOU DIDN'T LIE TO ME AS I BURIED MY PARENTS?!
HUH?
I'M SORRY, I'M SO, *SO* SORRY. I WAS TRYING TO PROTECT YOU.
PROTECT ME? EVERYONE I LOVE IS DYING. HOW IS THAT PROTECTING ME?!
LISTEN HONEY, I KNOW YOU'RE MAD AND I PROMISE TO TELL YOU EVERYTHING, JUST AS SOON AS I STOP BLEEDING.
HOW BADLY ARE YOU HURT?
IT'S MY PRIDE MORE THAN ANYTHING, *I'M* SUPPOSED TO BE THE ONE WHO SAVES YOU.
FRANK...

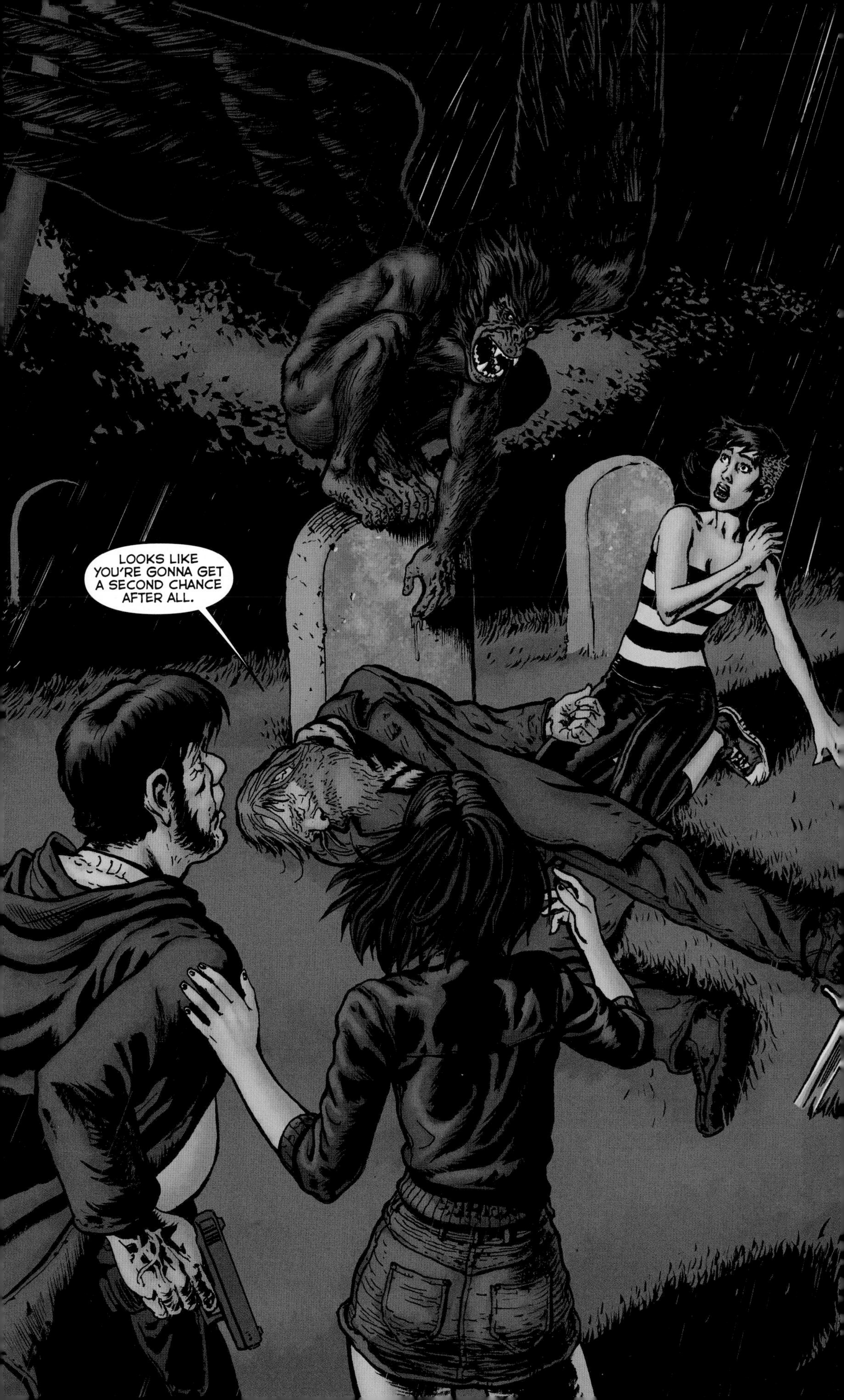
LOOKS LIKE YOU'RE GONNA GET A SECOND CHANCE AFTER ALL.

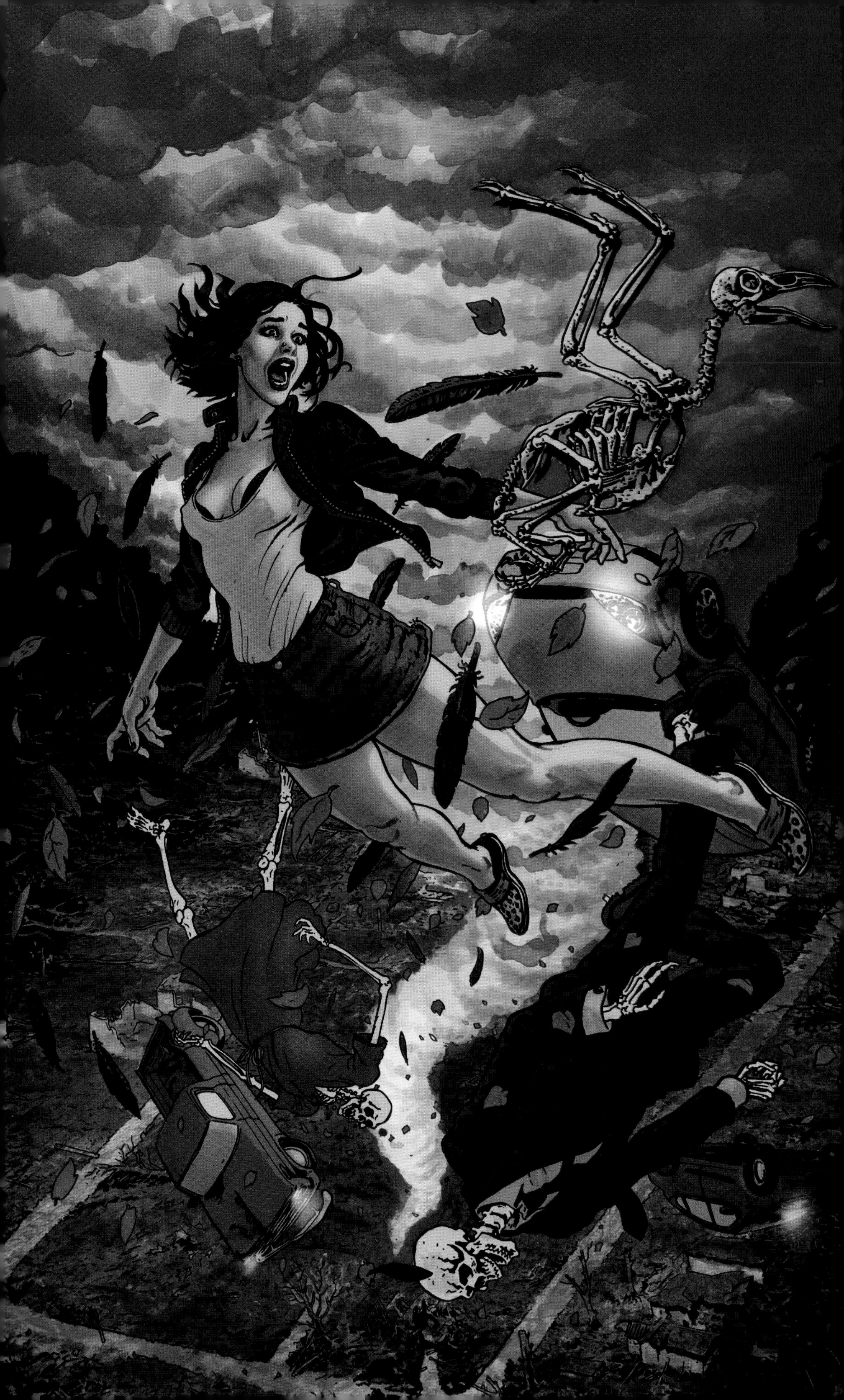

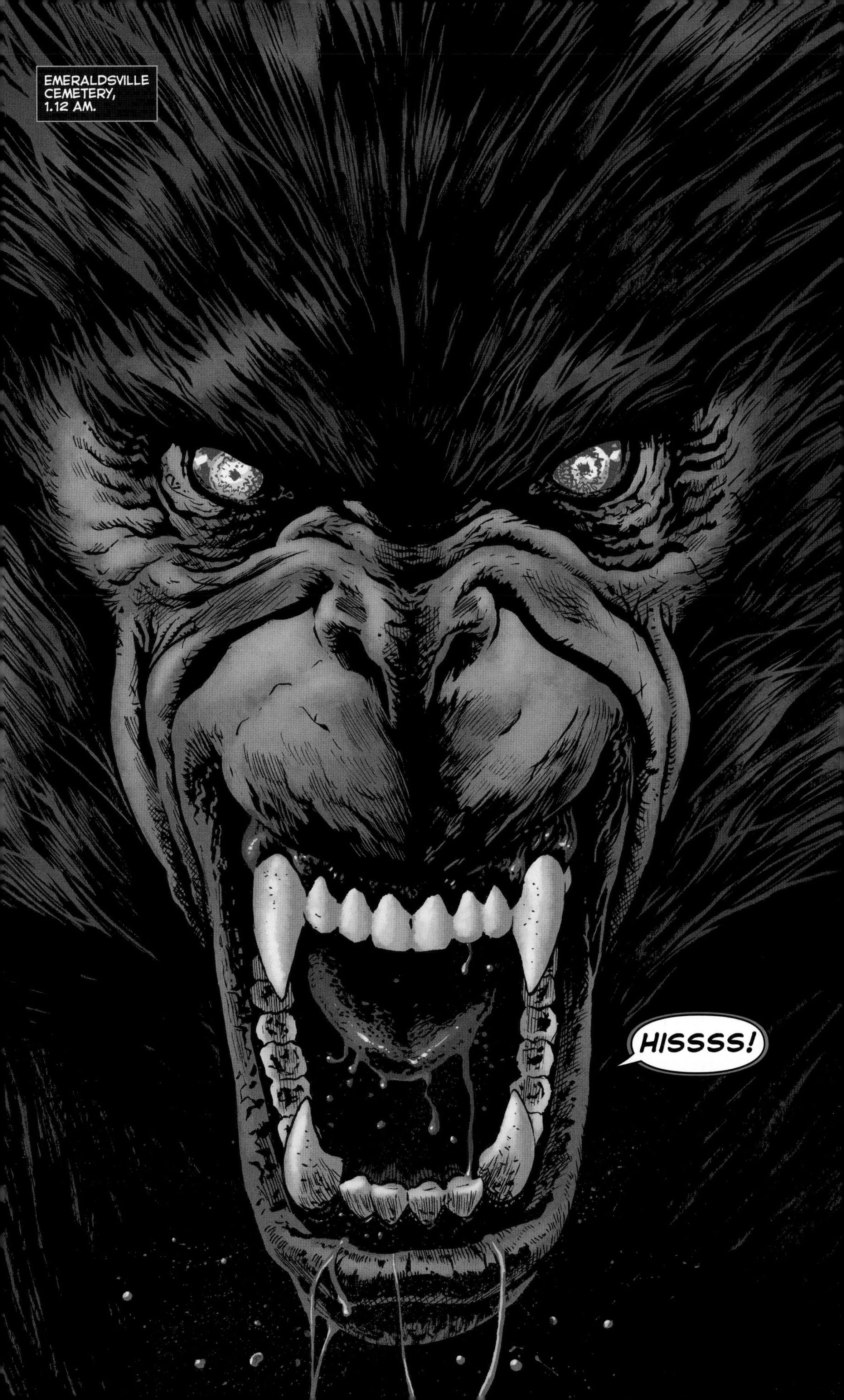
EMERALDSVILLE CEMETERY, 1.12 AM.
HISSSS!

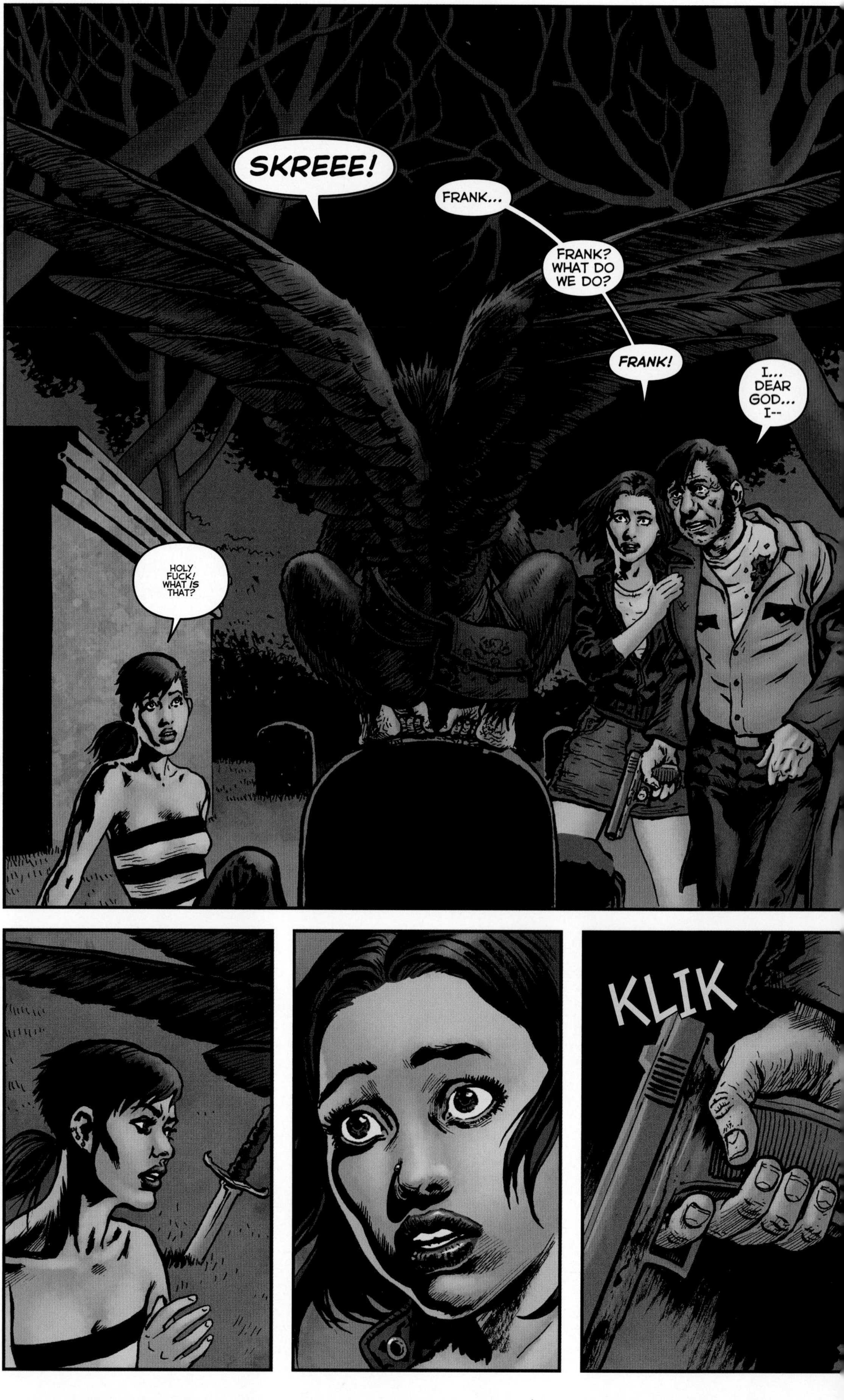
SKREEE!
FRANK...
FRANK? WHAT DO WE DO?
FRANK!
I... DEAR GOD... I--
HOLY FUCK! WHAT IS THAT?
KLIK

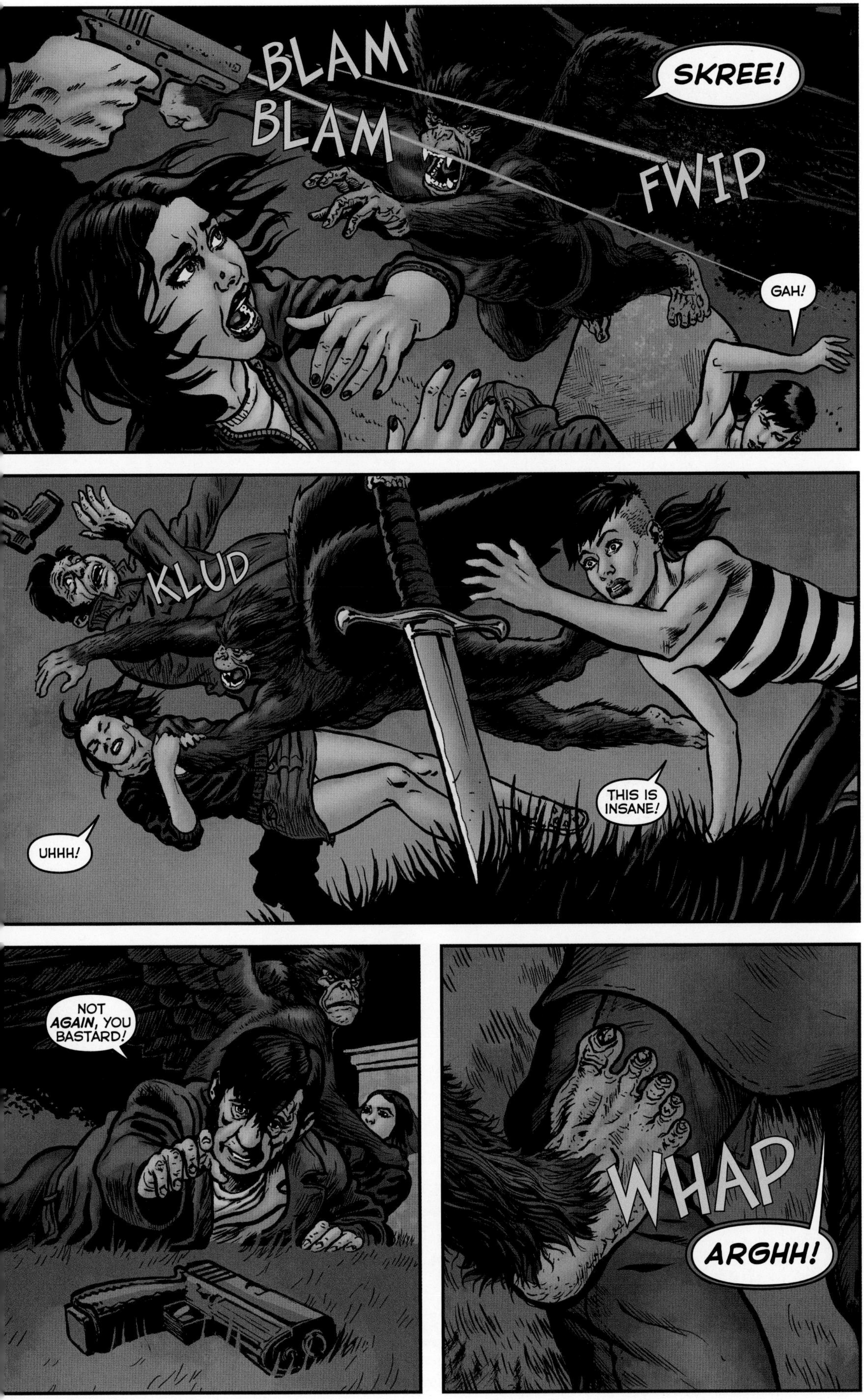
BLAM
BLAM
SKREE!
FWIP
GAH!
KLUD
THIS IS INSANE!
UHHH!
NOT AGAIN, YOU BASTARD!
WHAP
ARGHH!

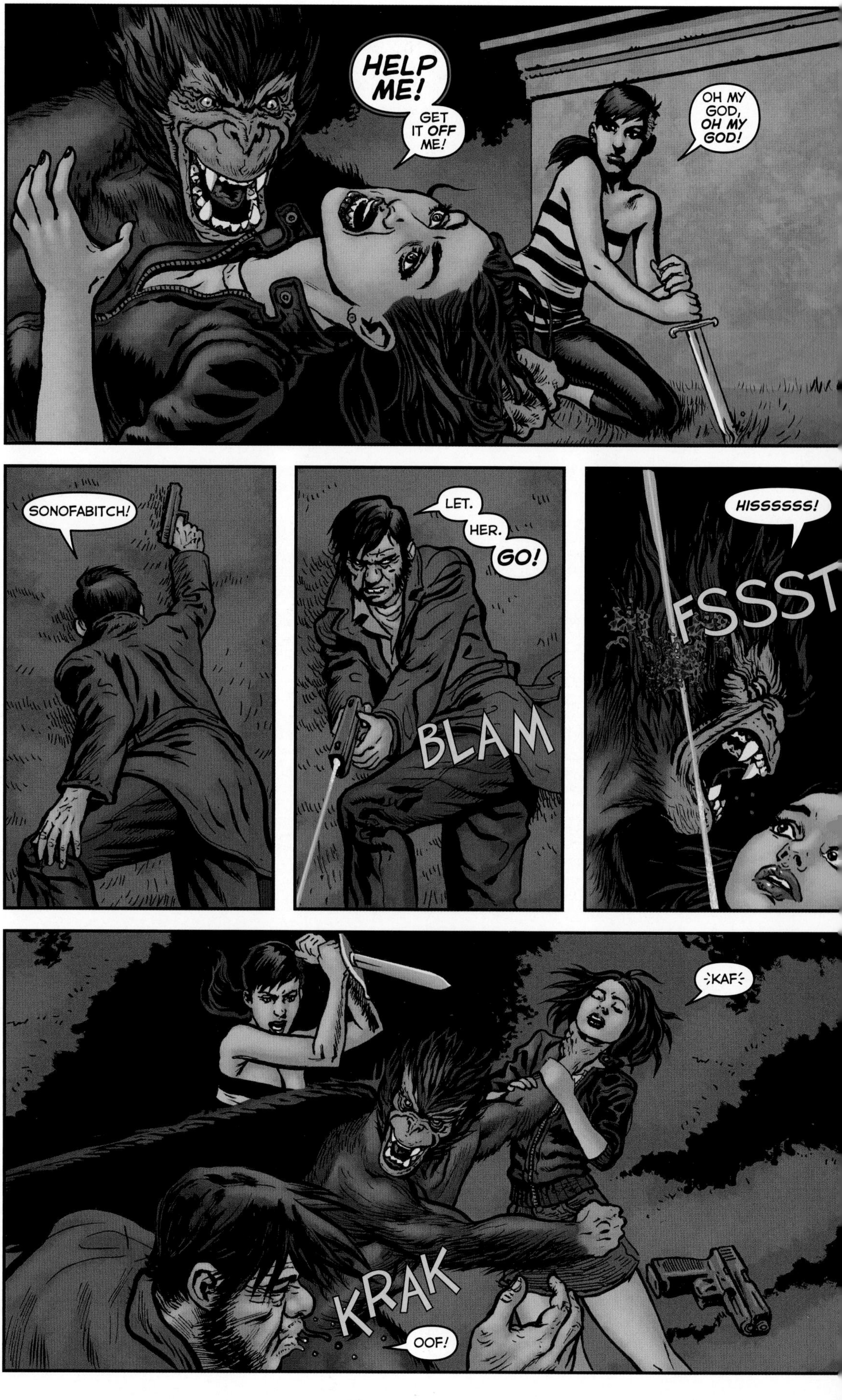
HELP ME!
GET IT OFF ME!
OH MY GOD, OH MY GOD!
SONOFABITCH!
LET. HER. GO!
BLAM
HISSSSSS!
FSSST
KAF
KRAK
OOF!

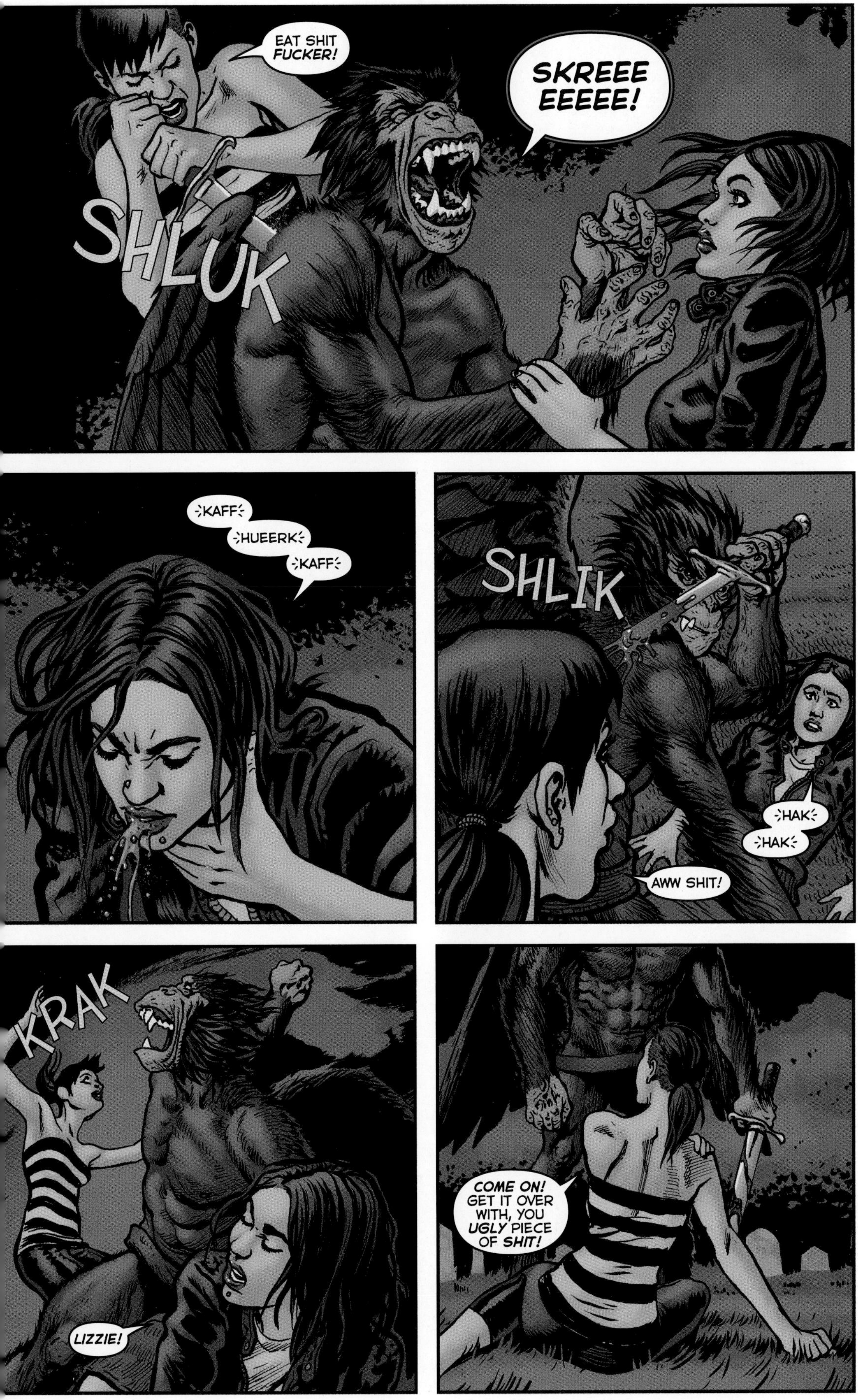
EAT SHIT FUCKER!
SKREEE EEEEE!
SHLUK
KAFF
HUEERK
KAFF
SHLIK
HAK
HAK
AWW SHIT!
KRAK
LIZZIE!
COME ON! GET IT OVER WITH, YOU UGLY PIECE OF SHIT!

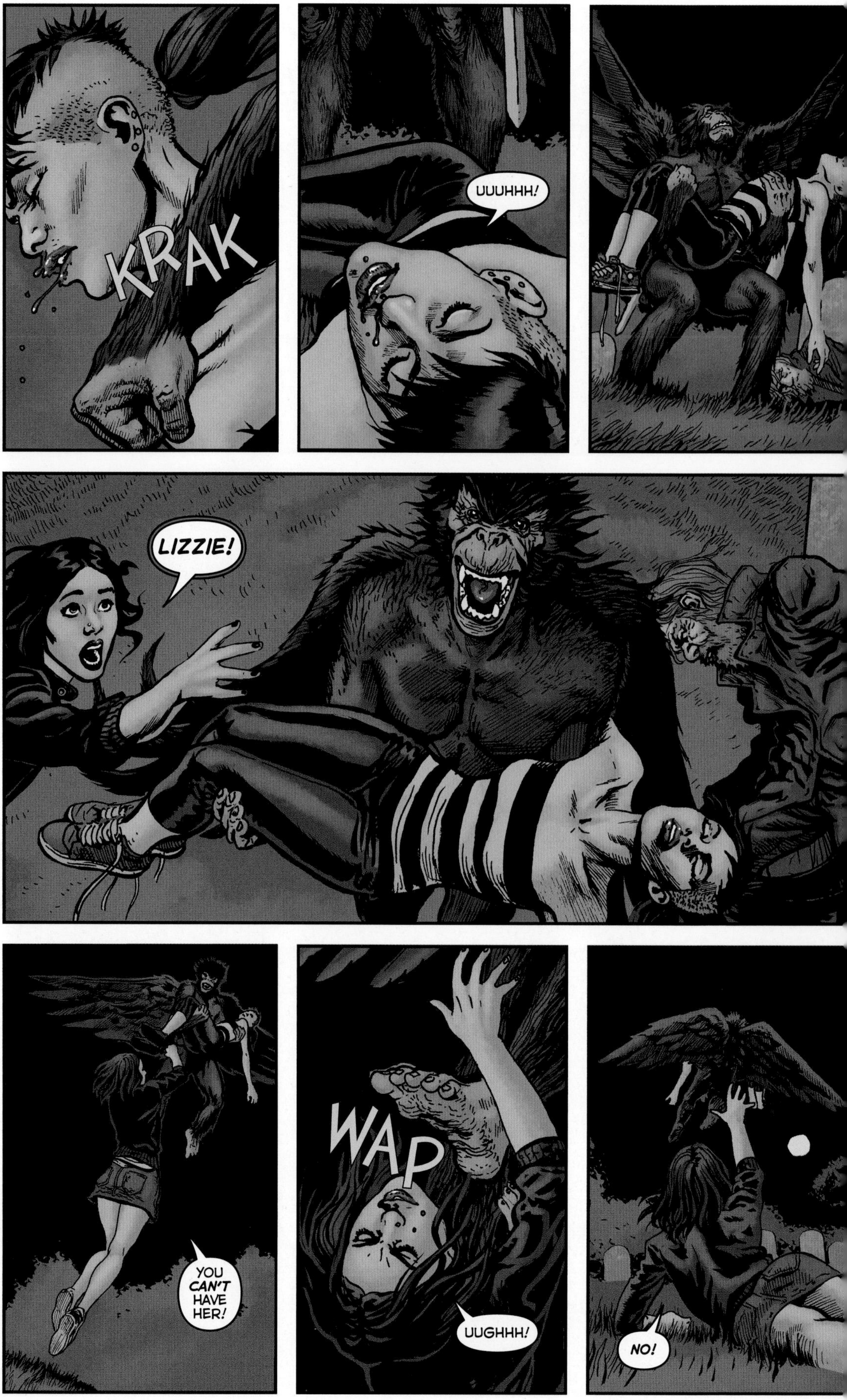
KRAK
UUUHHH!
LIZZIE!
YOU CAN'T HAVE HER!
WAP
UUGHHH!
NO!

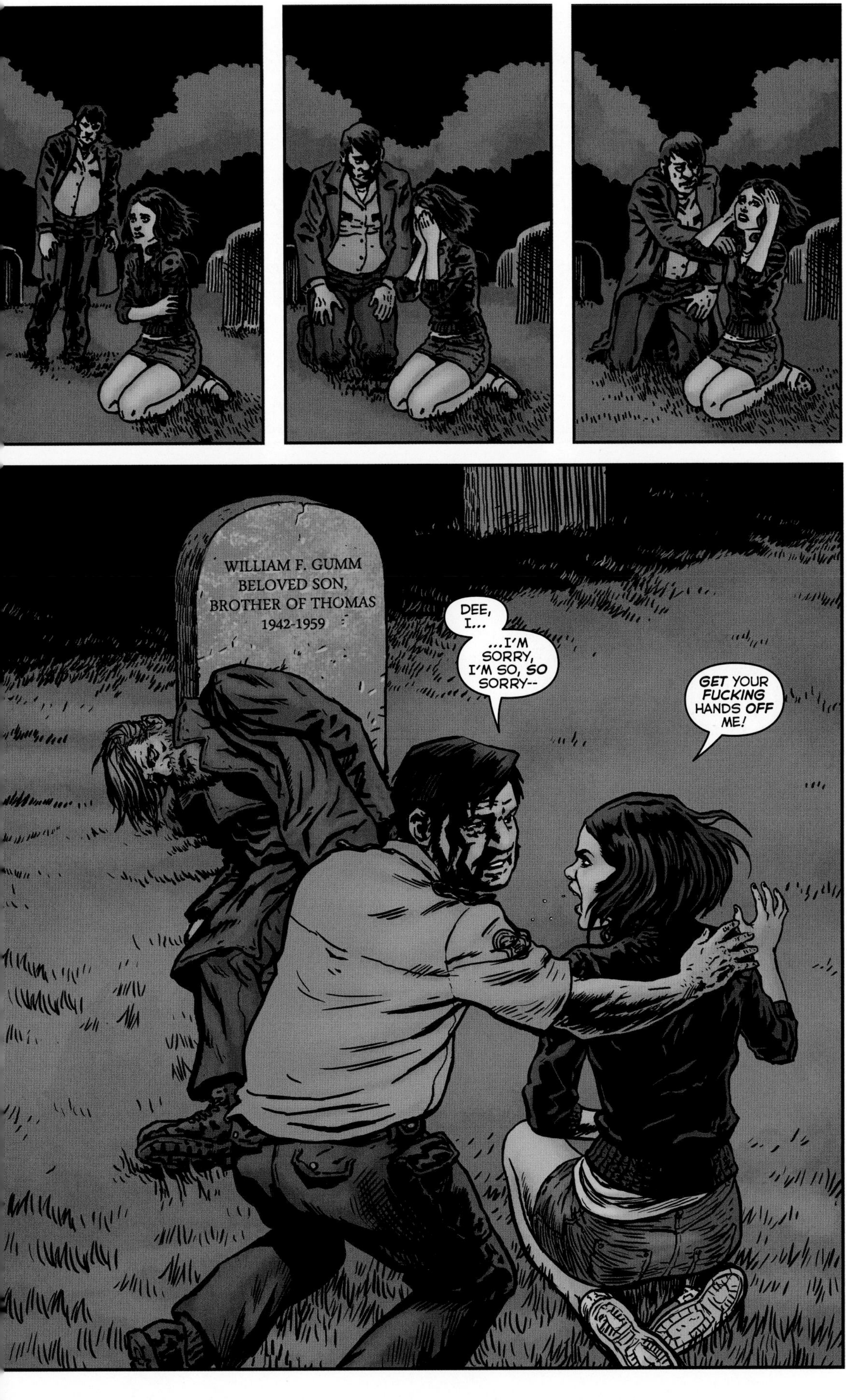
WILLIAM F. GUMM
BELOVED SON,
BROTHER OF THOMAS
1942-1959
DEE, I...
...I'M SORRY, I'M SO, SO SORRY--
GET YOUR FUCKING HANDS OFF ME!

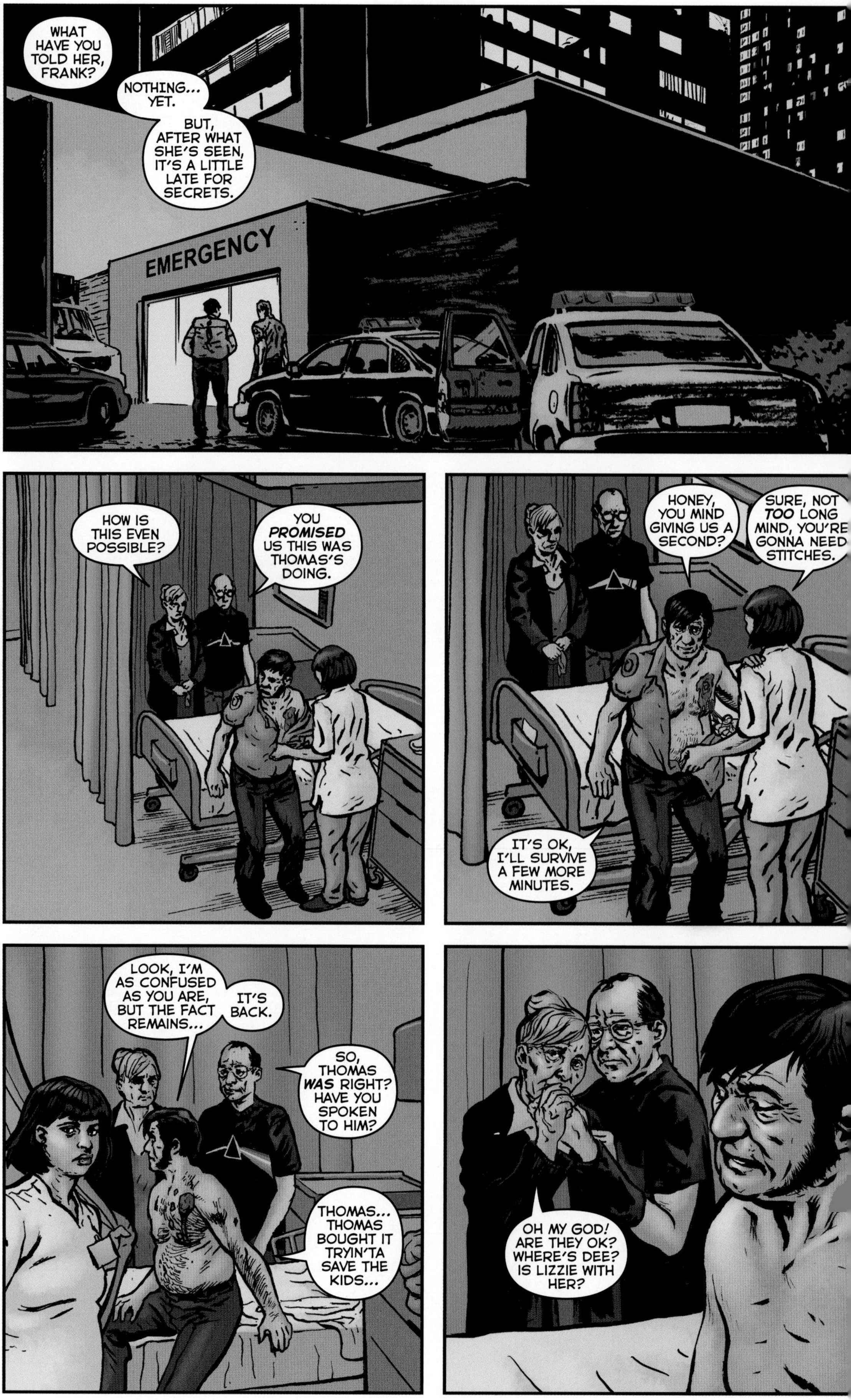
WHAT HAVE YOU TOLD HER, FRANK?
NOTHING... YET.
BUT, AFTER WHAT SHE'S SEEN, IT'S A LITTLE LATE FOR SECRETS.
EMERGENCY
HOW IS THIS EVEN POSSIBLE?
YOU ***PROMISED*** US THIS WAS THOMAS'S DOING.
HONEY, YOU MIND GIVING US A SECOND?
SURE, NOT ***TOO*** LONG MIND, YOU'RE GONNA NEED STITCHES.
IT'S OK, I'LL SURVIVE A FEW MORE MINUTES.
LOOK, I'M AS CONFUSED AS YOU ARE, BUT THE FACT REMAINS...
IT'S BACK.
SO, THOMAS ***WAS*** RIGHT? HAVE YOU SPOKEN TO HIM?
THOMAS... THOMAS BOUGHT IT TRYIN'TA SAVE THE KIDS...
OH MY GOD! ARE THEY OK? WHERE'S DEE? IS LIZZIE WITH HER?

DEE'S JUST FINE, SHE'S DOWN THE HALL, BUT LIZZIE...

...LIZZIE'S GONE.

GONE? GONE HOW?

IT TOOK HER AND I COULDN'T STOP IT.

WE'RE THE ONLY ONES LEFT NOW.

YOU *CAN'T* BE SERIOUS, WHAT DO YOU MEAN?

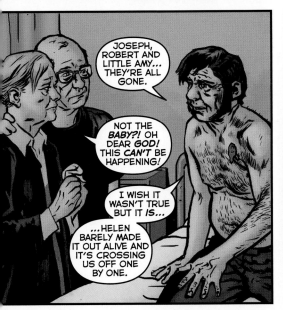

JOSEPH, ROBERT AND LITTLE AMY... THEY'RE ALL GONE.

NOT THE *BABY?!* OH DEAR *GOD!* THIS *CAN'T* BE HAPPENING!

I WISH IT WASN'T TRUE BUT IT *IS*...

...HELEN BARELY MADE IT OUT ALIVE AND IT'S CROSSING US OFF ONE BY ONE.

AND PATTY?

DON'T WORRY ABOUT HER, JUST GO HOME AND LOCK YOUR DOORS. NICK WILL DRIVE YOU.

IT'S HAPPENING AGAIN ISN'T IT? BECAUSE OF WHAT WE DID!

WE'RE ALL GOING TO DIE.

BETTY! *TRUST ME*, I KILLED IT THE FIRST TIME, I CAN DO IT AGAIN.

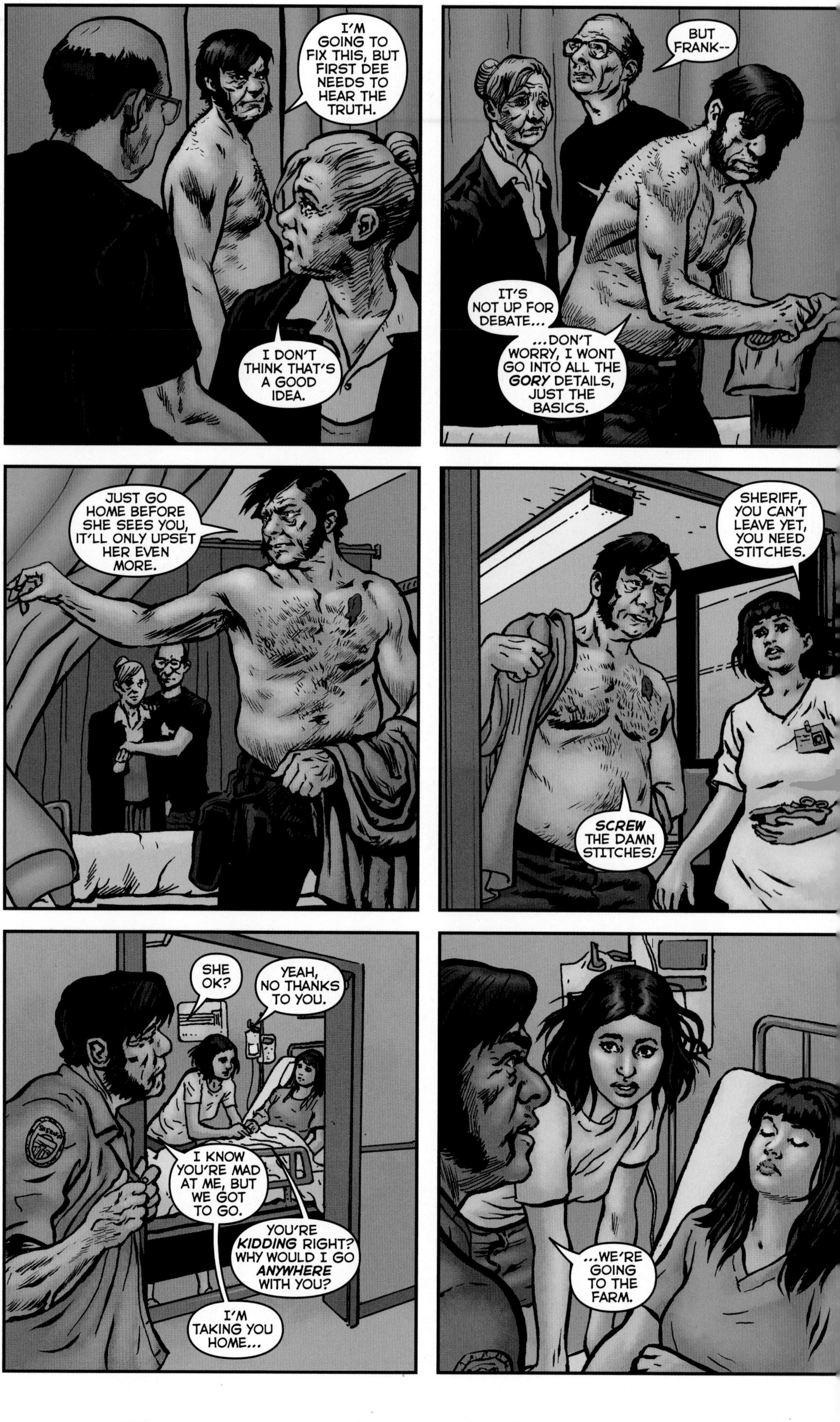
I'M GOING TO FIX THIS, BUT FIRST DEE NEEDS TO HEAR THE TRUTH.
I DON'T THINK THAT'S A GOOD IDEA.
BUT FRANK--
IT'S NOT UP FOR DEBATE...
...DON'T WORRY, I WONT GO INTO ALL THE GORY DETAILS, JUST THE BASICS.
JUST GO HOME BEFORE SHE SEES YOU, IT'LL ONLY UPSET HER EVEN MORE.
SHERIFF, YOU CAN'T LEAVE YET, YOU NEED STITCHES.
SCREW THE DAMN STITCHES!
SHE OK?
YEAH, NO THANKS TO YOU.
I KNOW YOU'RE MAD AT ME, BUT WE GOT TO GO.
YOU'RE KIDDING RIGHT? WHY WOULD I GO ANYWHERE WITH YOU?
I'M TAKING YOU HOME...
...WE'RE GOING TO THE FARM.

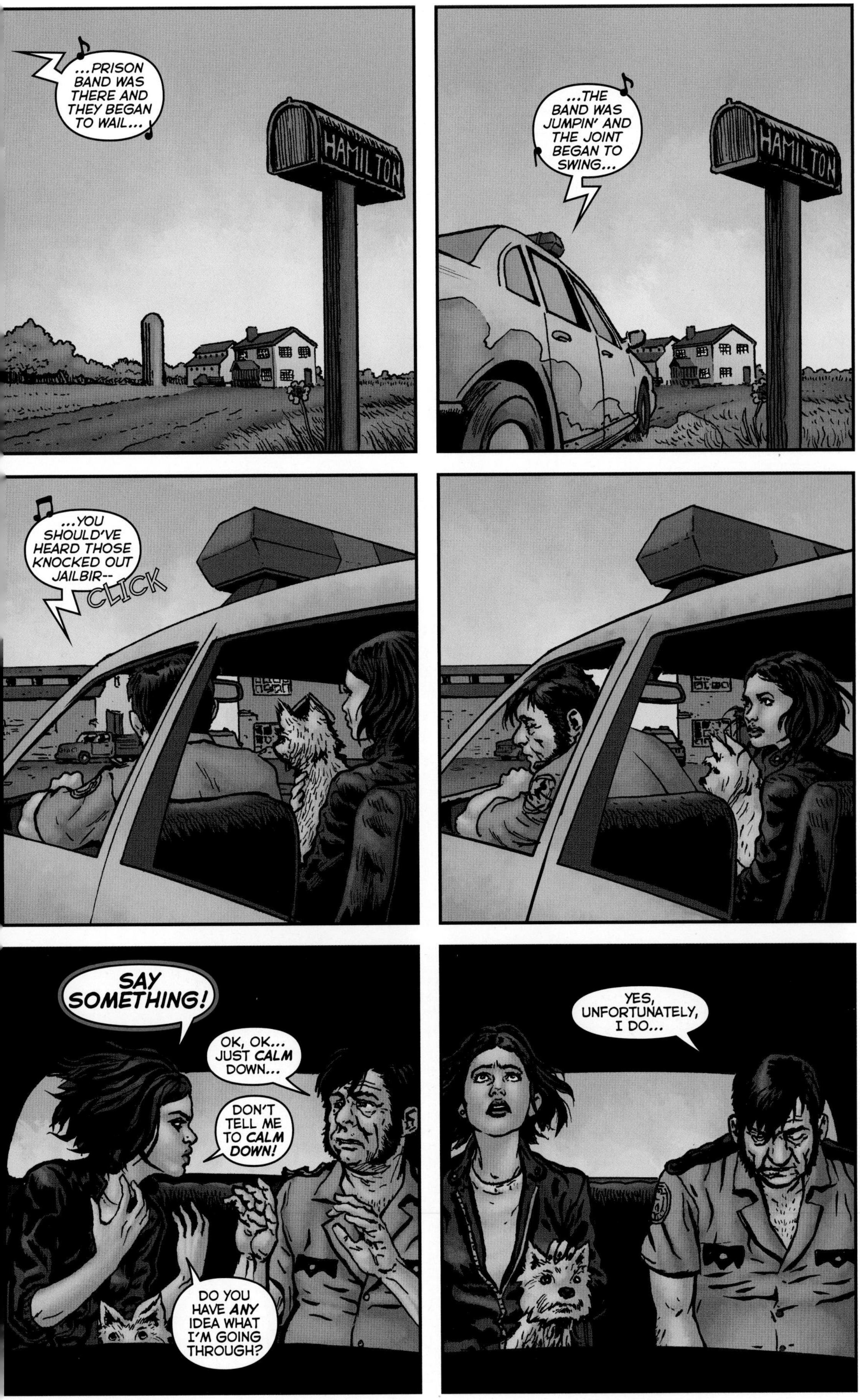
...PRISON BAND WAS THERE AND THEY BEGAN TO WAIL...
HAMILTON
...THE BAND WAS JUMPIN' AND THE JOINT BEGAN TO SWING...
HAMILTON
...YOU SHOULD'VE HEARD THOSE KNOCKED OUT JAILBIR--
CLICK
SAY SOMETHING!
OK, OK... JUST CALM DOWN...
DON'T TELL ME TO CALM DOWN!
DO YOU HAVE ANY IDEA WHAT I'M GOING THROUGH?
YES, UNFORTUNATELY, I DO...

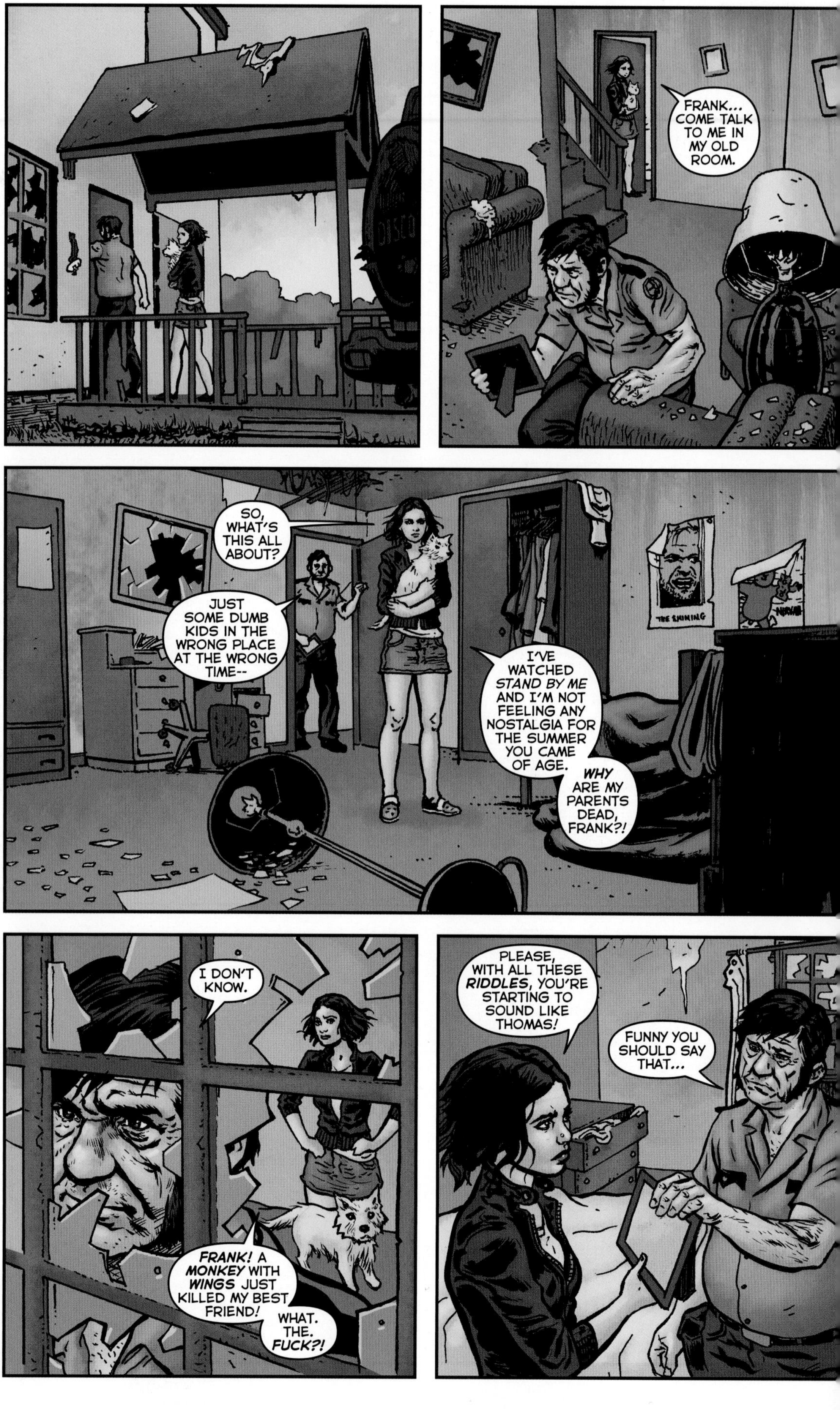
FRANK... COME TALK TO ME IN MY OLD ROOM.
SO, WHAT'S THIS ALL ABOUT?
JUST SOME DUMB KIDS IN THE WRONG PLACE AT THE WRONG TIME--
I'VE WATCHED STAND BY ME AND I'M NOT FEELING ANY NOSTALGIA FOR THE SUMMER YOU CAME OF AGE.
WHY ARE MY PARENTS DEAD, FRANK?!
THE SHINING
I DON'T KNOW.
FRANK! A MONKEY WITH WINGS JUST KILLED MY BEST FRIEND!
WHAT. THE. FUCK?!
PLEASE, WITH ALL THESE RIDDLES, YOU'RE STARTING TO SOUND LIKE THOMAS!
FUNNY YOU SHOULD SAY THAT...

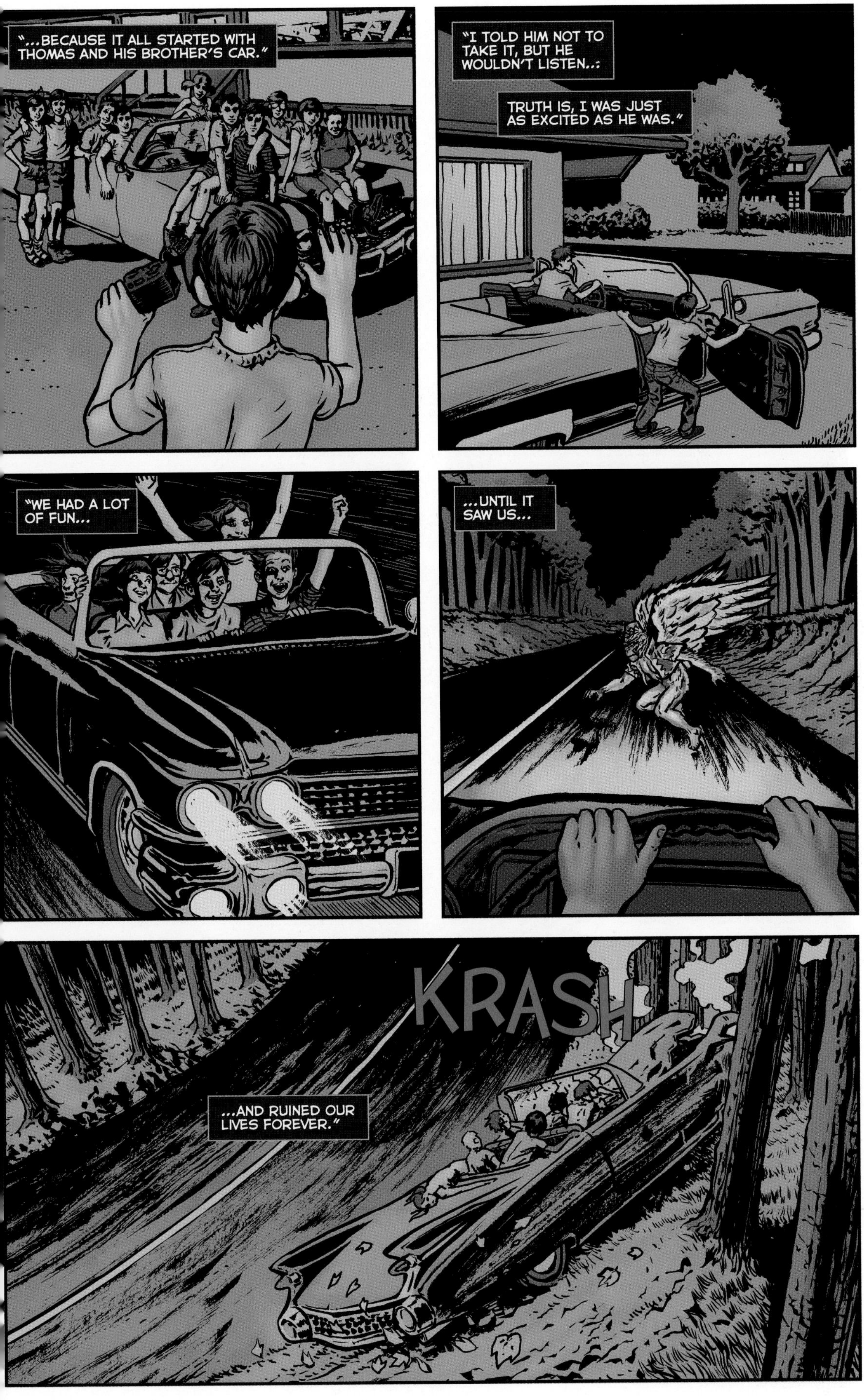
"...BECAUSE IT ALL STARTED WITH THOMAS AND HIS BROTHER'S CAR."
"I TOLD HIM NOT TO TAKE IT, BUT HE WOULDN'T LISTEN...
TRUTH IS, I WAS JUST AS EXCITED AS HE WAS."
"WE HAD A LOT OF FUN...
...UNTIL IT SAW US...
KRASH
...AND RUINED OUR LIVES FOREVER."

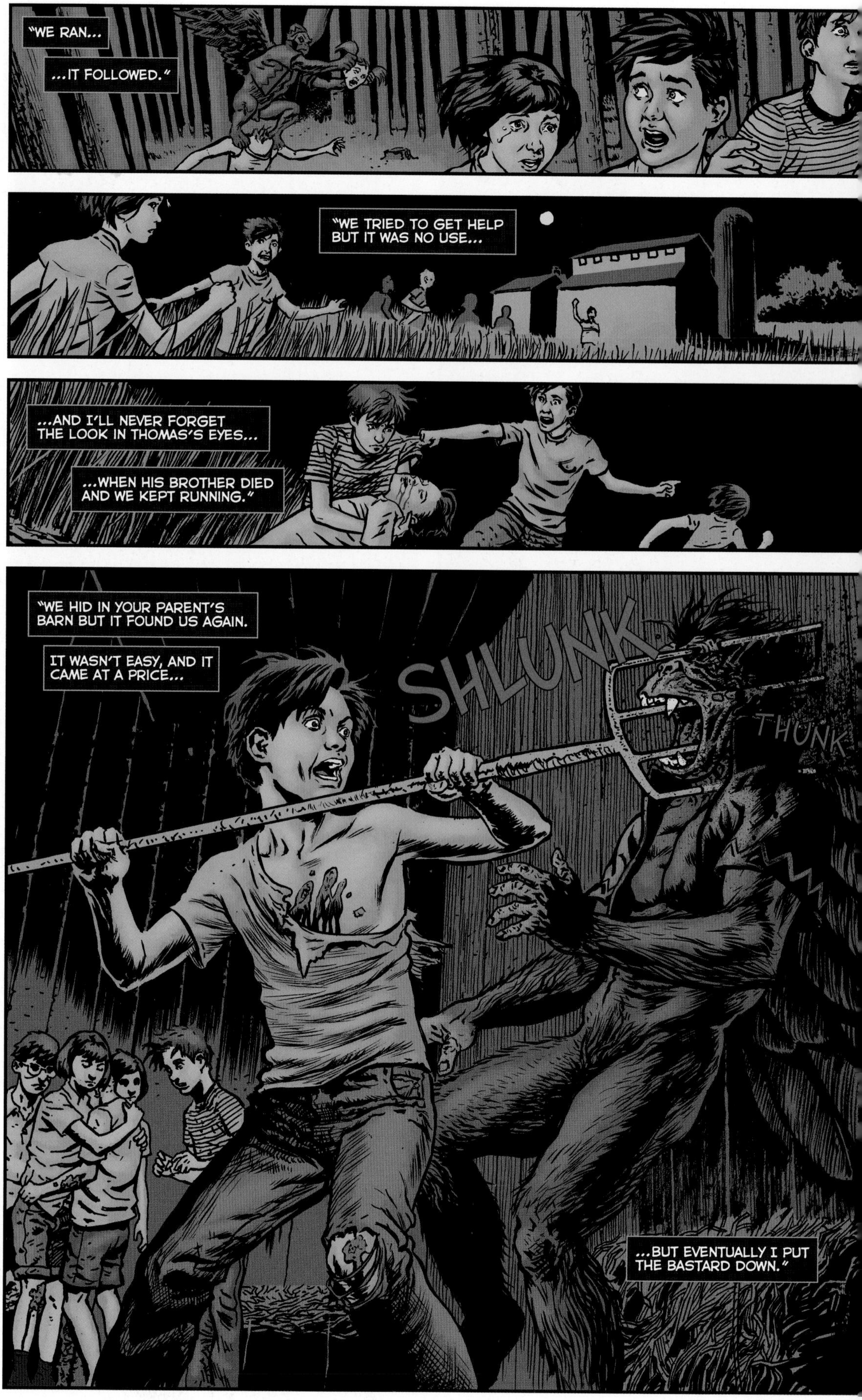
"WE RAN...
...IT FOLLOWED."
"WE TRIED TO GET HELP BUT IT WAS NO USE...
...AND I'LL NEVER FORGET THE LOOK IN THOMAS'S EYES...
...WHEN HIS BROTHER DIED AND WE KEPT RUNNING."
"WE HID IN YOUR PARENT'S BARN BUT IT FOUND US AGAIN.
IT WASN'T EASY, AND IT CAME AT A PRICE...
SHLUNK
THUNK
...BUT EVENTUALLY I PUT THE BASTARD DOWN."

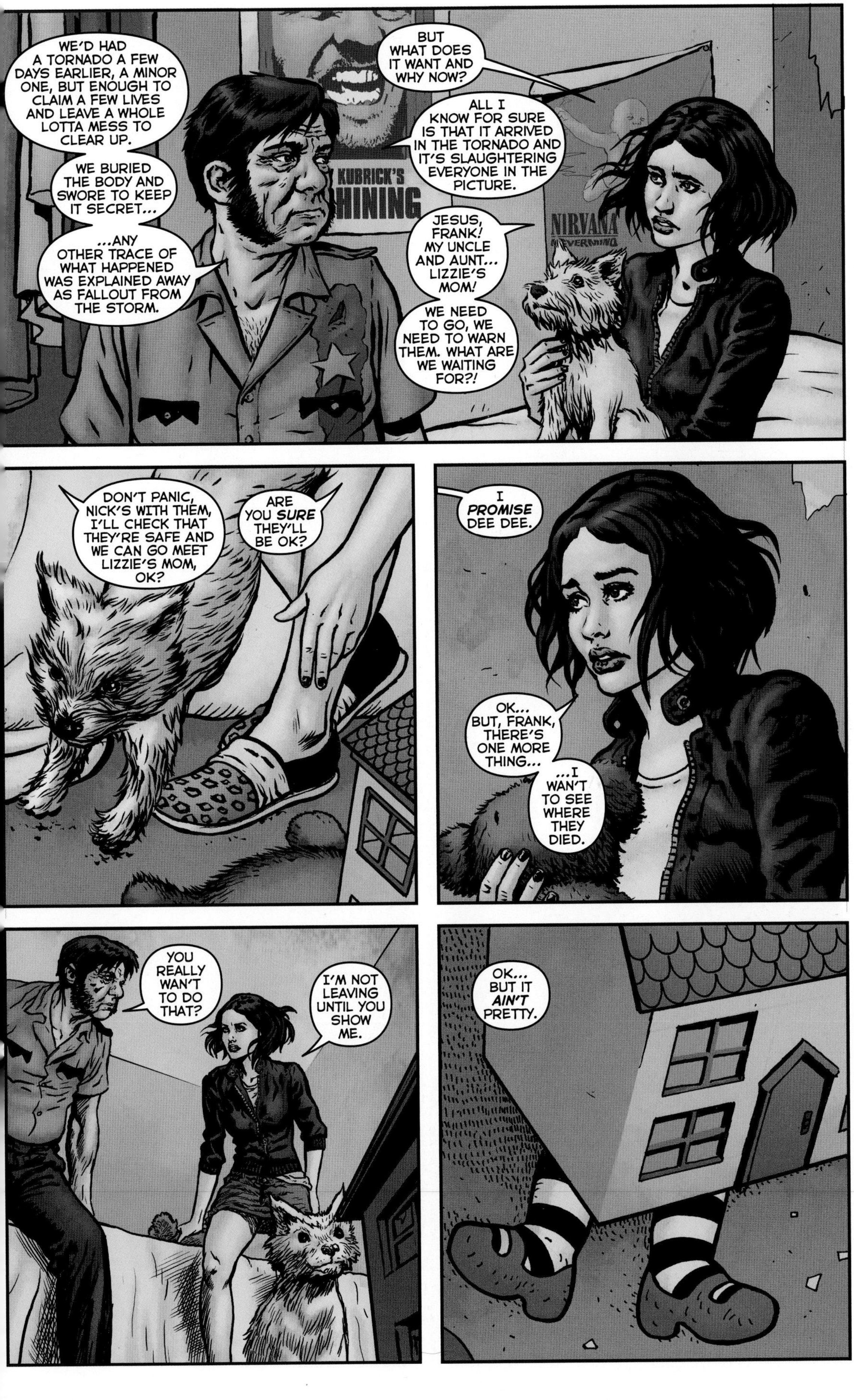
WE'D HAD A TORNADO A FEW DAYS EARLIER, A MINOR ONE, BUT ENOUGH TO CLAIM A FEW LIVES AND LEAVE A WHOLE LOTTA MESS TO CLEAR UP.
WE BURIED THE BODY AND SWORE TO KEEP IT SECRET...
...ANY OTHER TRACE OF WHAT HAPPENED WAS EXPLAINED AWAY AS FALLOUT FROM THE STORM.
BUT WHAT DOES IT WANT AND WHY NOW?
ALL I KNOW FOR SURE IS THAT IT ARRIVED IN THE TORNADO AND IT'S SLAUGHTERING EVERYONE IN THE PICTURE.
JESUS, FRANK! MY UNCLE AND AUNT... LIZZIE'S MOM!
WE NEED TO GO, WE NEED TO WARN THEM. WHAT ARE WE WAITING FOR?!
KUBRICK'S
HINING
NIRVANA
DON'T PANIC, NICK'S WITH THEM, I'LL CHECK THAT THEY'RE SAFE AND WE CAN GO MEET LIZZIE'S MOM, OK?
ARE YOU **SURE** THEY'LL BE OK?
I **PROMISE** DEE DEE.
OK... BUT, FRANK, THERE'S ONE MORE THING...
...I WAN'T TO SEE WHERE THEY DIED.
YOU REALLY WAN'T TO DO THAT?
I'M NOT LEAVING UNTIL YOU SHOW ME.
OK... BUT IT **AIN'T** PRETTY.

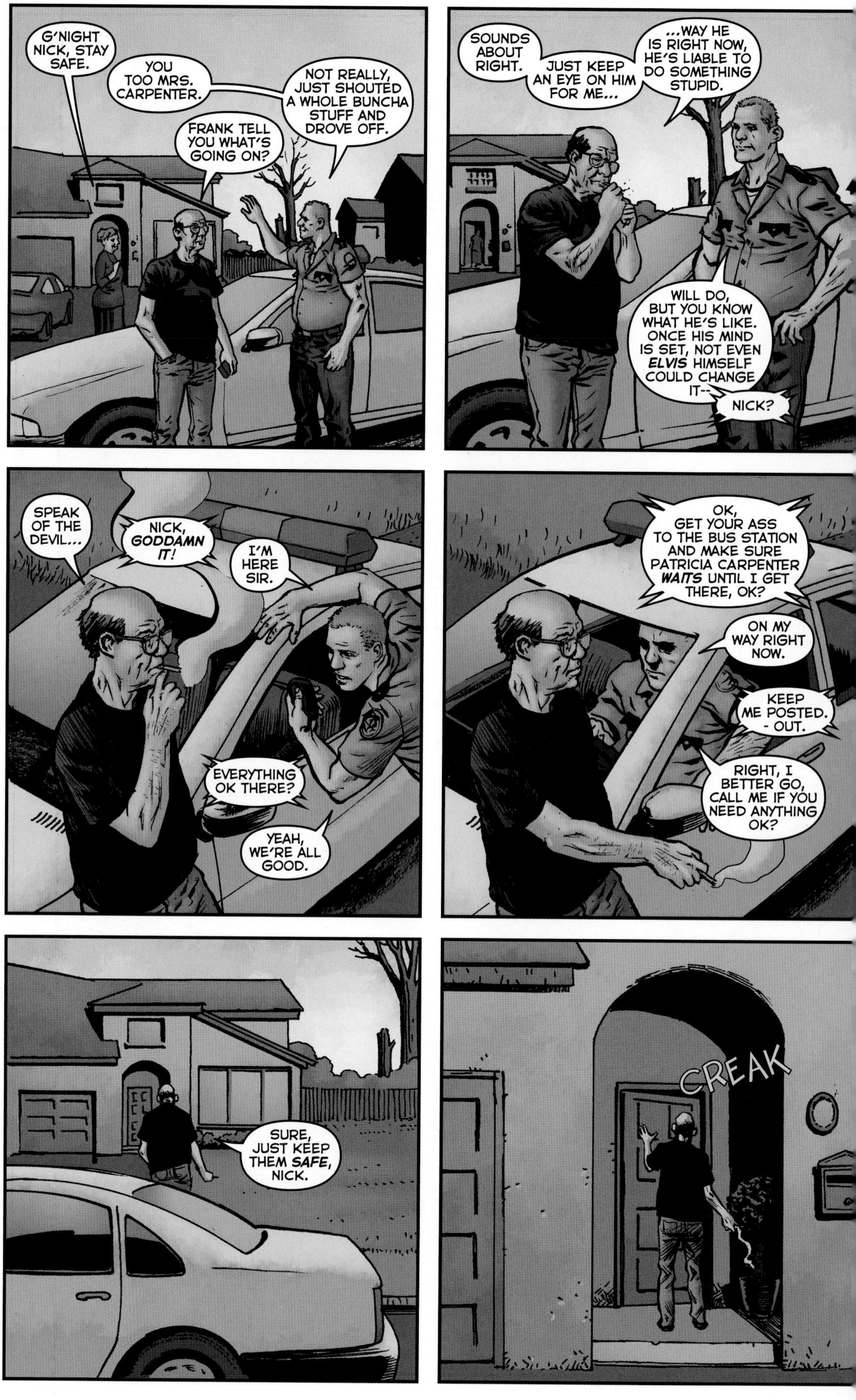
G'NIGHT NICK, STAY SAFE.
YOU TOO MRS. CARPENTER.
FRANK TELL YOU WHAT'S GOING ON?
NOT REALLY, JUST SHOUTED A WHOLE BUNCHA STUFF AND DROVE OFF.
SOUNDS ABOUT RIGHT.
JUST KEEP AN EYE ON HIM FOR ME...
...WAY HE IS RIGHT NOW, HE'S LIABLE TO DO SOMETHING STUPID.
WILL DO, BUT YOU KNOW WHAT HE'S LIKE. ONCE HIS MIND IS SET, NOT EVEN ELVIS HIMSELF COULD CHANGE IT--
NICK?
SPEAK OF THE DEVIL...
NICK, GODDAMN IT!
I'M HERE SIR.
EVERYTHING OK THERE?
YEAH, WE'RE ALL GOOD.
OK, GET YOUR ASS TO THE BUS STATION AND MAKE SURE PATRICIA CARPENTER WAITS UNTIL I GET THERE, OK?
ON MY WAY RIGHT NOW.
KEEP ME POSTED. - OUT.
RIGHT, I BETTER GO, CALL ME IF YOU NEED ANYTHING OK?
SURE, JUST KEEP THEM SAFE, NICK.
CREAK

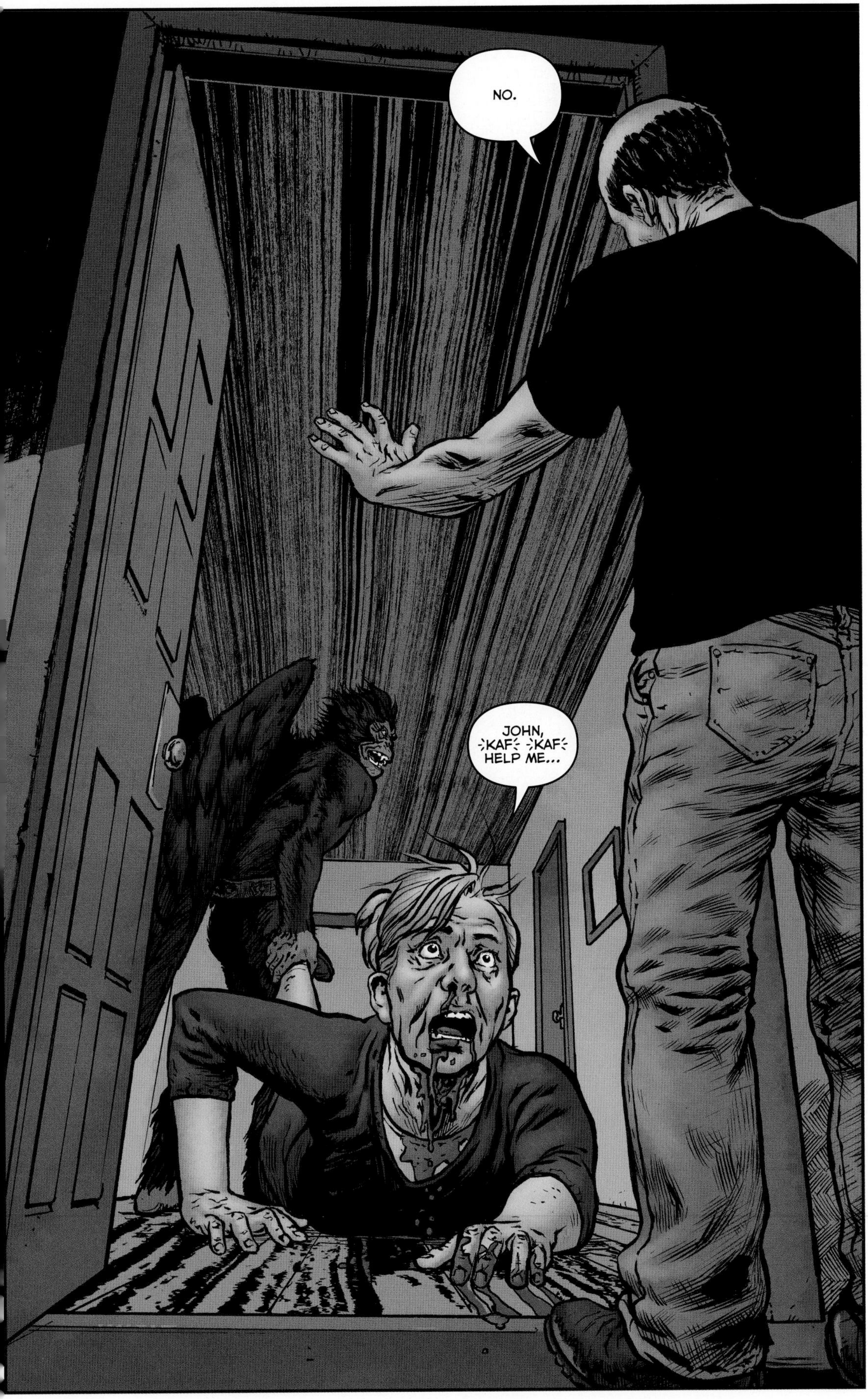
NO.
JOHN, *KAF* *KAF* HELP ME...

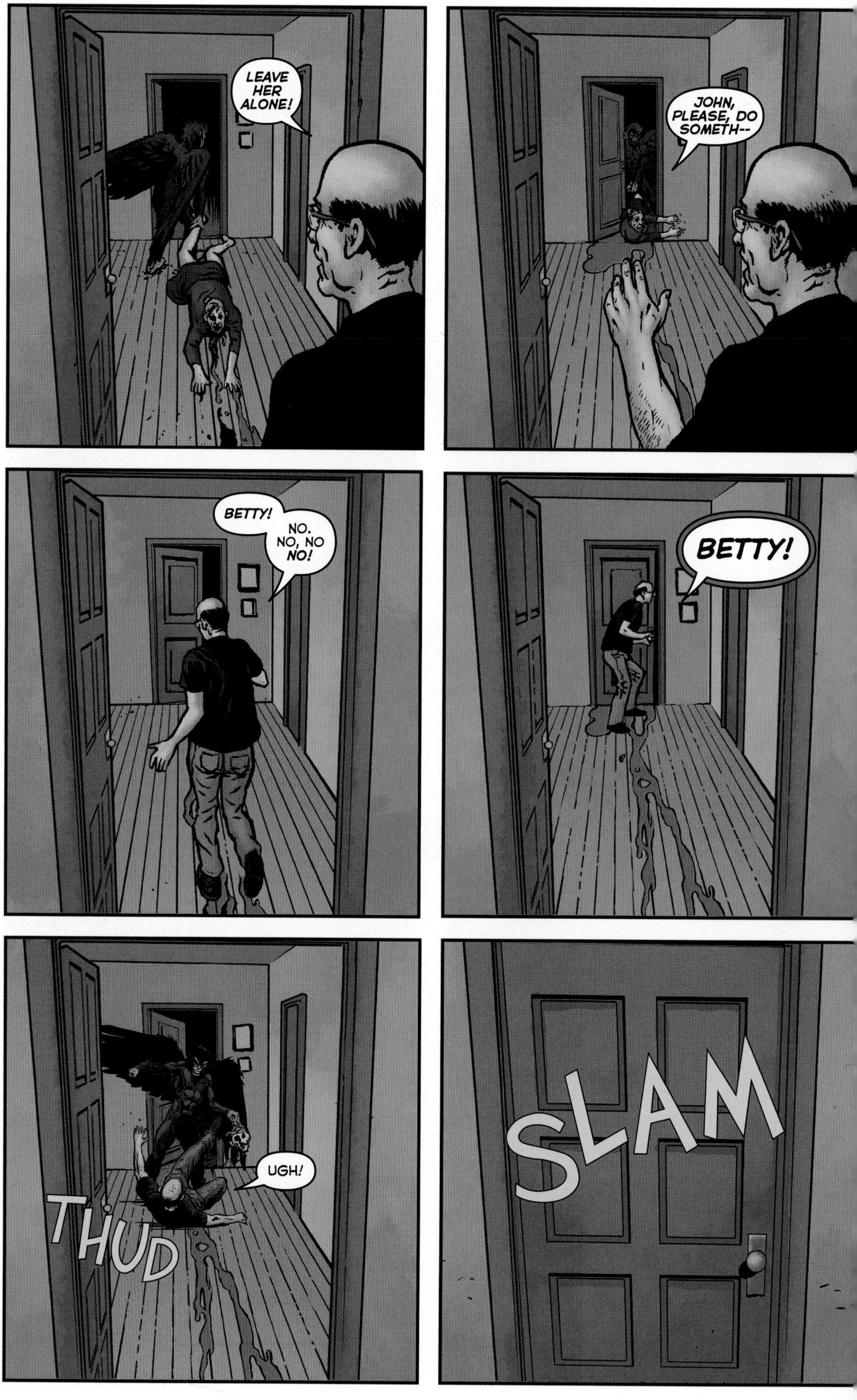
LEAVE HER ALONE!
JOHN, PLEASE, DO SOMETH--
BETTY!
NO. NO, NO NO!
BETTY!
THUD
UGH!
SLAM

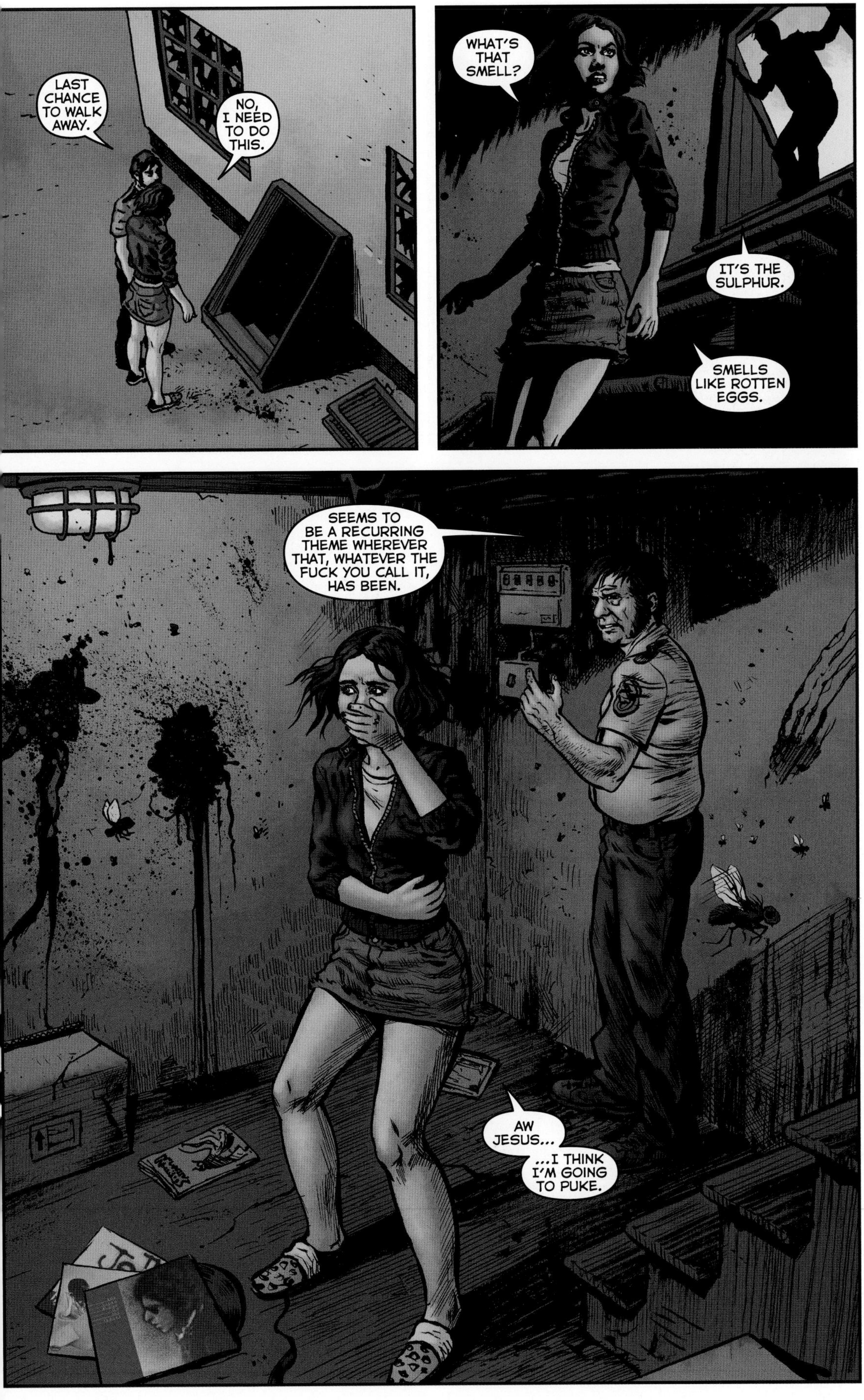
LAST CHANCE TO WALK AWAY.
NO, I NEED TO DO THIS.
WHAT'S THAT SMELL?
IT'S THE SULPHUR.
SMELLS LIKE ROTTEN EGGS.
SEEMS TO BE A RECURRING THEME WHEREVER THAT, WHATEVER THE FUCK YOU CALL IT, HAS BEEN.
AW JESUS...
...I THINK I'M GOING TO PUKE.

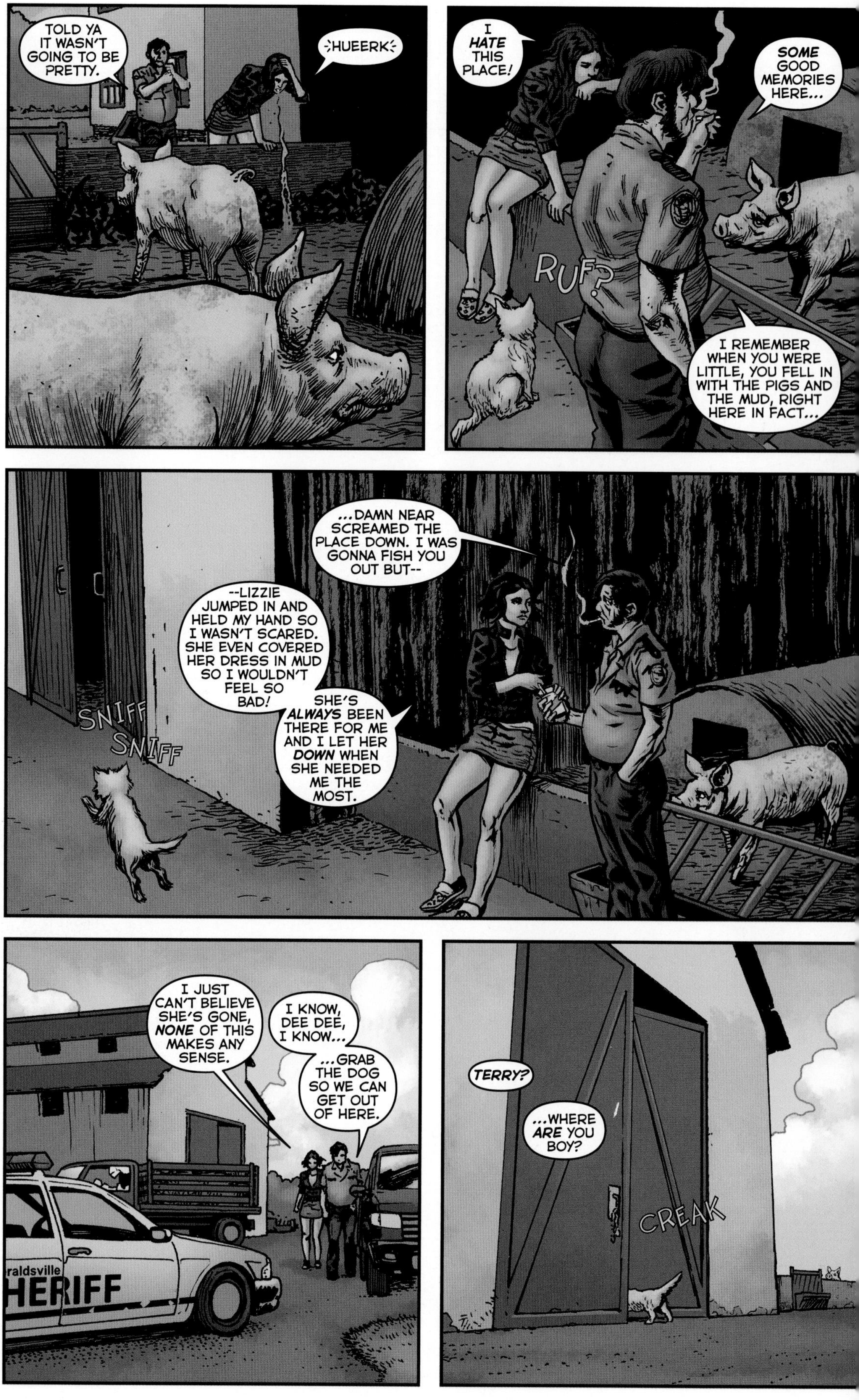
TOLD YA IT WASN'T GOING TO BE PRETTY.
HUEERK
I HATE THIS PLACE!
SOME GOOD MEMORIES HERE...
RUF?
I REMEMBER WHEN YOU WERE LITTLE, YOU FELL IN WITH THE PIGS AND THE MUD, RIGHT HERE IN FACT...
...DAMN NEAR SCREAMED THE PLACE DOWN. I WAS GONNA FISH YOU OUT BUT--
--LIZZIE JUMPED IN AND HELD MY HAND SO I WASN'T SCARED. SHE EVEN COVERED HER DRESS IN MUD SO I WOULDN'T FEEL SO BAD!
SHE'S ALWAYS BEEN THERE FOR ME AND I LET HER DOWN WHEN SHE NEEDED ME THE MOST.
SNIFF
SNIFF
I JUST CAN'T BELIEVE SHE'S GONE, NONE OF THIS MAKES ANY SENSE.
I KNOW, DEE DEE, I KNOW...
...GRAB THE DOG SO WE CAN GET OUT OF HERE.
SHERIFF
TERRY?
...WHERE ARE YOU BOY?
CREAK

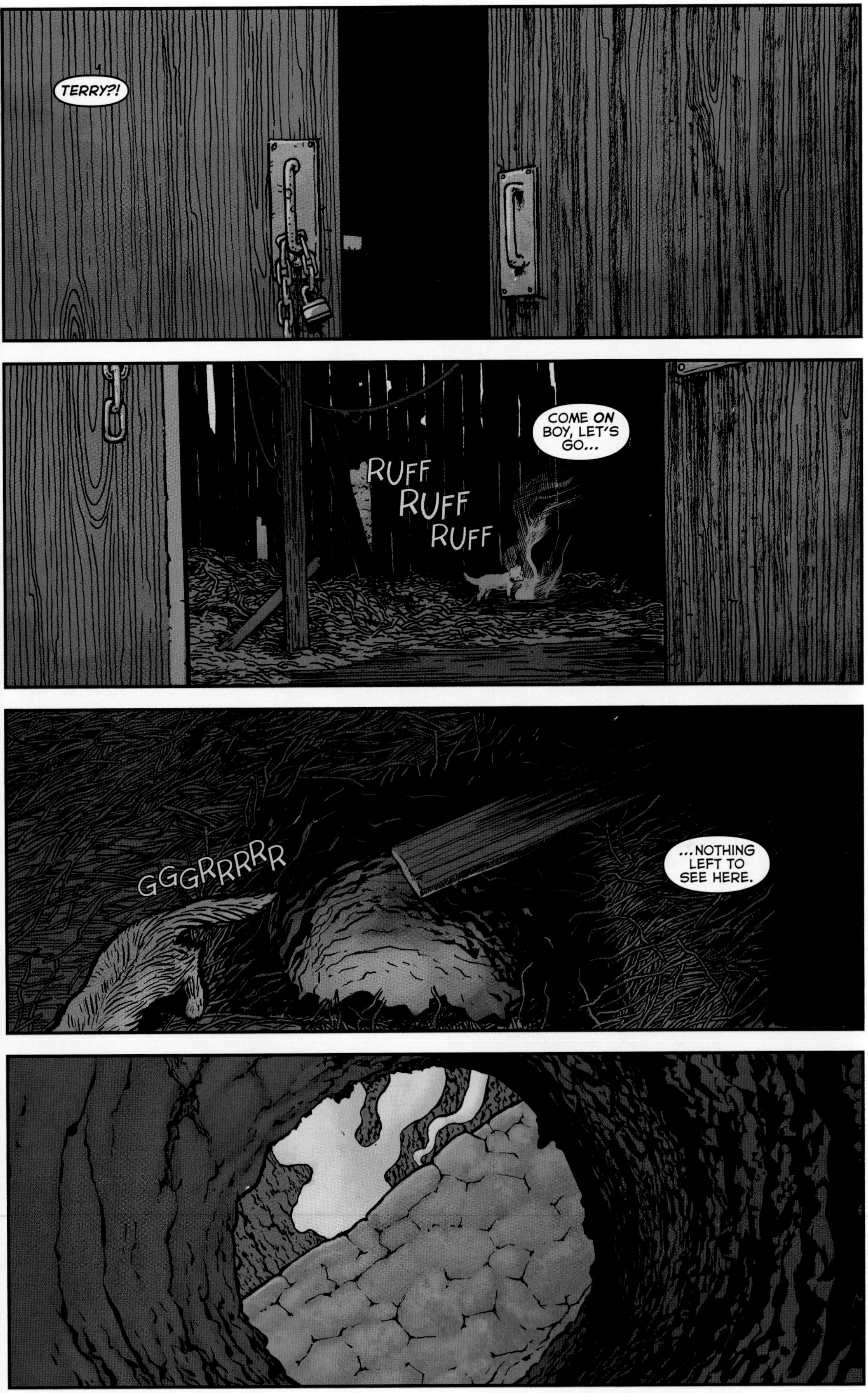
TERRY?!
RUFF
RUFF
RUFF
COME ON BOY, LET'S GO...
GGGRRRRR
...NOTHING LEFT TO SEE HERE.

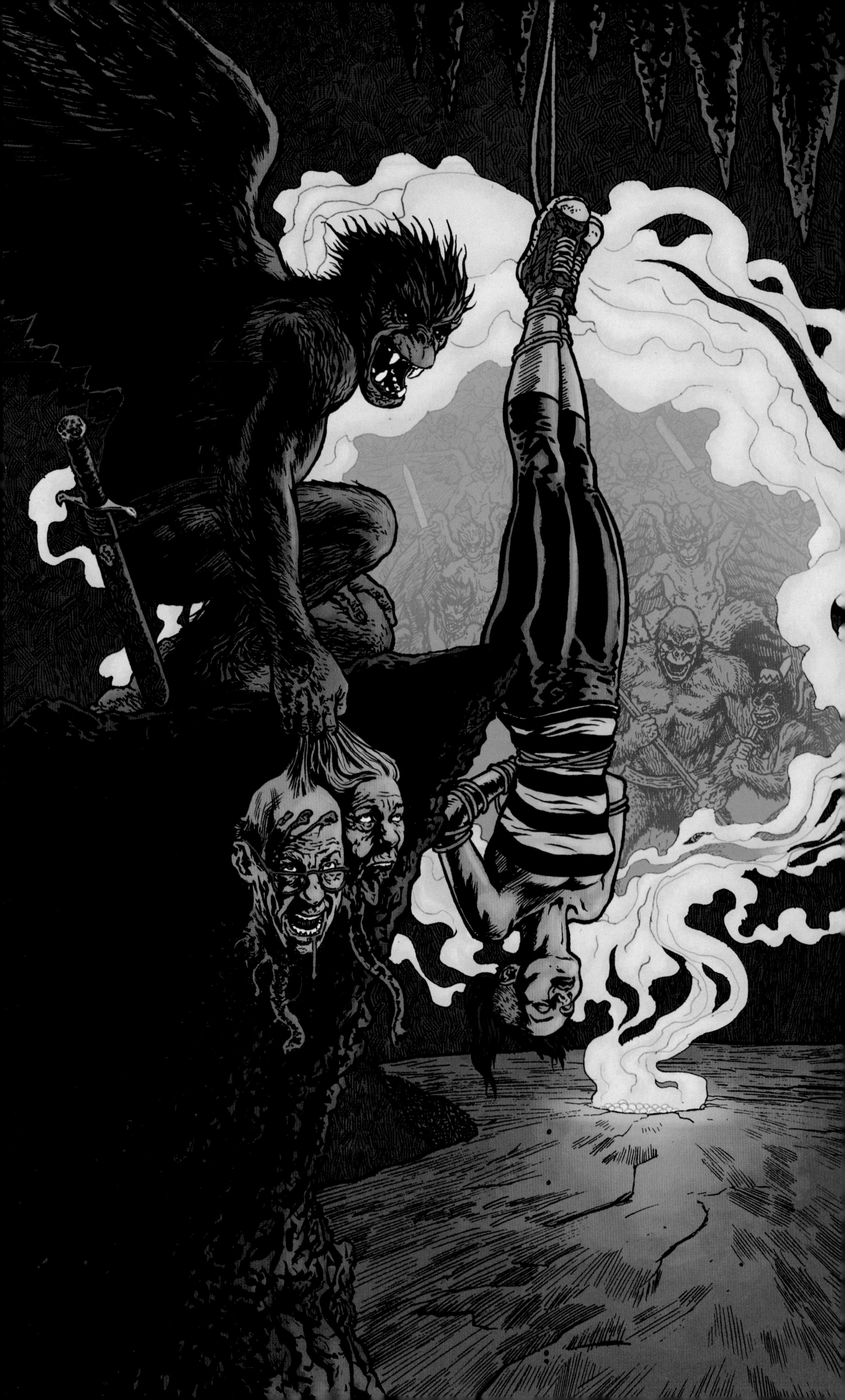

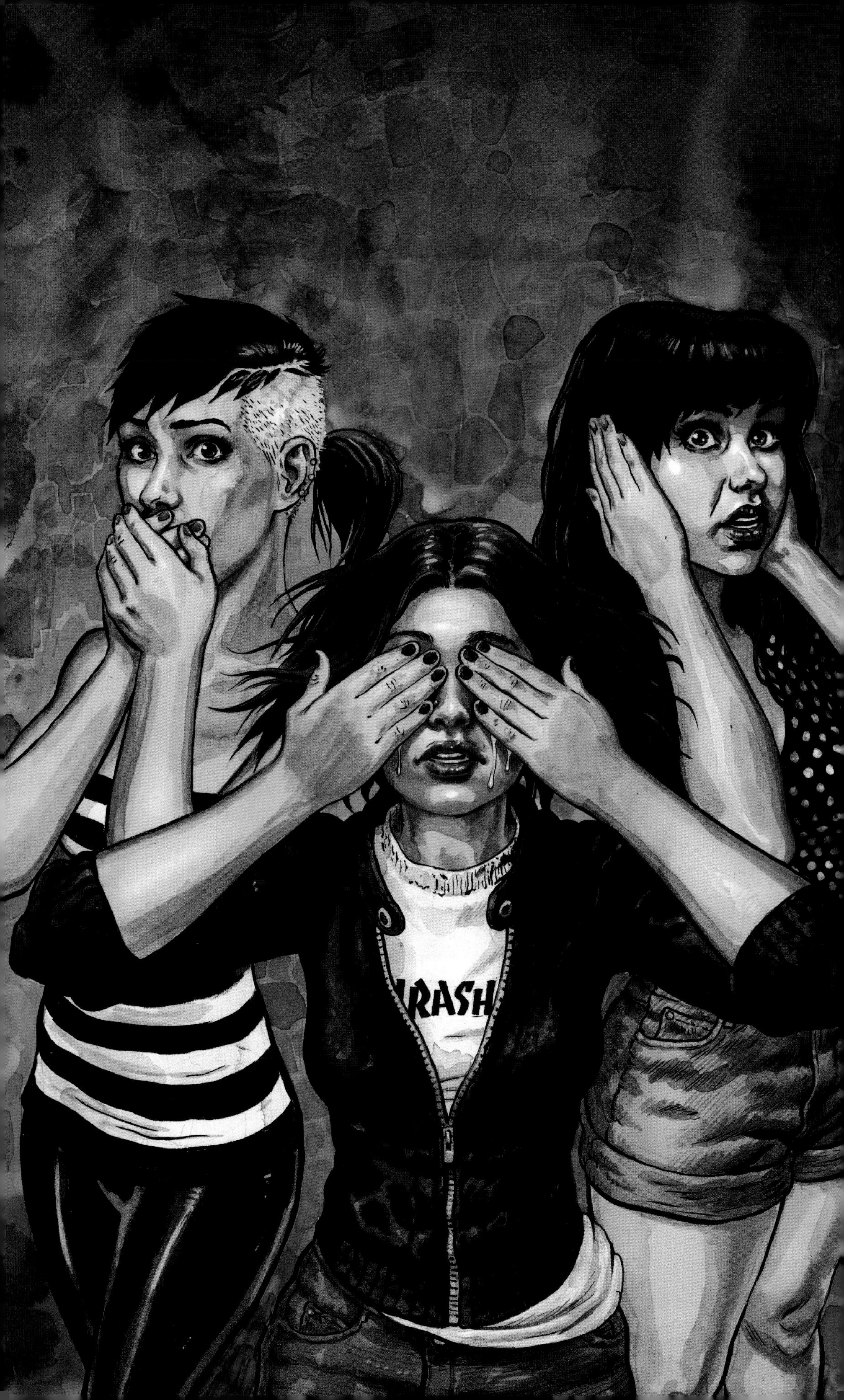
RASH

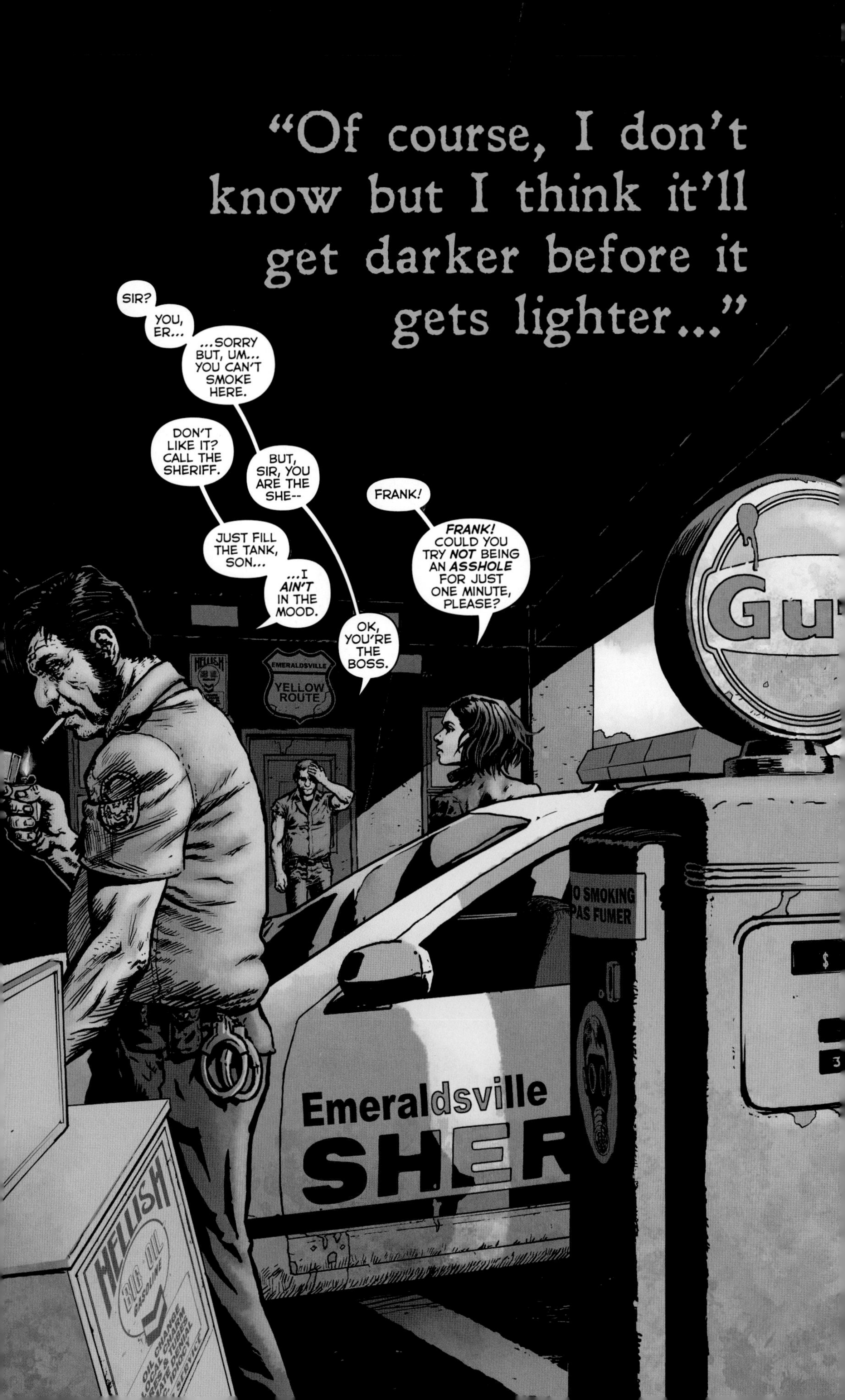
"Of course, I don't know but I think it'll get darker before it gets lighter..."
SIR?
YOU, ER...
...SORRY BUT, UM... YOU CAN'T SMOKE HERE.
DON'T LIKE IT? CALL THE SHERIFF.
BUT, SIR, YOU ARE THE SHE--
JUST FILL THE TANK, SON...
...I *AIN'T* IN THE MOOD.
OK, YOU'RE THE BOSS.
FRANK!
FRANK! COULD YOU TRY *NOT* BEING AN *ASSHOLE* FOR JUST ONE MINUTE, PLEASE?
EMERALDSVILLE YELLOW ROUTE
Emeraldsville

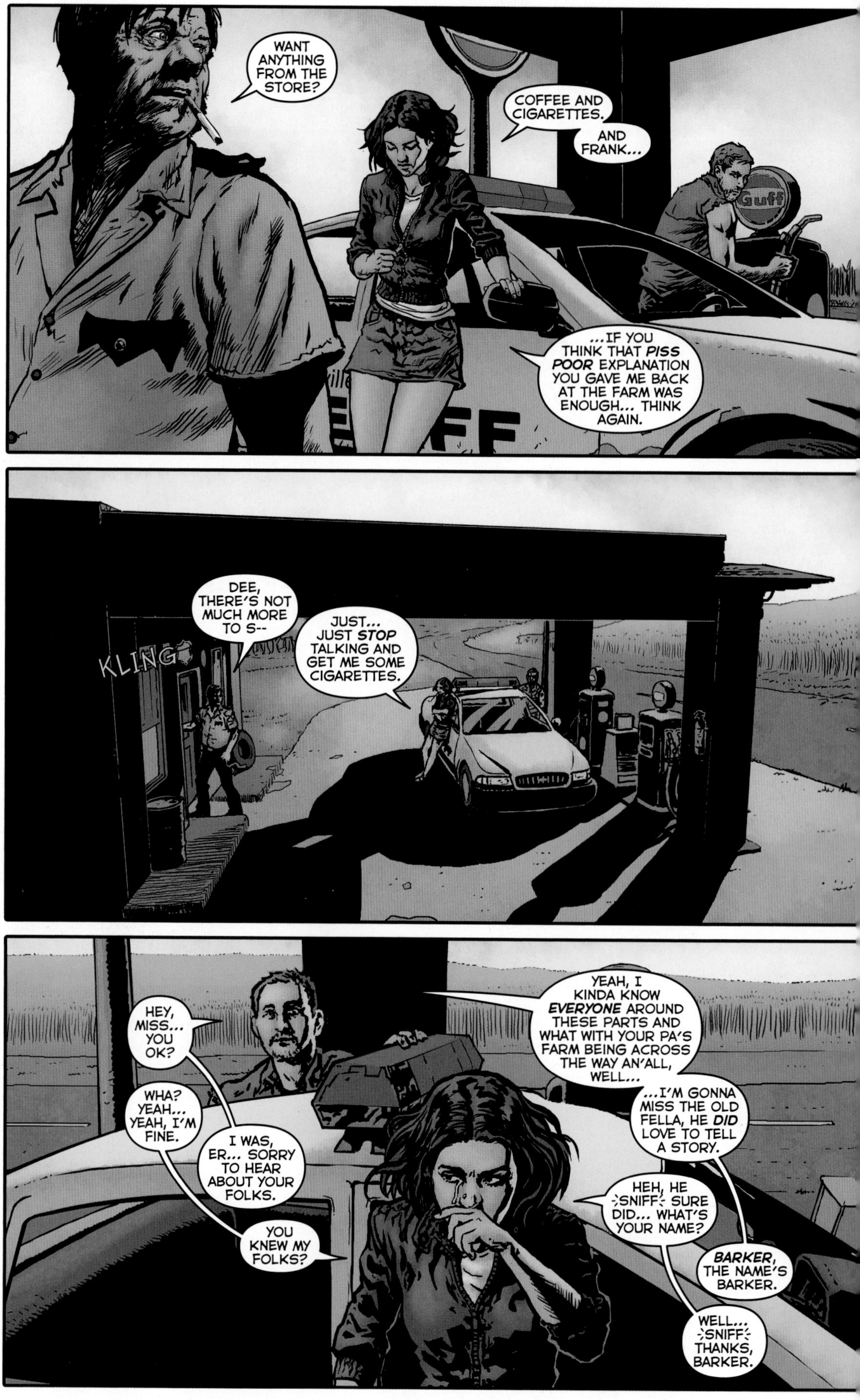
WANT ANYTHING FROM THE STORE?
COFFEE AND CIGARETTES.
AND FRANK...
...IF YOU THINK THAT PISS POOR EXPLANATION YOU GAVE ME BACK AT THE FARM WAS ENOUGH... THINK AGAIN.
DEE, THERE'S NOT MUCH MORE TO S--
KLING
JUST... JUST STOP TALKING AND GET ME SOME CIGARETTES.
HEY, MISS... YOU OK?
WHA? YEAH... YEAH, I'M FINE.
I WAS, ER... SORRY TO HEAR ABOUT YOUR FOLKS.
YOU KNEW MY FOLKS?
YEAH, I KINDA KNOW EVERYONE AROUND THESE PARTS AND WHAT WITH YOUR PA'S FARM BEING ACROSS THE WAY AN'ALL, WELL...
...I'M GONNA MISS THE OLD FELLA, HE DID LOVE TO TELL A STORY.
HEH, HE SNIFF SURE DID... WHAT'S YOUR NAME?
BARKER, THE NAME'S BARKER.
WELL... SNIFF THANKS, BARKER.

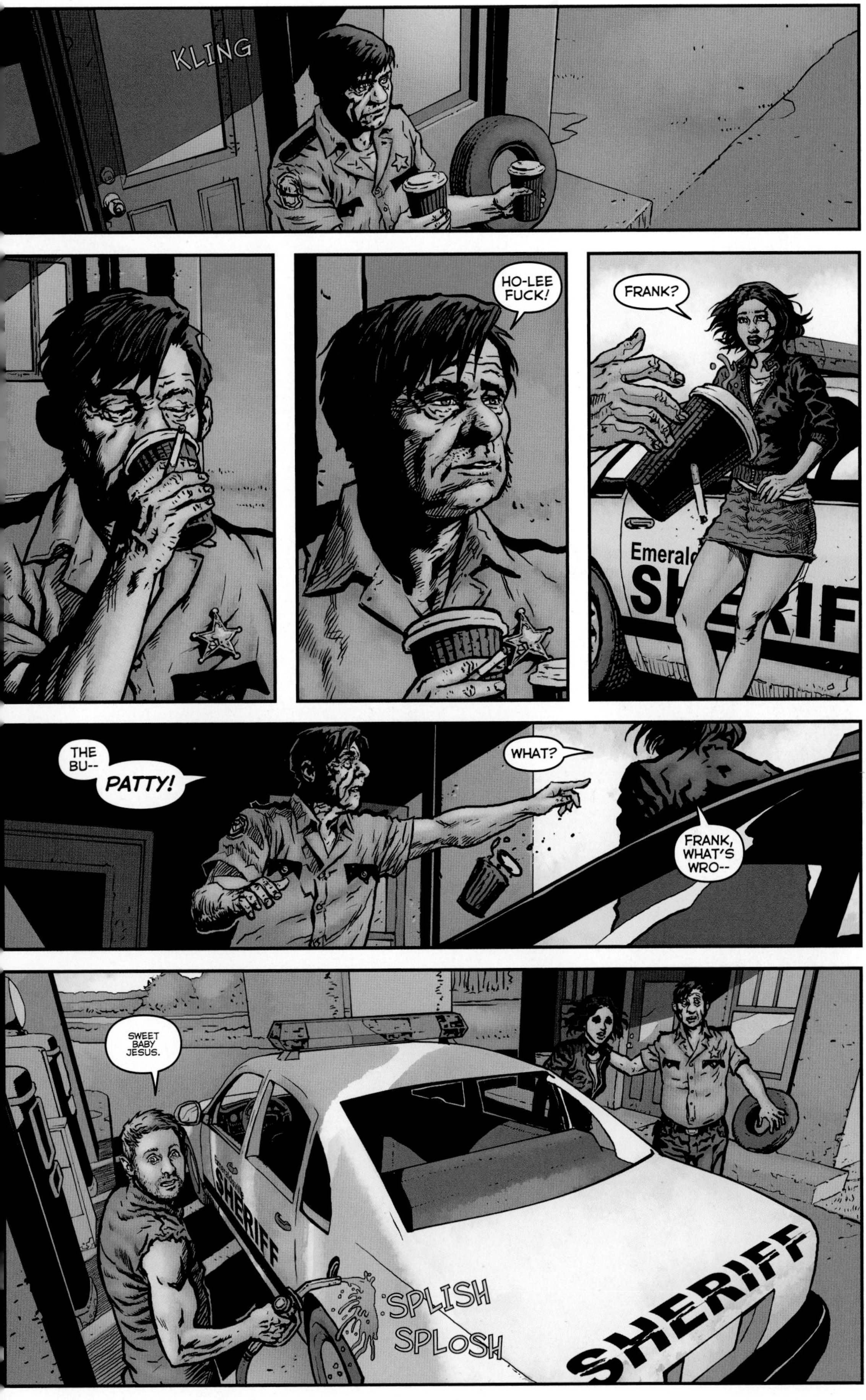
KLING
HO-LEE FUCK!
FRANK?
Emerald
SHERIFF
THE BU-- PATTY!
WHAT?
FRANK, WHAT'S WRO--
SWEET BABY JESUS.
SHERIFF
SPLISH SPLOSH
SHERIFF

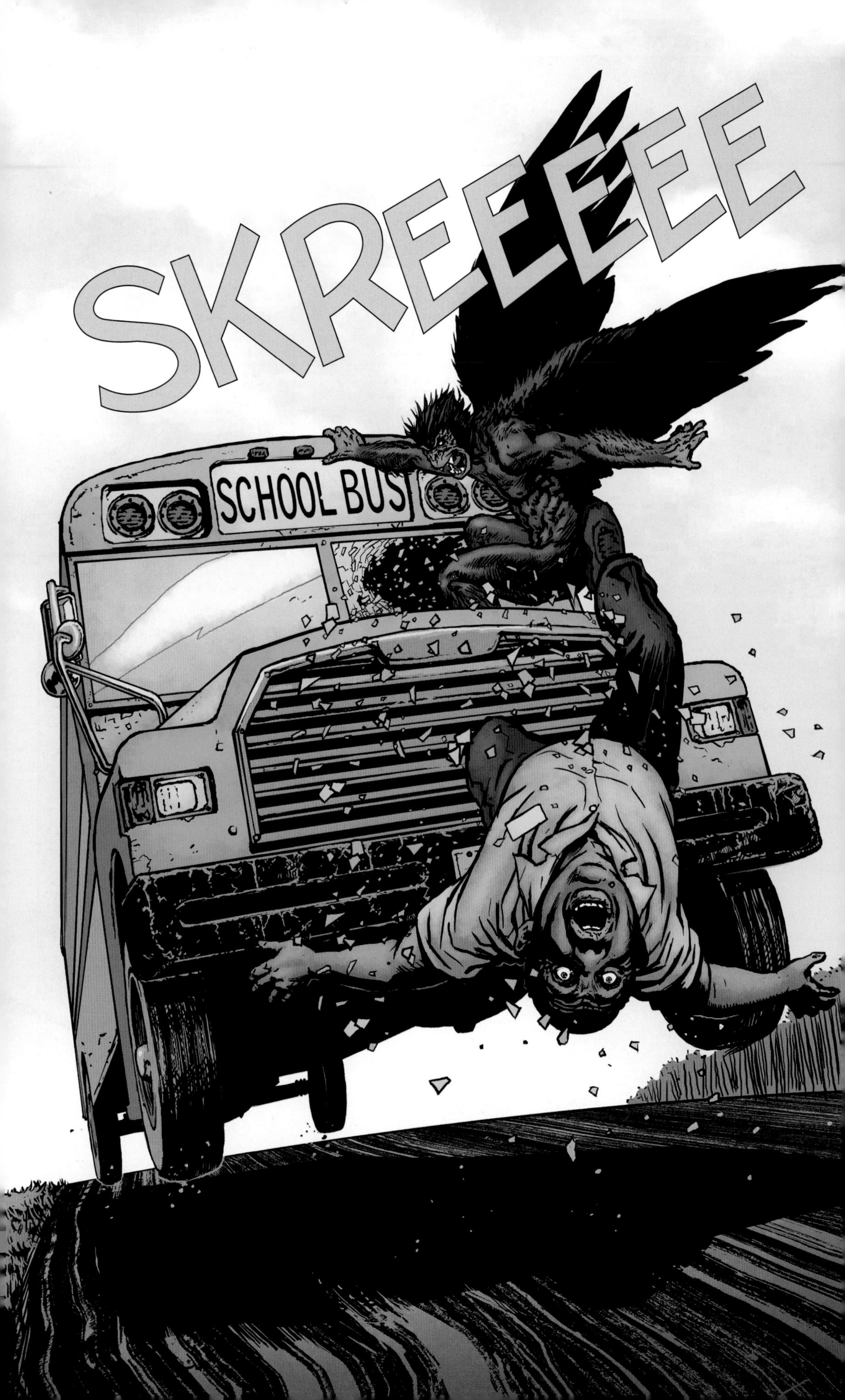
SKREEEEEE
SCHOOL BUS

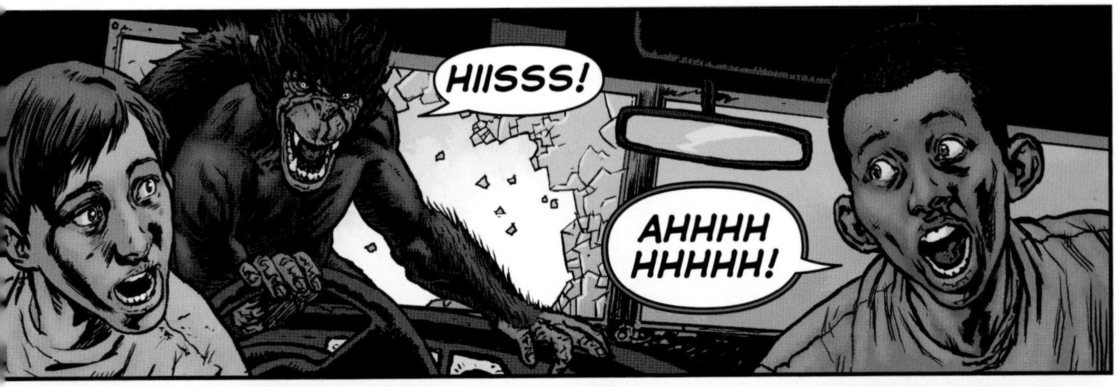
HIISSS!
AHHHH HHHHH!

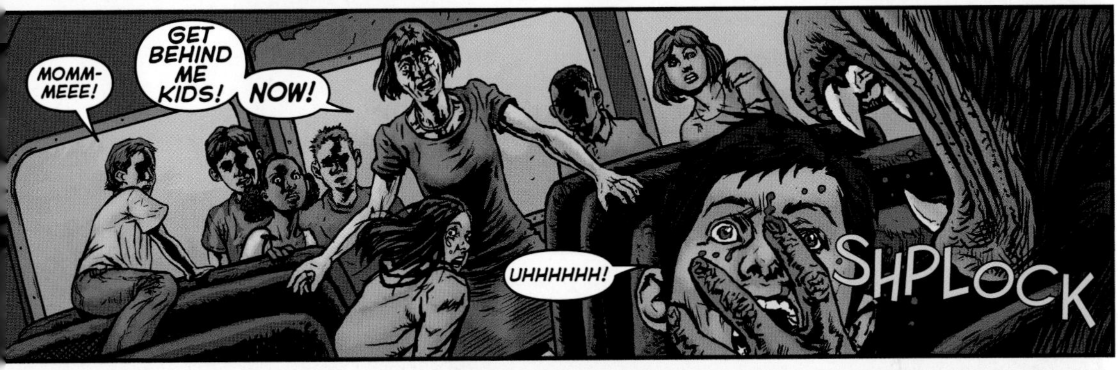
MOMM-MEEE!
GET BEHIND ME KIDS!
NOW!
UHHHHHH!
SHPLOCK

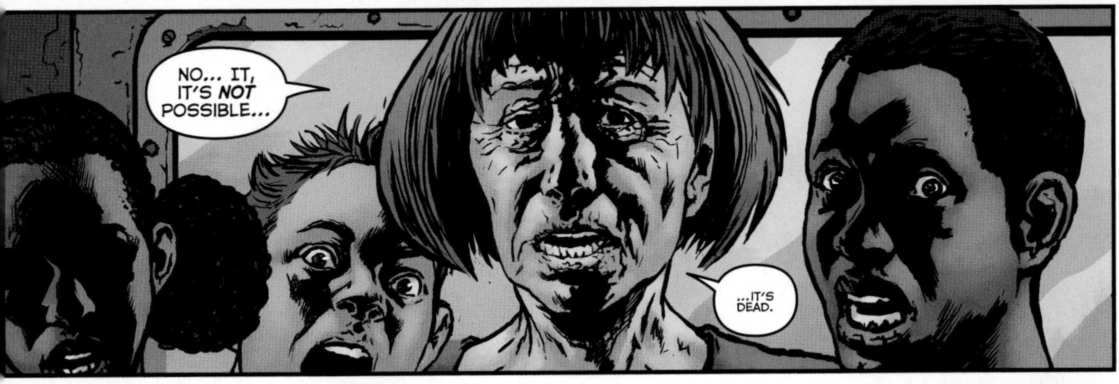
NO... IT, IT'S NOT POSSIBLE...
...IT'S DEAD.

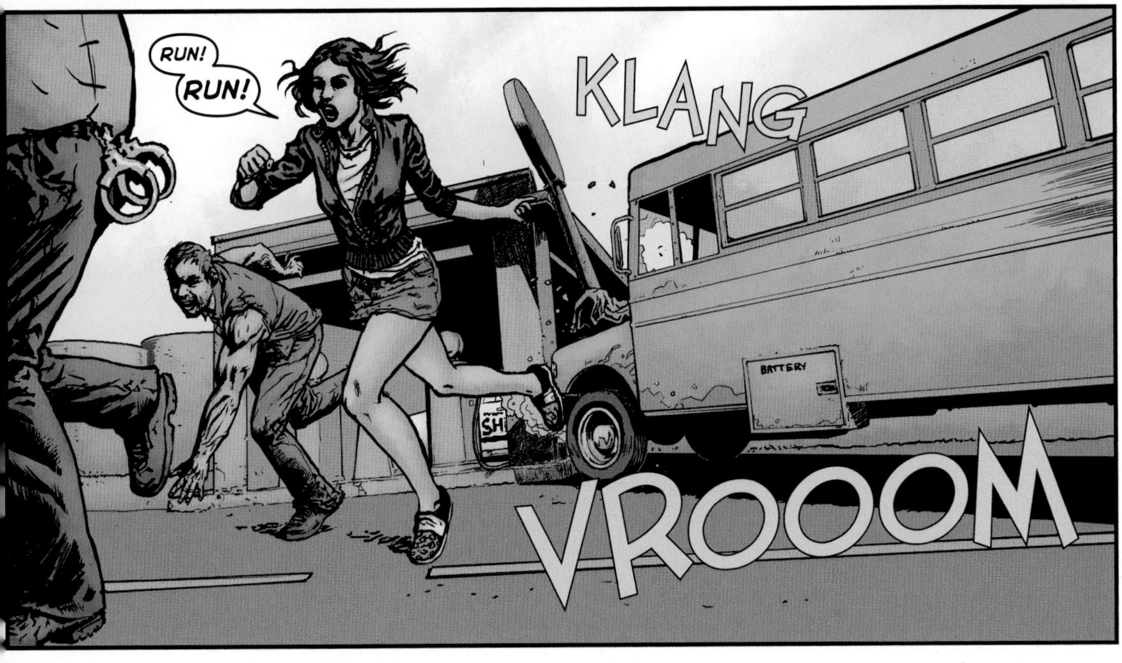
RUN!
RUN!
KLANG
BATTERY
VROOOM

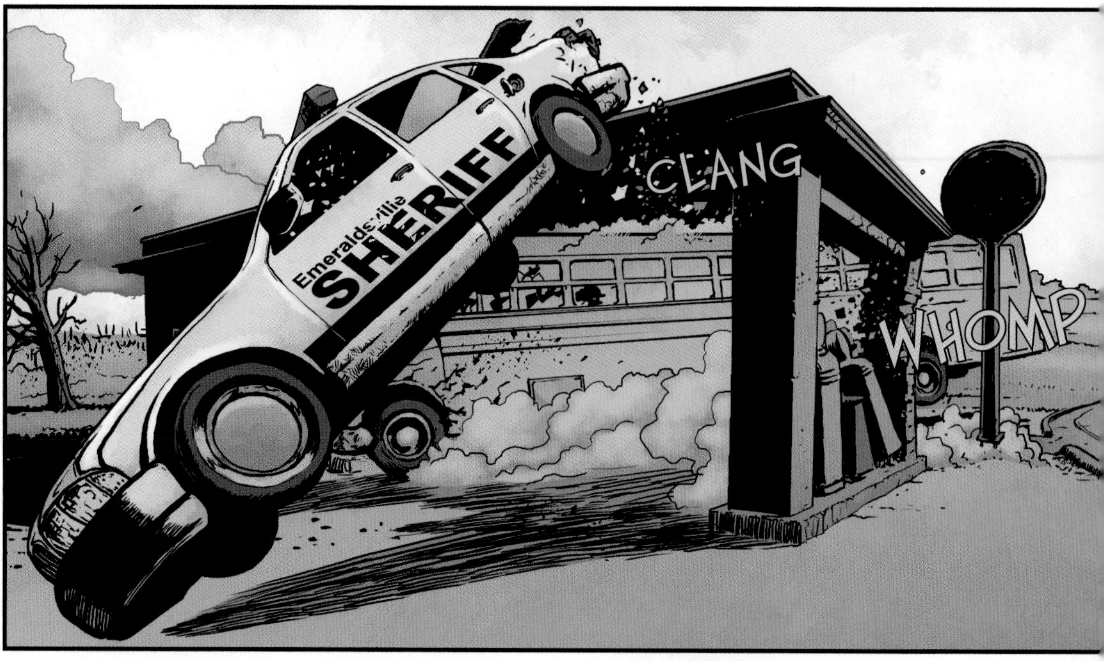
Emeraldsville
SHERIFF
CLANG
WHOMP

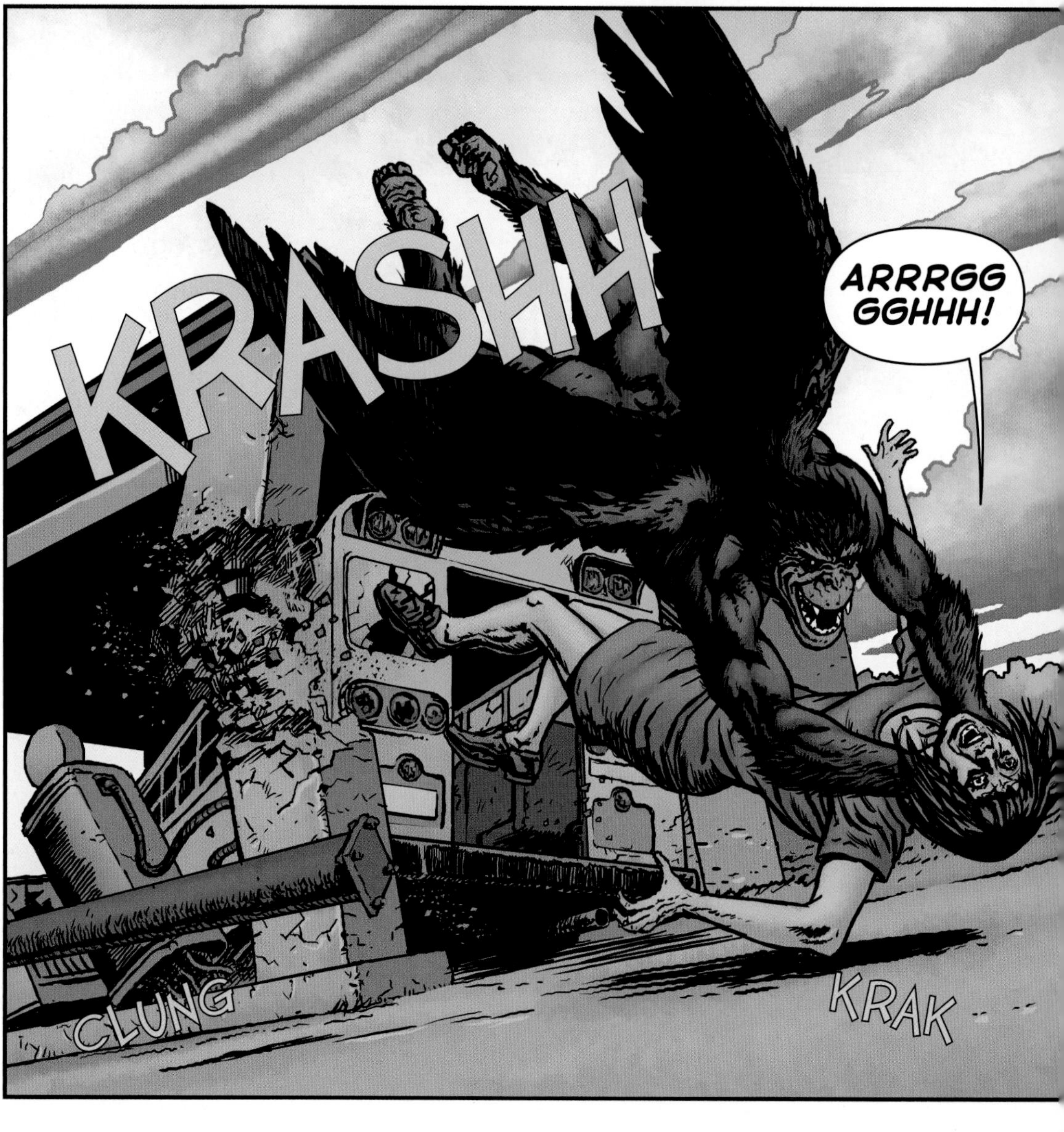
KRASHH
ARRRGG GGHHH!
CLUNG
KRAK

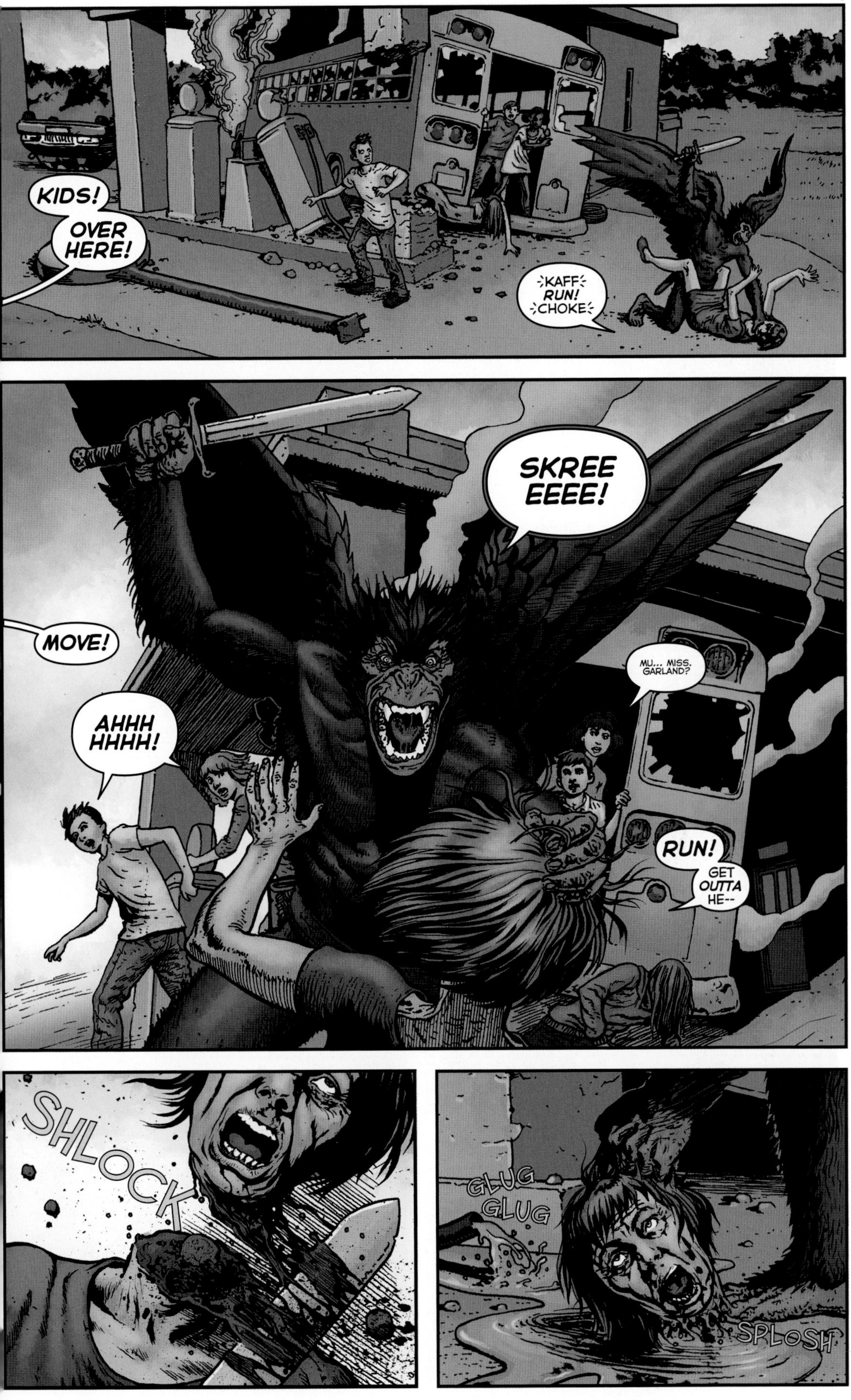
KIDS!
OVER HERE!
KAFF RUN! CHOKE
SKREE EEEE!
MOVE!
AHHH HHHH!
MU... MISS. GARLAND?
RUN!
GET OUTTA HE--
SHLOCK
GLUG GLUG
SPLOSH

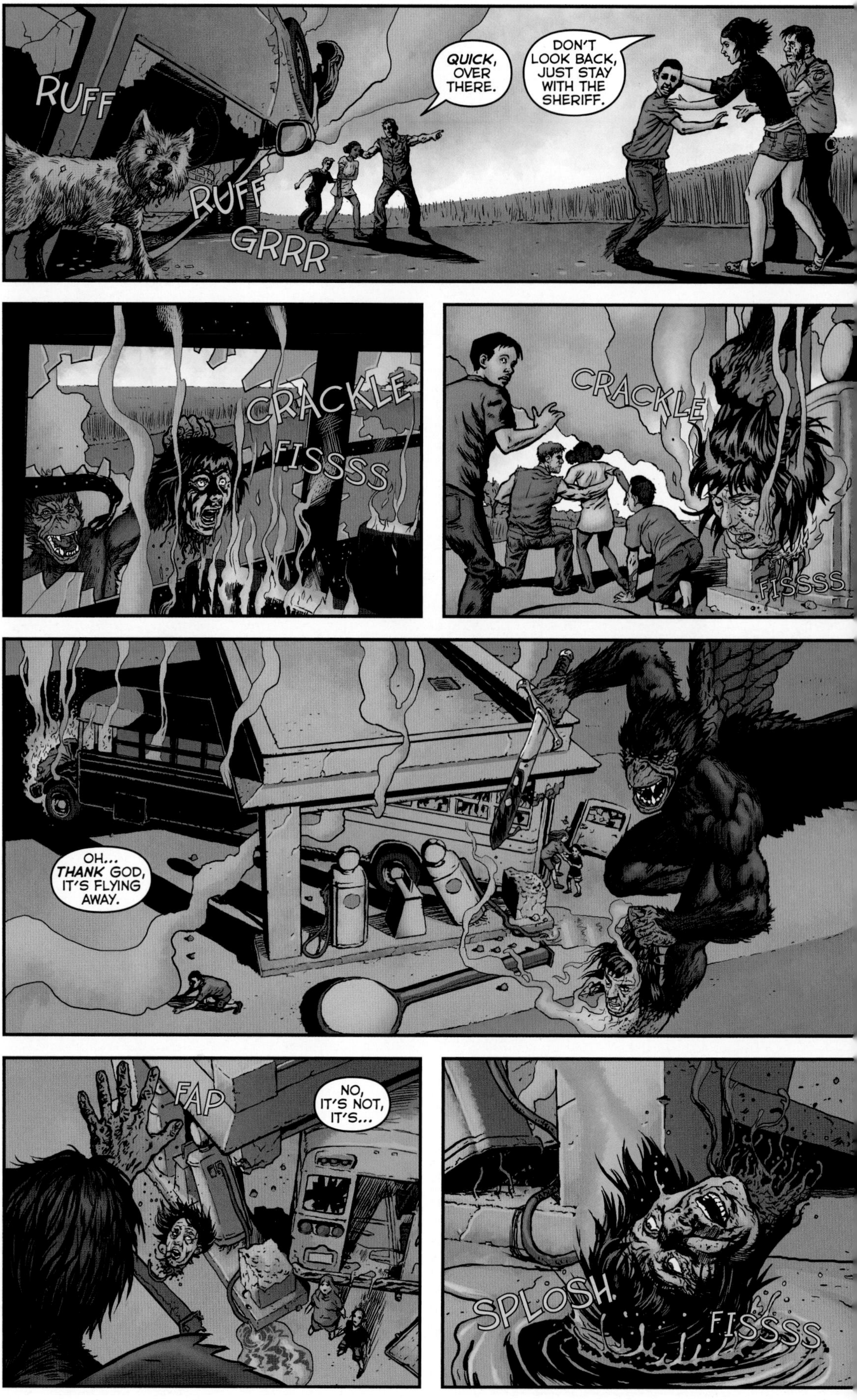
RUFF
RUFF
GRRR
QUICK, OVER THERE.
DON'T LOOK BACK, JUST STAY WITH THE SHERIFF.
CRACKLE
FISSSS
CRACKLE
FISSSS
OH... THANK GOD, IT'S FLYING AWAY.
FAP
NO, IT'S NOT, IT'S...
SPLOSH
FISSSS

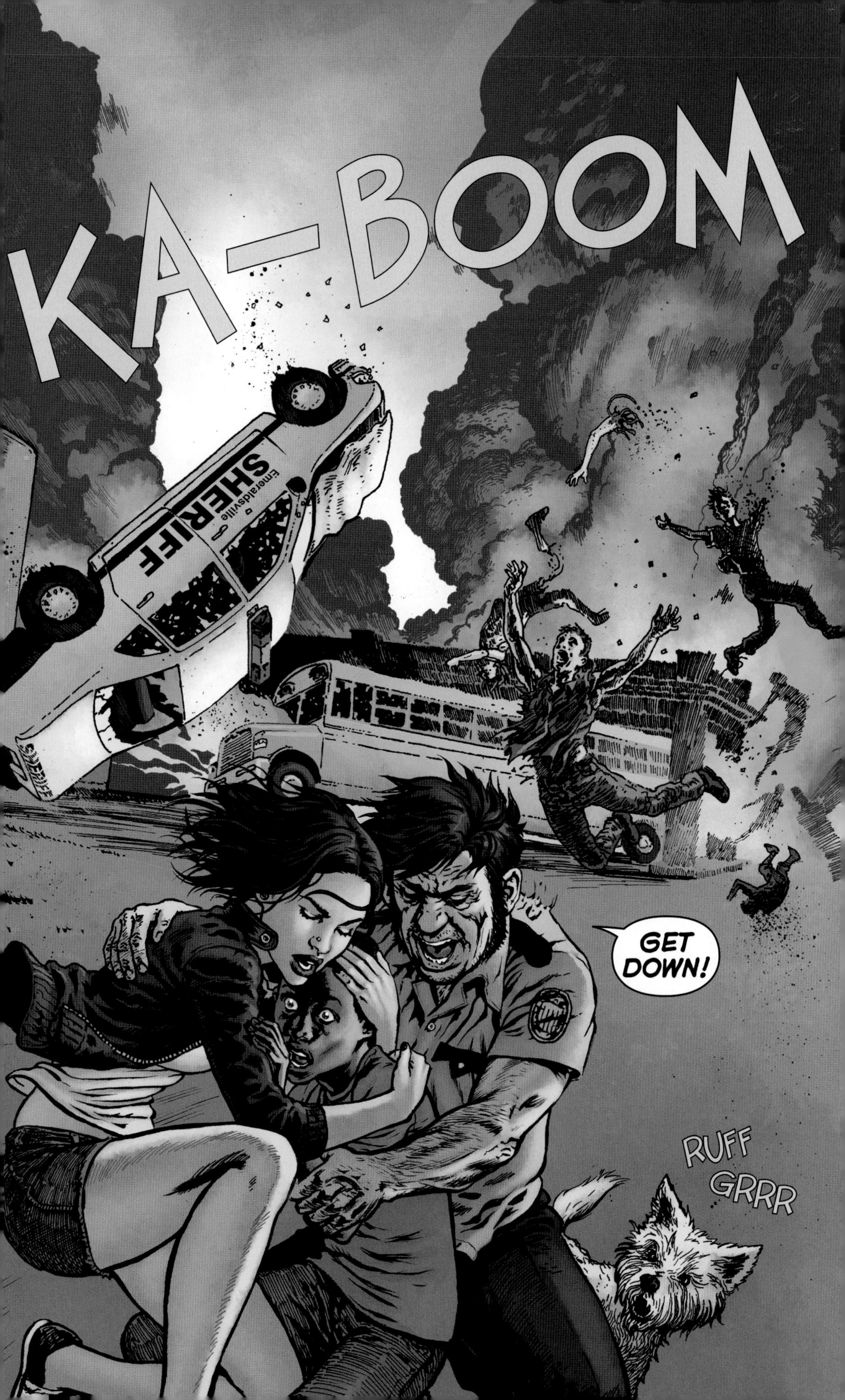
KA-BOOM
SHERIFF
Emeraldsville
GET DOWN!
RUFF
GRRR

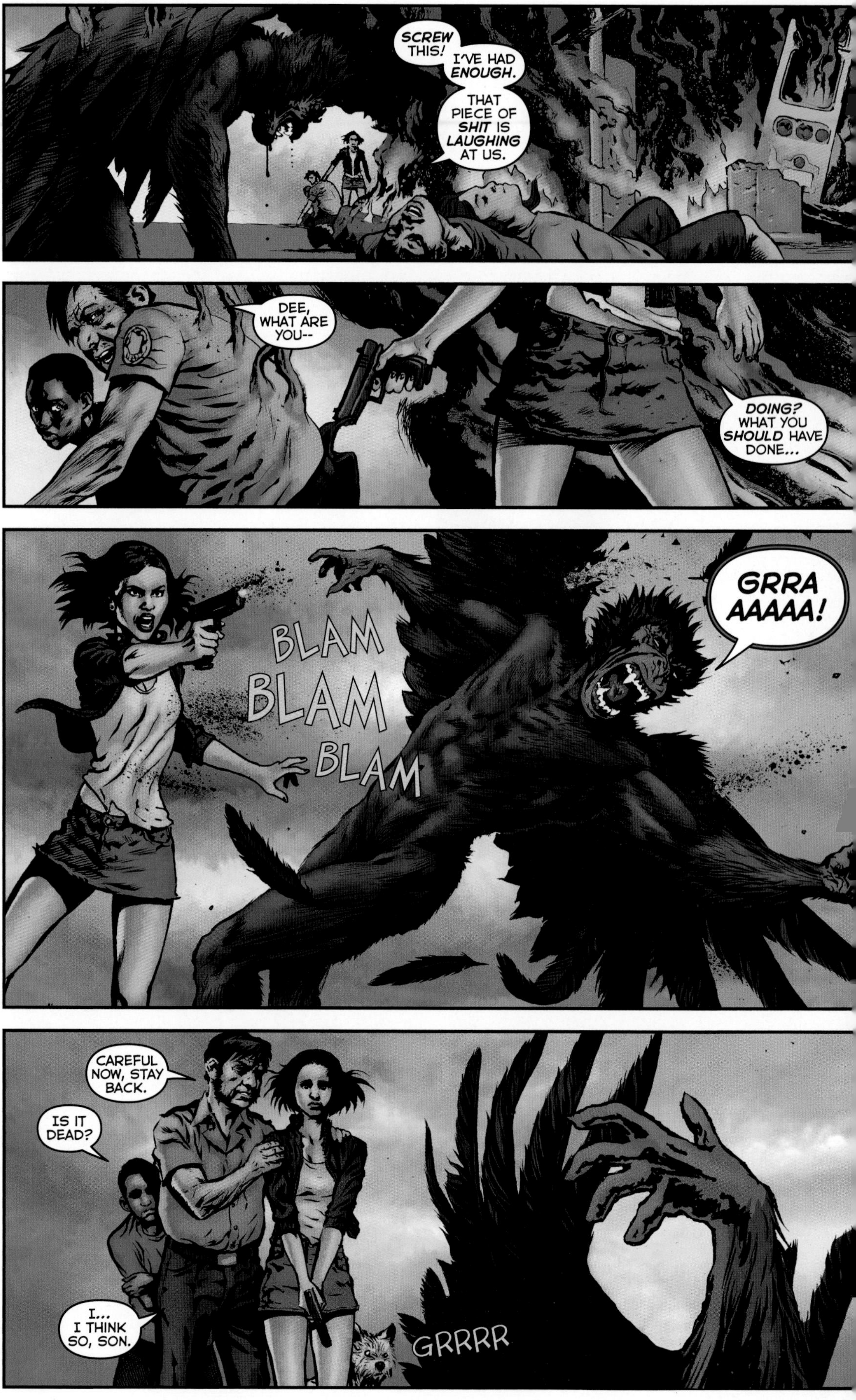

SCREW THIS!
I'VE HAD ENOUGH.
THAT PIECE OF SHIT IS LAUGHING AT US.
DEE, WHAT ARE YOU--
DOING? WHAT YOU SHOULD HAVE DONE...
BLAM
BLAM
BLAM
GRRA AAAAA!
CAREFUL NOW, STAY BACK.
IS IT DEAD?
I... I THINK SO, SON.
GRRRR

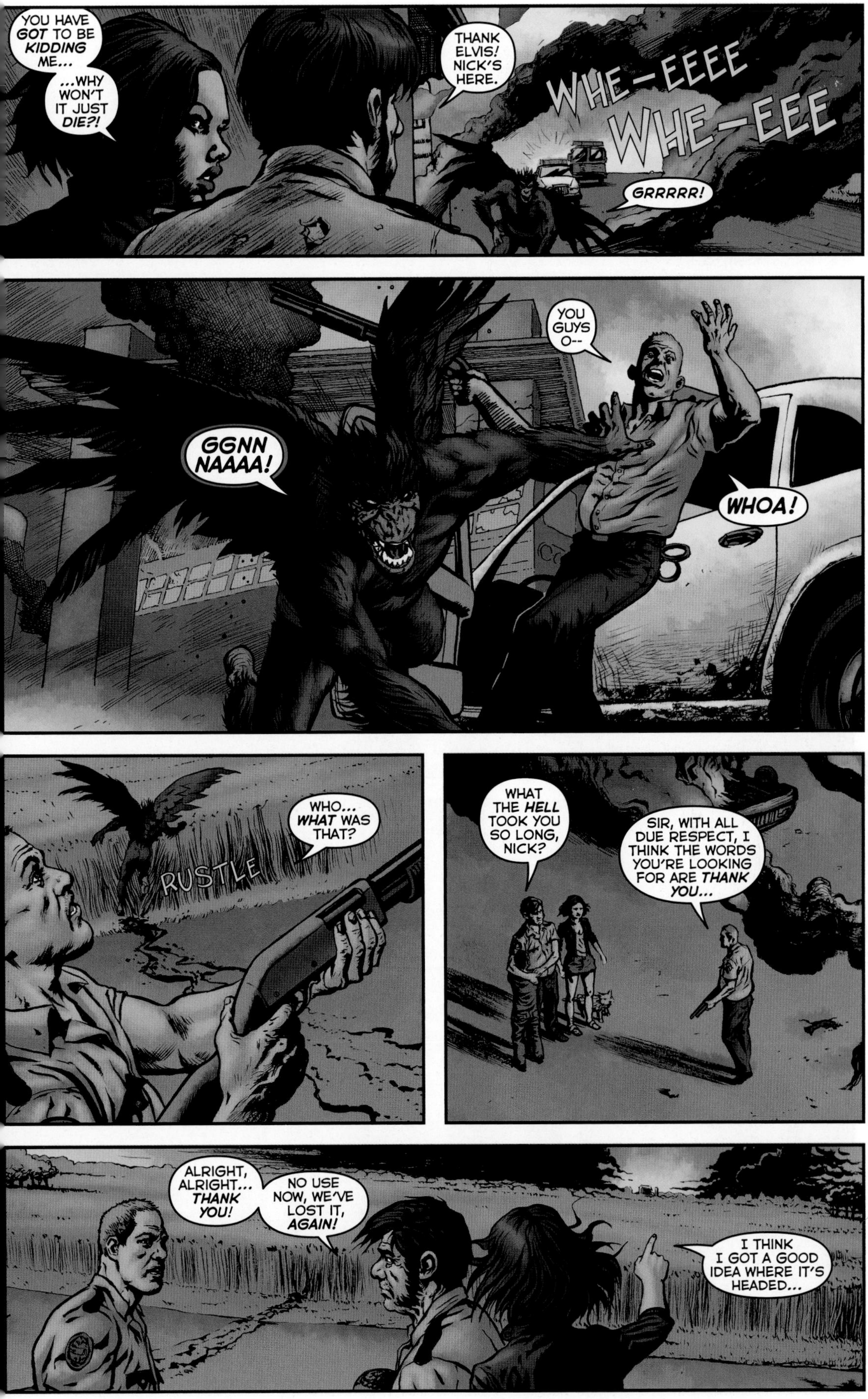
YOU HAVE GOT TO BE KIDDING ME...
...WHY WON'T IT JUST DIE?!
THANK ELVIS! NICK'S HERE.
WHE-EEEE
WHE-EEE
GRRRRR!
YOU GUYS O--
GGNN NAAAA!
WHOA!
WHO... WHAT WAS THAT?
RUSTLE
WHAT THE HELL TOOK YOU SO LONG, NICK?
SIR, WITH ALL DUE RESPECT, I THINK THE WORDS YOU'RE LOOKING FOR ARE THANK YOU...
ALRIGHT, ALRIGHT... THANK YOU!
NO USE NOW, WE'VE LOST IT, AGAIN!
I THINK I GOT A GOOD IDEA WHERE IT'S HEADED...

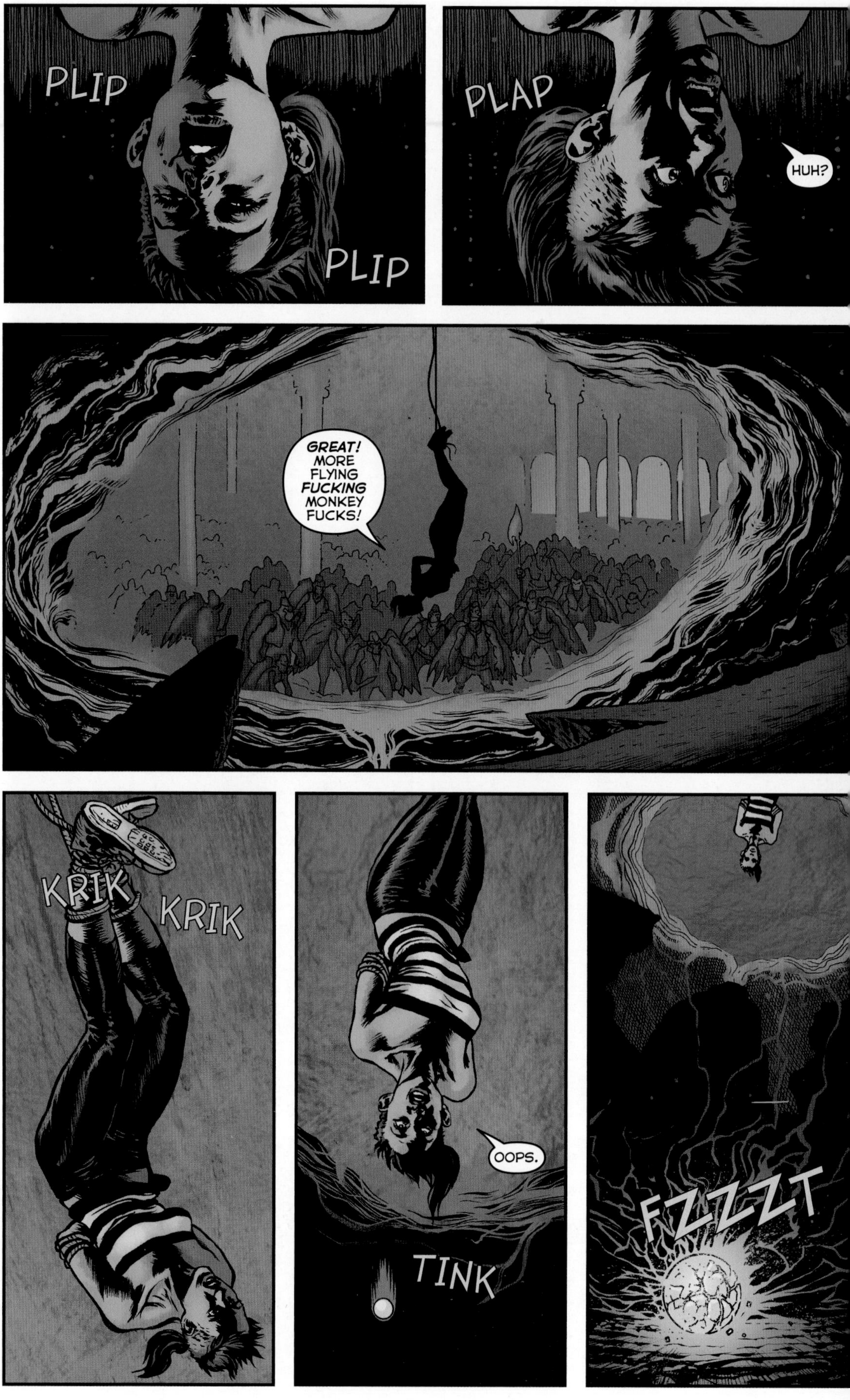
PLIP
PLIP
PLAP
HUH?
GREAT! MORE FLYING FUCKING MONKEY FUCKS!
KRIK
KRIK
OOPS.
TINK
FZZZZT

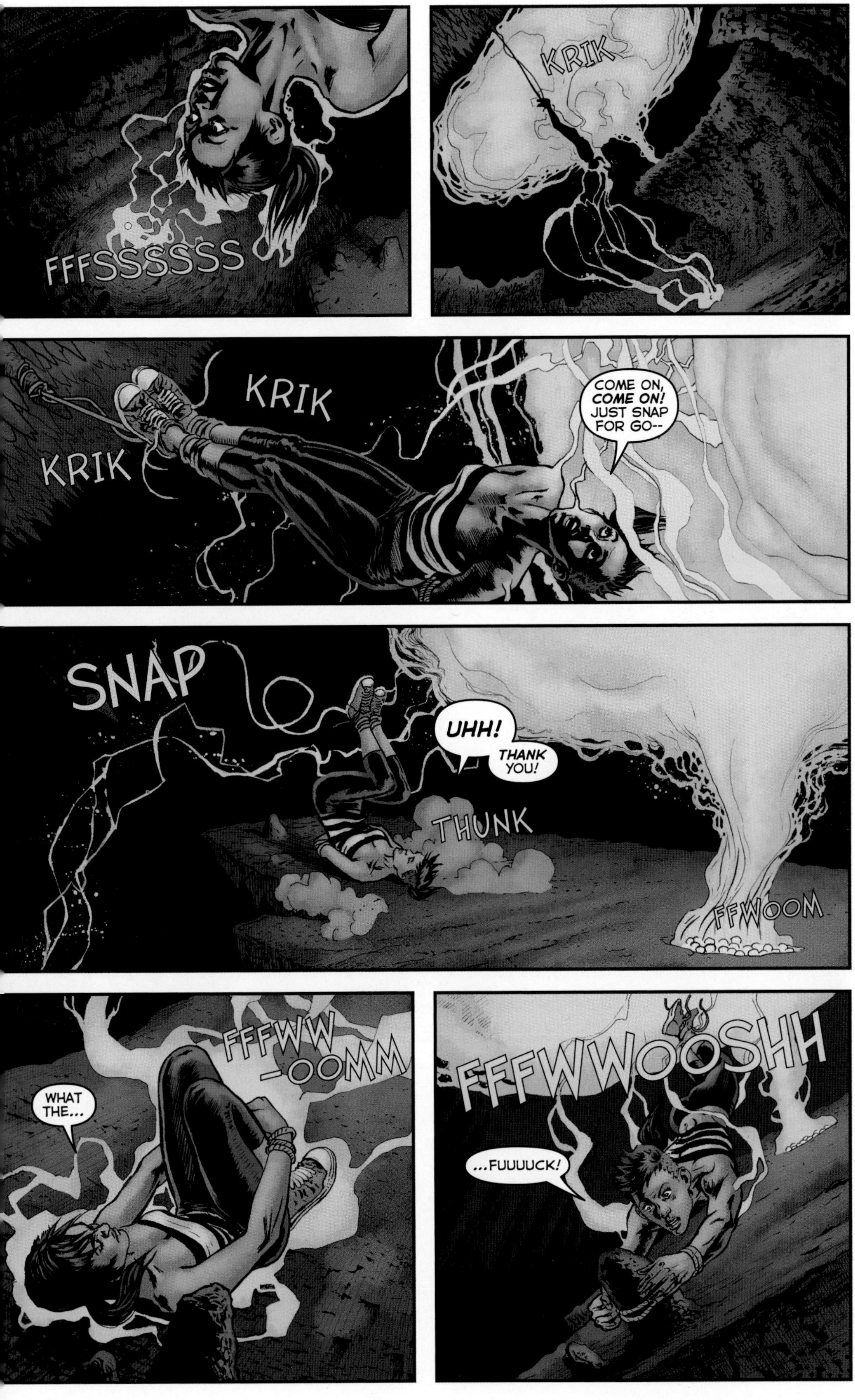
FFFSSSSSS
KRIK
KRIK
KRIK
COME ON, COME ON! JUST SNAP FOR GO--
SNAP
UHH!
THANK YOU!
THUNK
FFWOOM
FFFWW -OOMM
WHAT THE...
FFFWWOOSHH
...FUUUUCK!

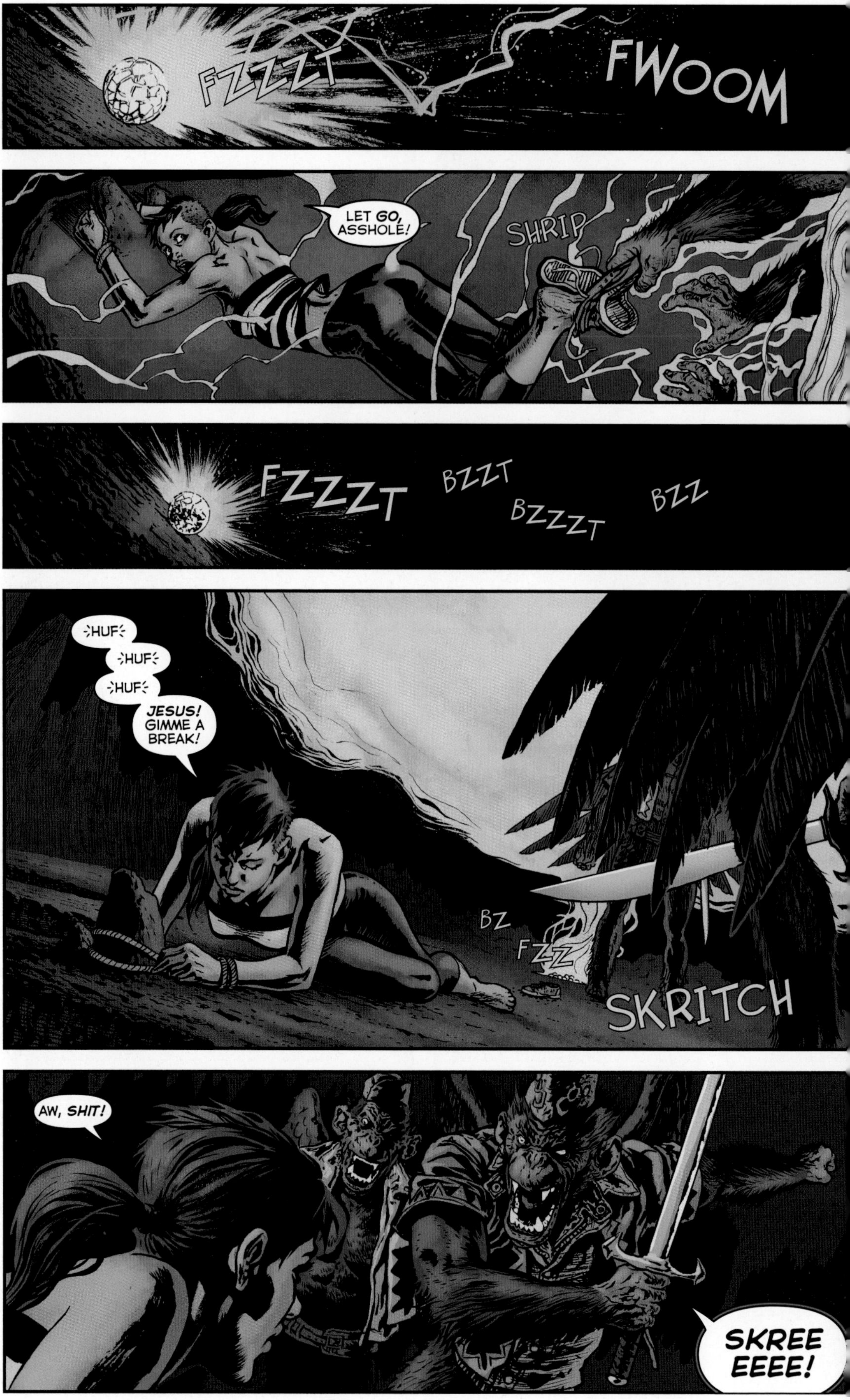
FZZZT
FWOOM
LET GO, ASSHOLE!
SHRIP
FZZZT
BZZT
BZZZT
BZZ
HUF
HUF
HUF
JESUS! GIMME A BREAK!
BZ
FZZ
SKRITCH
AW, SHIT!
SKREE EEEE!

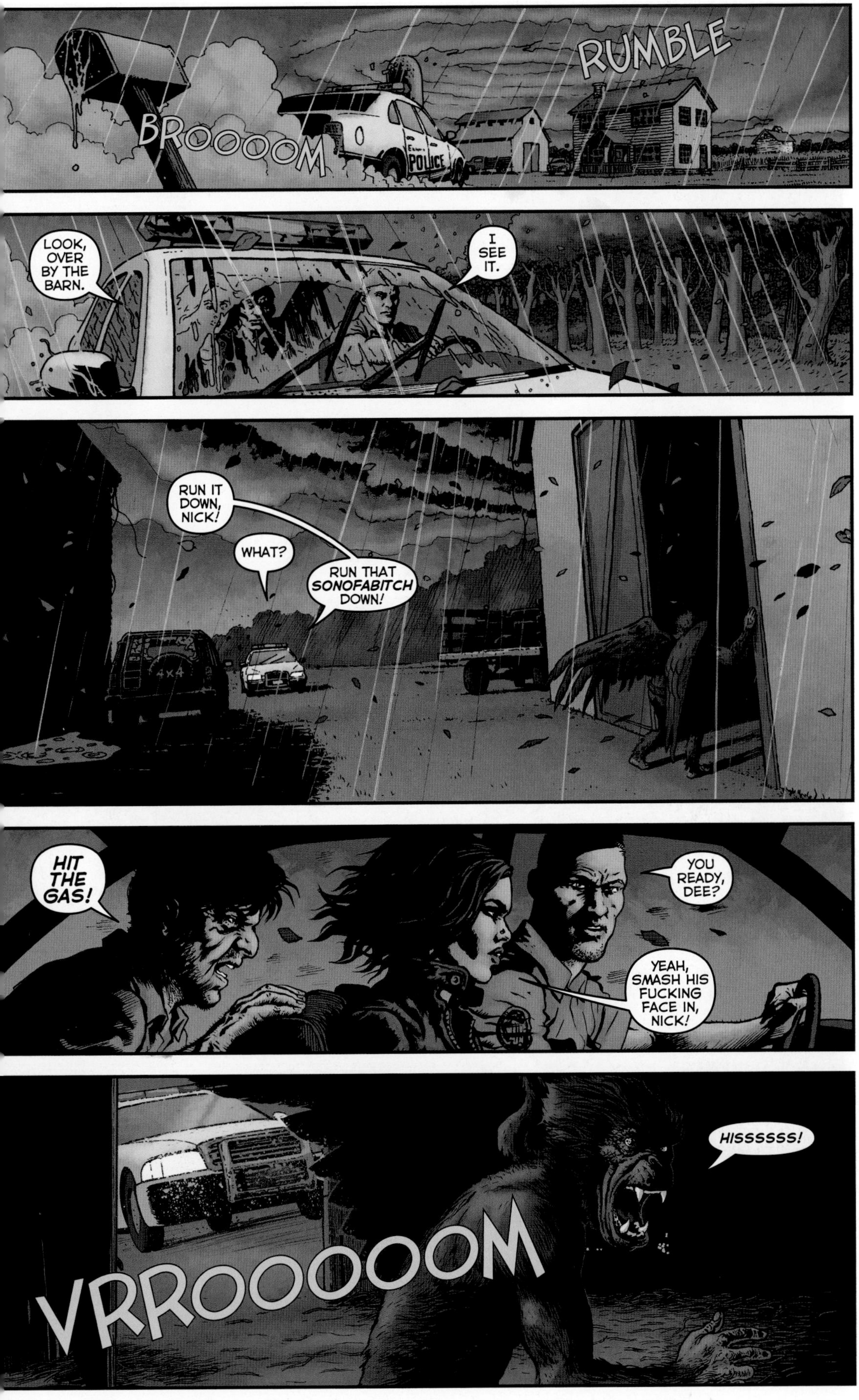
BROOOOM
RUMBLE
POLICE
LOOK, OVER BY THE BARN.
I SEE IT.
RUN IT DOWN, NICK!
WHAT?
RUN THAT SONOFABITCH DOWN!
4X4
HIT THE GAS!
YOU READY, DEE?
YEAH, SMASH HIS FUCKING FACE IN, NICK!
HISSSSSS!
VRROOOOOM

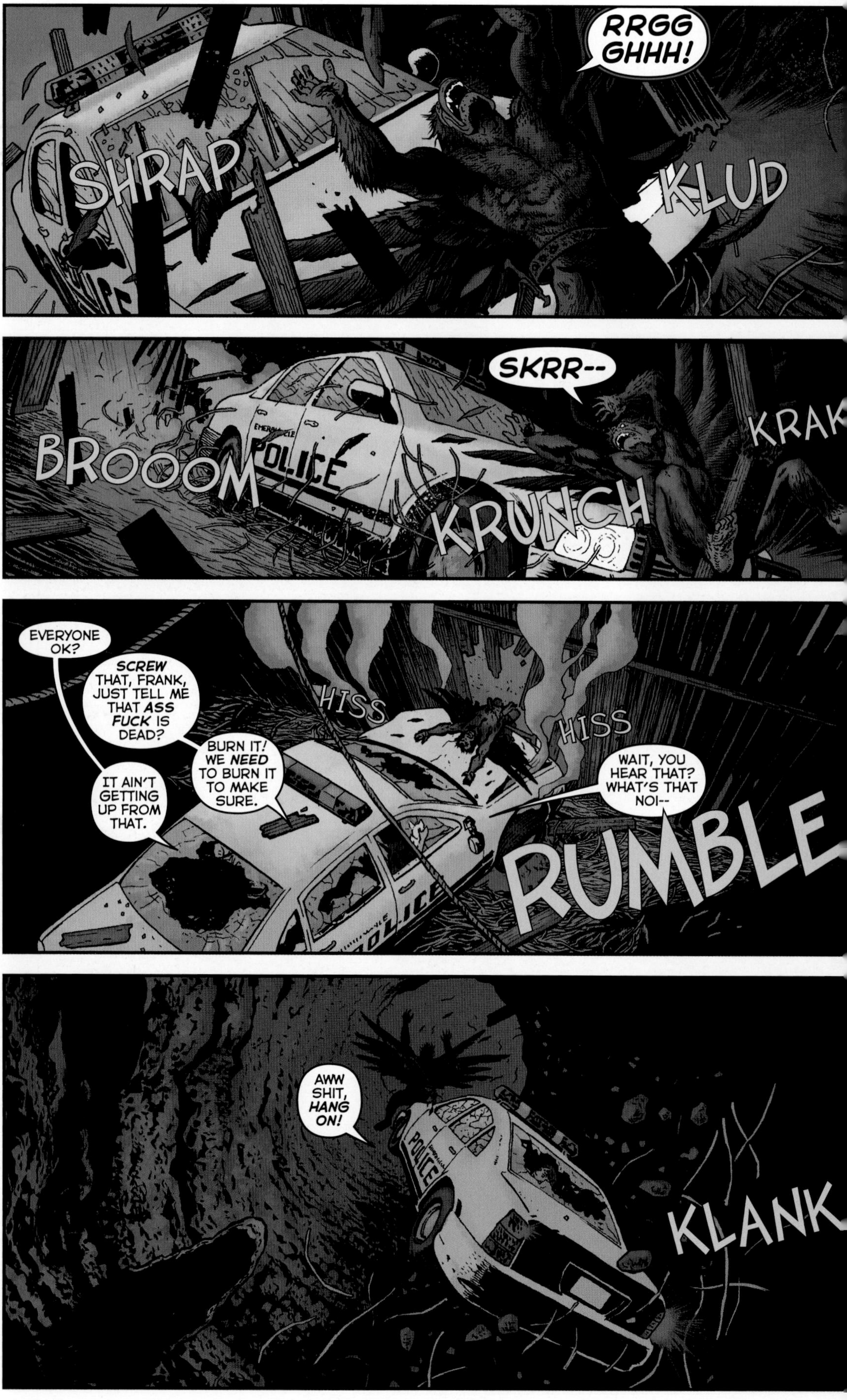
RRGG GHHH!
SHRAP
KLUD
SKRR--
BROOOM
KRUNCH
KRAK
EVERYONE OK?
SCREW THAT, FRANK, JUST TELL ME THAT ASS FUCK IS DEAD?
IT AIN'T GETTING UP FROM THAT.
BURN IT! WE NEED TO BURN IT TO MAKE SURE.
HISS
HISS
WAIT, YOU HEAR THAT? WHAT'S THAT NOI--
RUMBLE
AWW SHIT, HANG ON!
KLANK

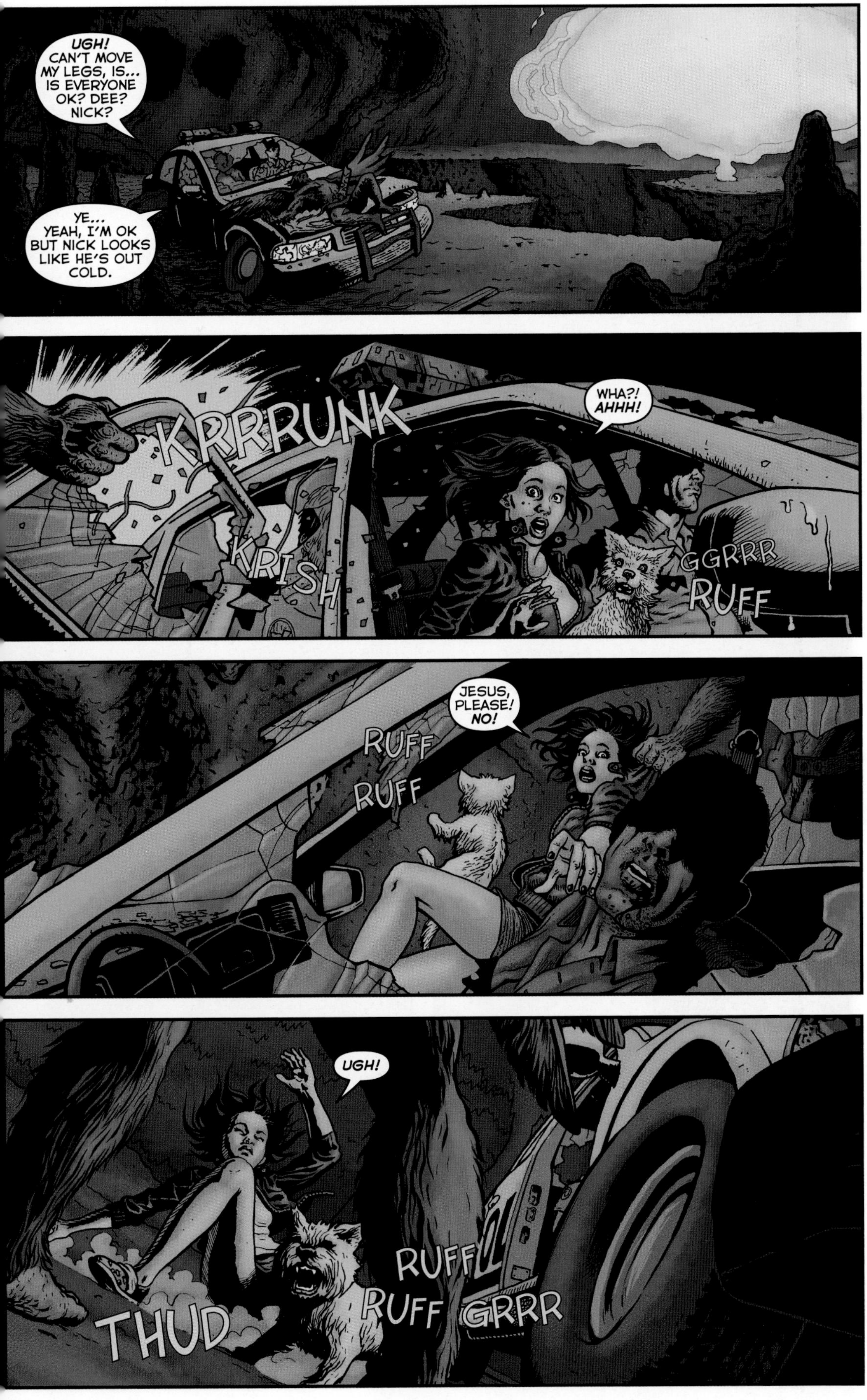
UGH! CAN'T MOVE MY LEGS, IS... IS EVERYONE OK? DEE? NICK?
YE... YEAH, I'M OK BUT NICK LOOKS LIKE HE'S OUT COLD.
KRRRUNK
KRISH
WHA?! AHHH!
GGRRR
RUFF
JESUS, PLEASE! NO!
RUFF
RUFF
UGH!
THUD
RUFF
RUFF
GRRR

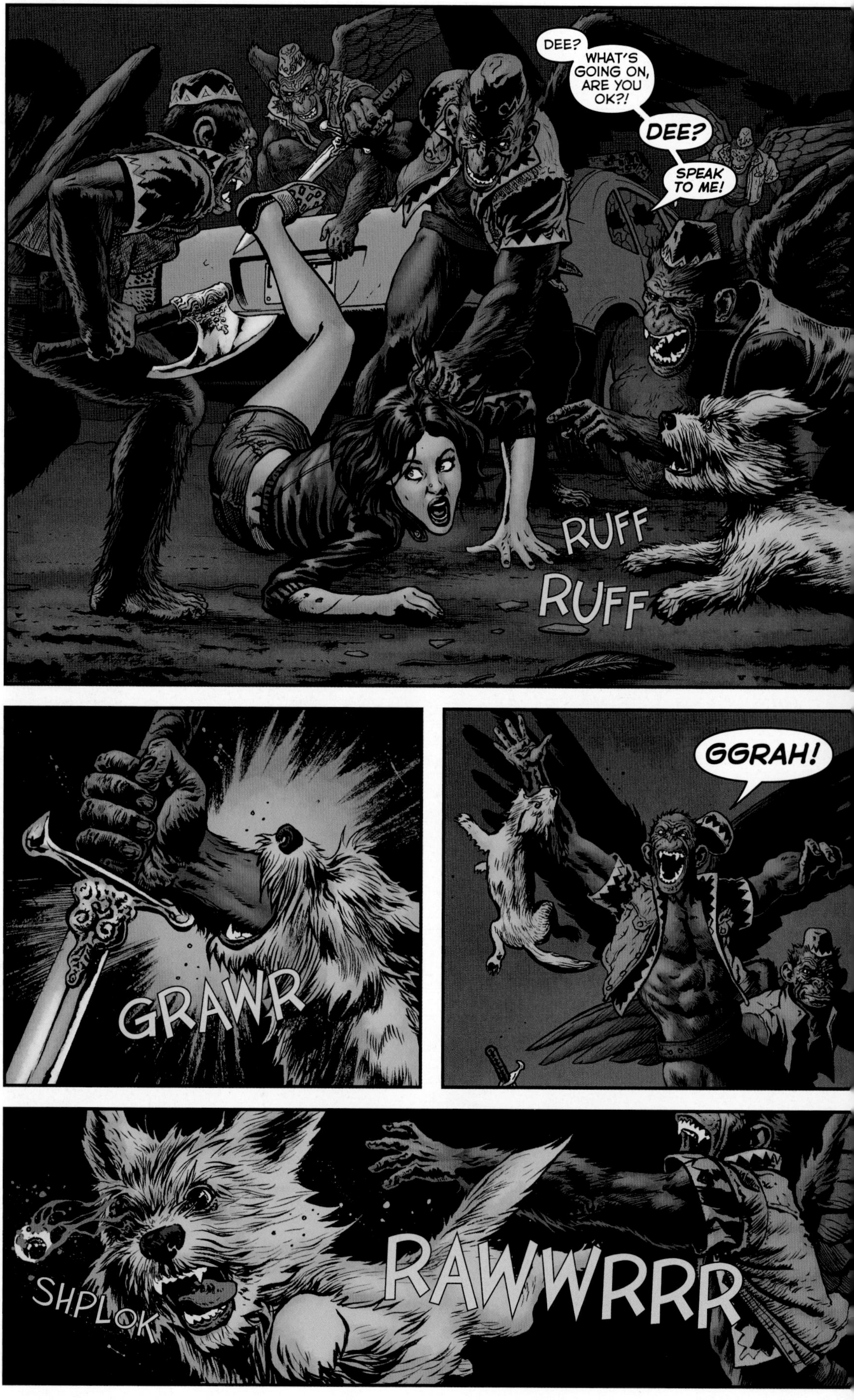

DEE? WHAT'S GOING ON, ARE YOU OK?!
DEE?
SPEAK TO ME!
RUFF
RUFF
GRAWR
GGRAH!
SHPLOK
RAWWRRR

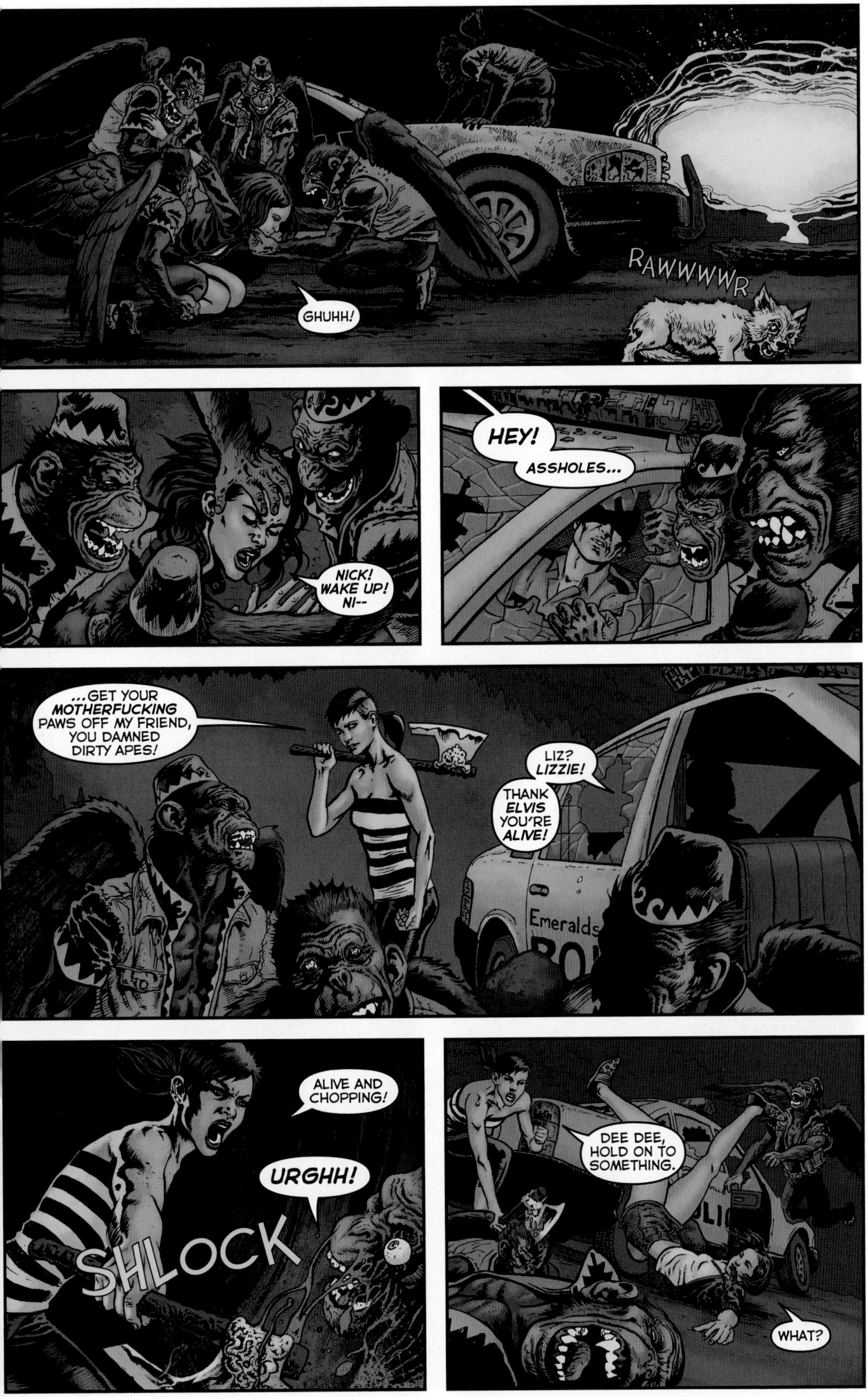
RAWWWWR
GHUHH!
NICK! WAKE UP! NI--
HEY!
ASSHOLES...
...GET YOUR MOTHERFUCKING PAWS OFF MY FRIEND, YOU DAMNED DIRTY APES!
LIZ? LIZZIE!
THANK ELVIS YOU'RE ALIVE!
Emeralds
ALIVE AND CHOPPING!
URGHH!
SHLOCK
DEE DEE, HOLD ON TO SOMETHING.
WHAT?

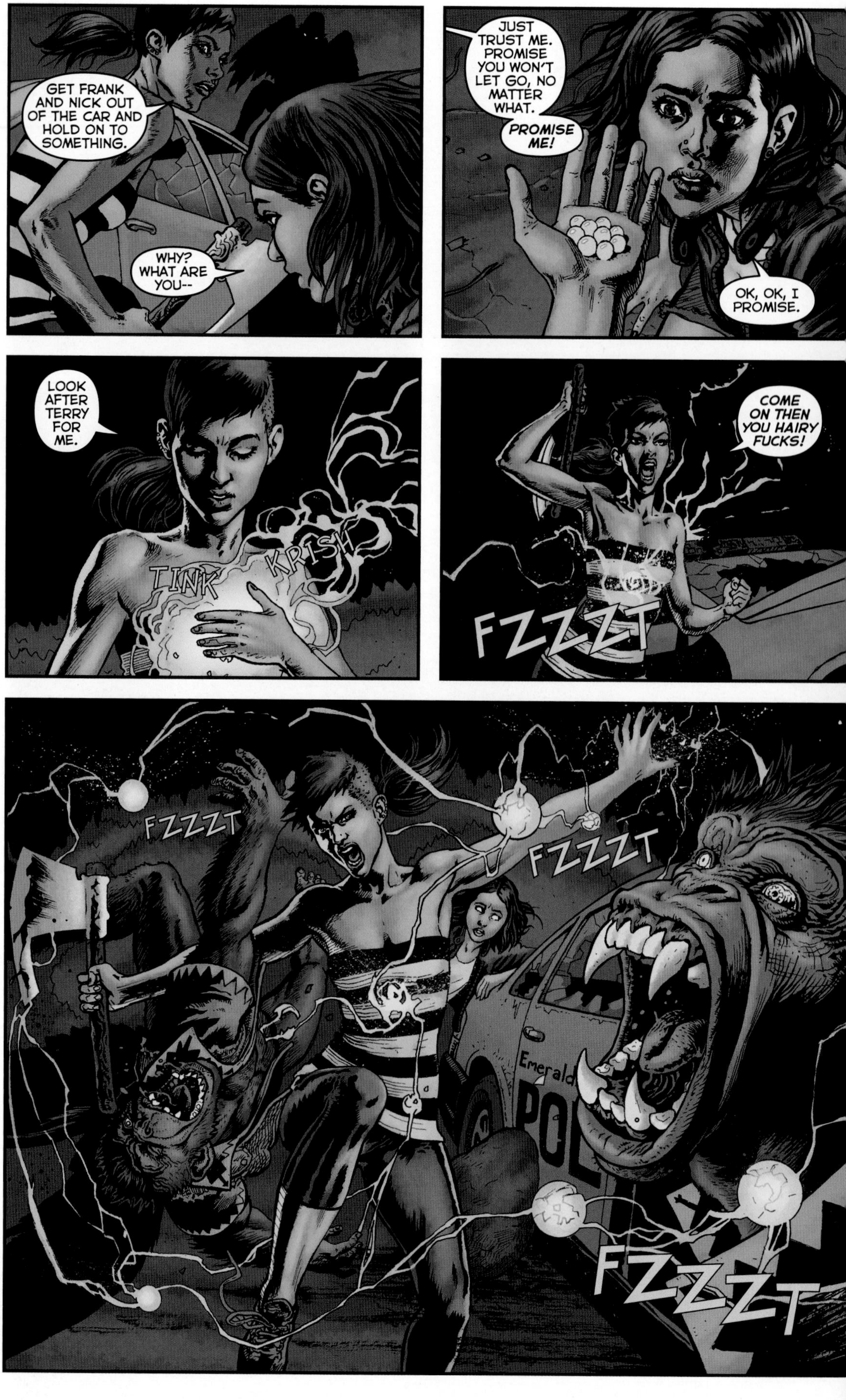
GET FRANK AND NICK OUT OF THE CAR AND HOLD ON TO SOMETHING.
WHY? WHAT ARE YOU--
JUST TRUST ME. PROMISE YOU WON'T LET GO, NO MATTER WHAT.
PROMISE ME!
OK, OK, I PROMISE.
LOOK AFTER TERRY FOR ME.
TINK
KRISH
COME ON THEN YOU HAIRY FUCKS!
FZZZT
FZZZT
FZZZT
Emerald
POL
FZZZZT

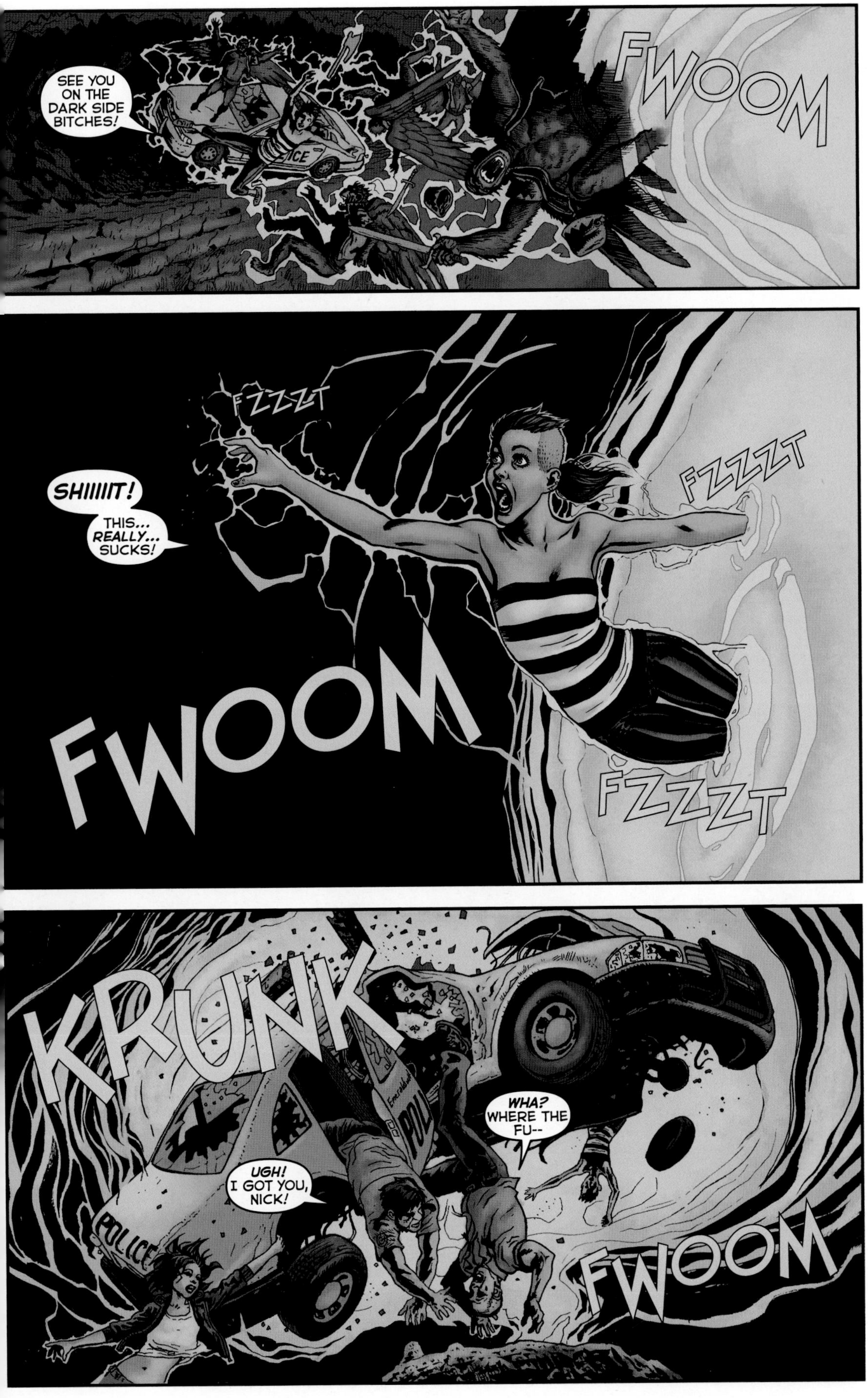
FWOOM
SEE YOU ON THE DARK SIDE BITCHES!
FZZZT
SHIIIIIT!
THIS... REALLY... SUCKS!
FZZZZT
FWOOM
FZZZZT
KRUNK
WHA? WHERE THE FU--
UGH! I GOT YOU, NICK!
FWOOM

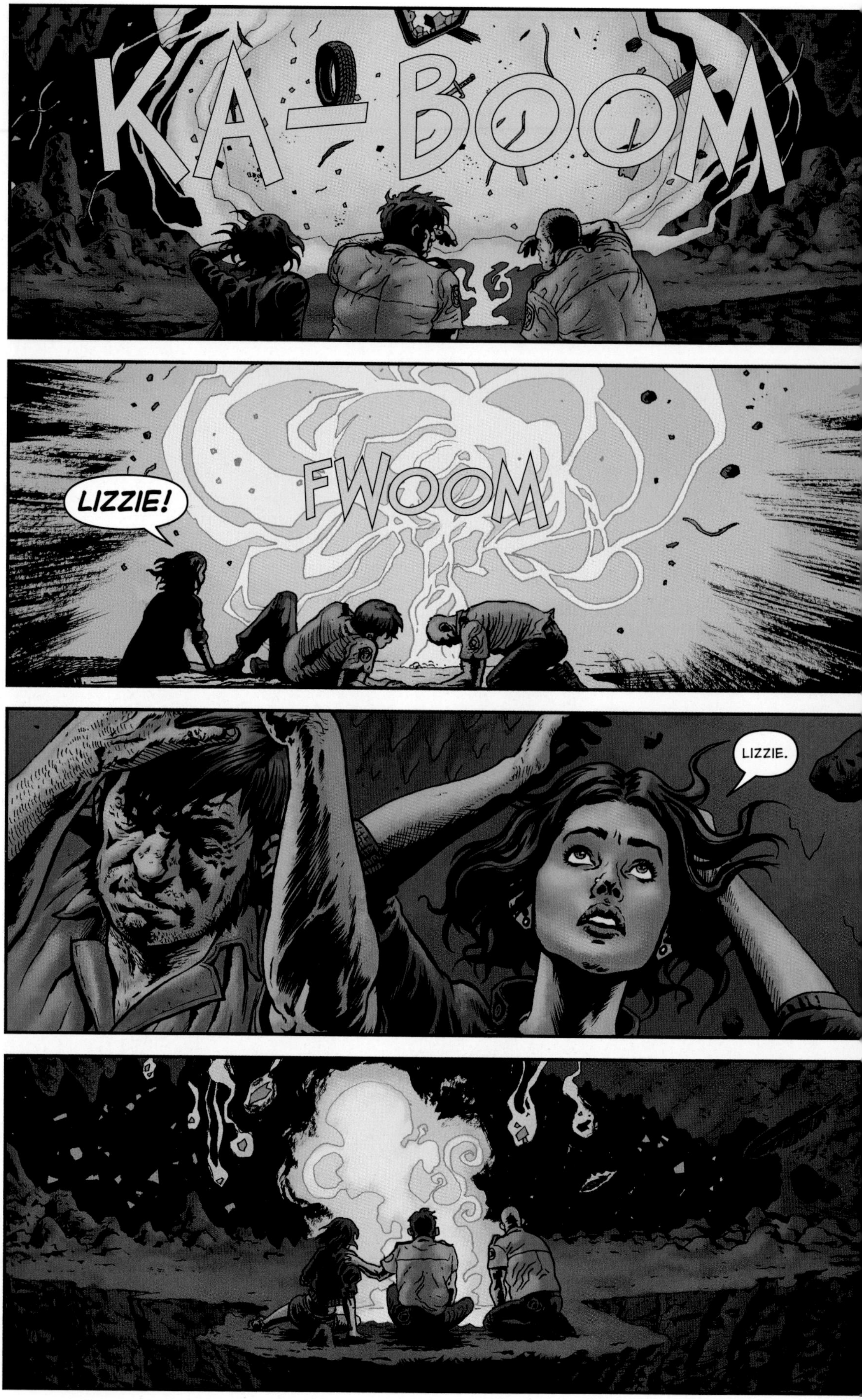
KA-BOOM
FWOOM
LIZZIE!
LIZZIE.

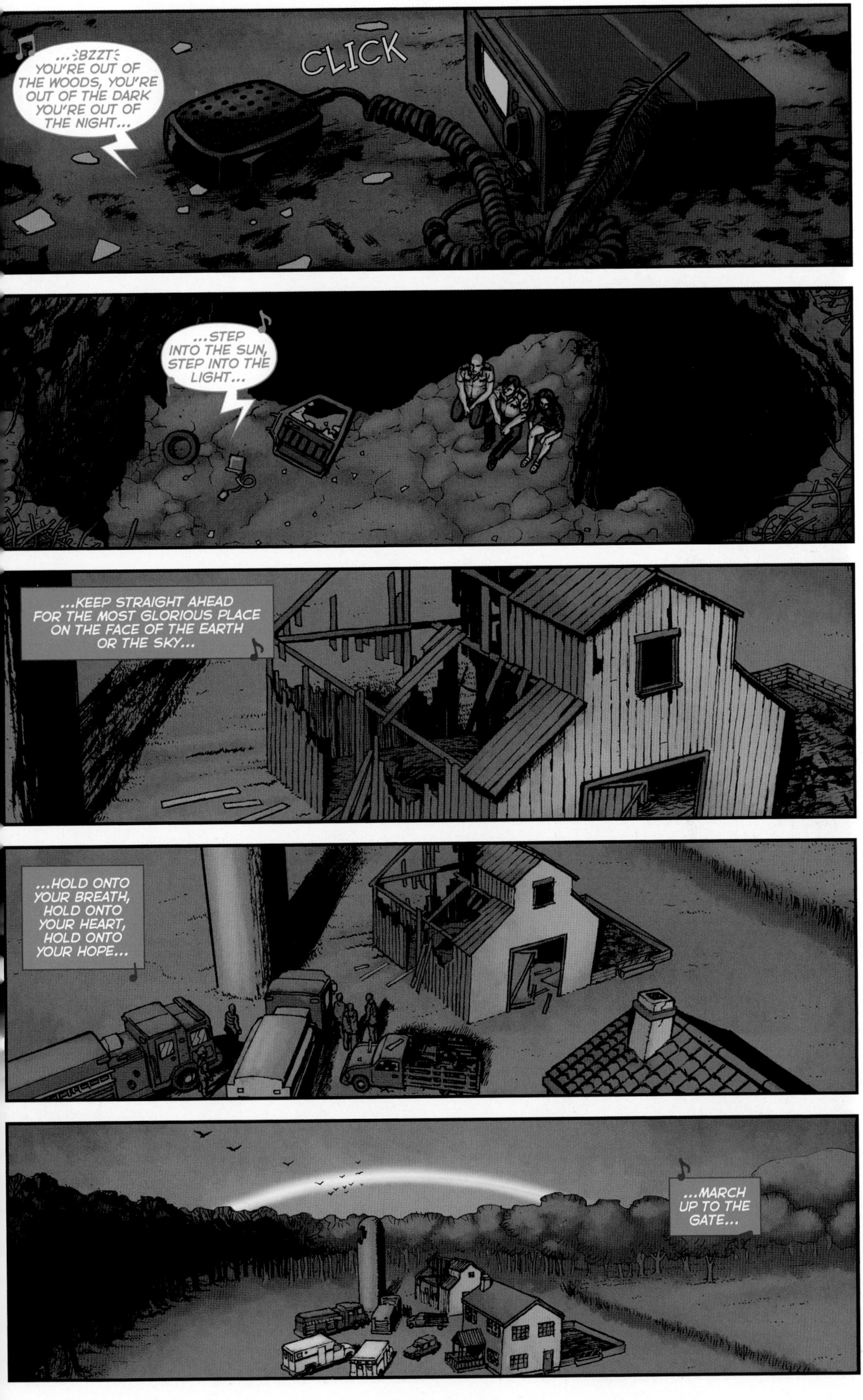
...BZZT YOU'RE OUT OF THE WOODS, YOU'RE OUT OF THE DARK YOU'RE OUT OF THE NIGHT...
CLICK
...STEP INTO THE SUN, STEP INTO THE LIGHT...
...KEEP STRAIGHT AHEAD FOR THE MOST GLORIOUS PLACE ON THE FACE OF THE EARTH OR THE SKY...
...HOLD ONTO YOUR BREATH, HOLD ONTO YOUR HEART, HOLD ONTO YOUR HOPE...
...MARCH UP TO THE GATE...

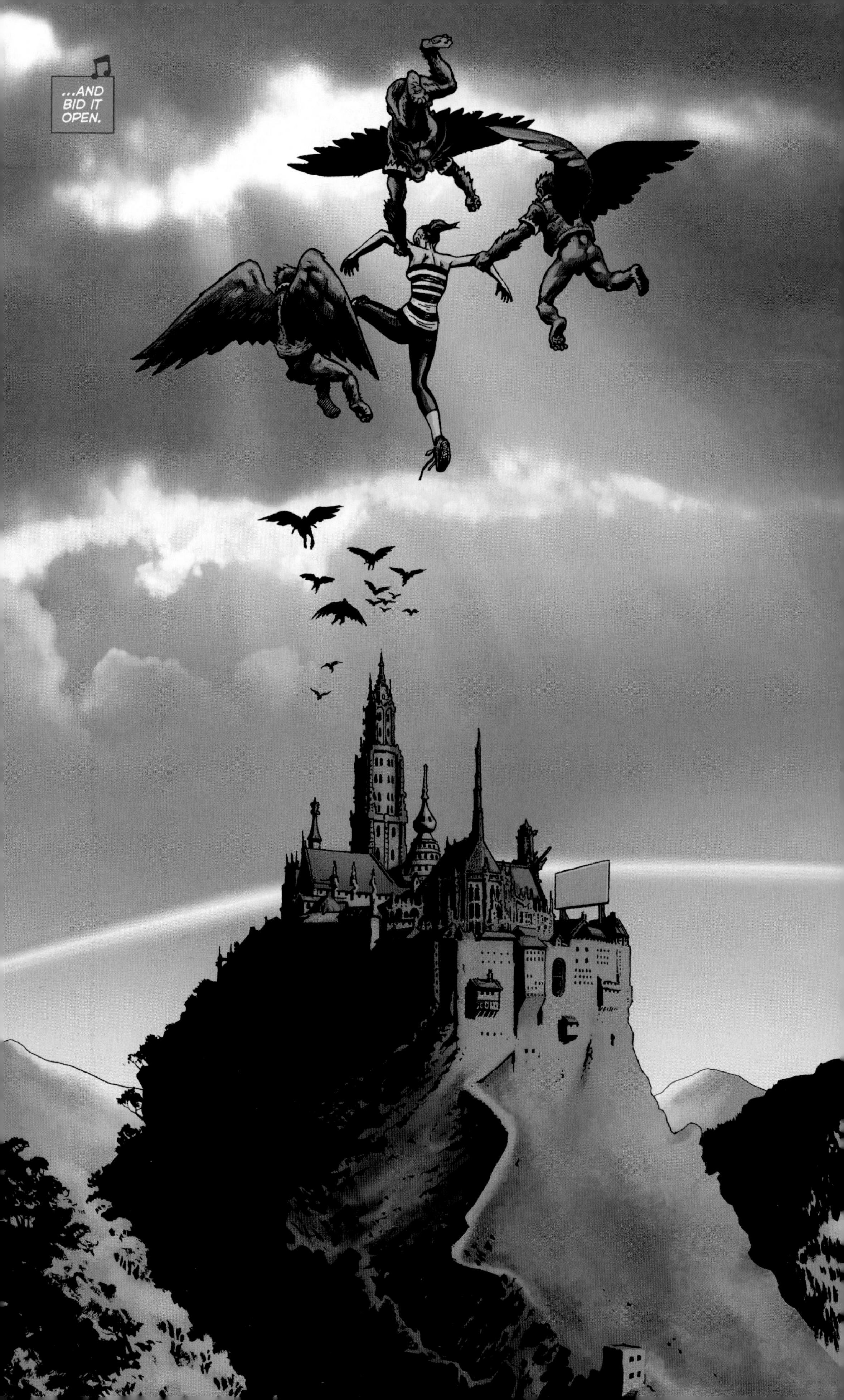
...AND
BID IT
OPEN.

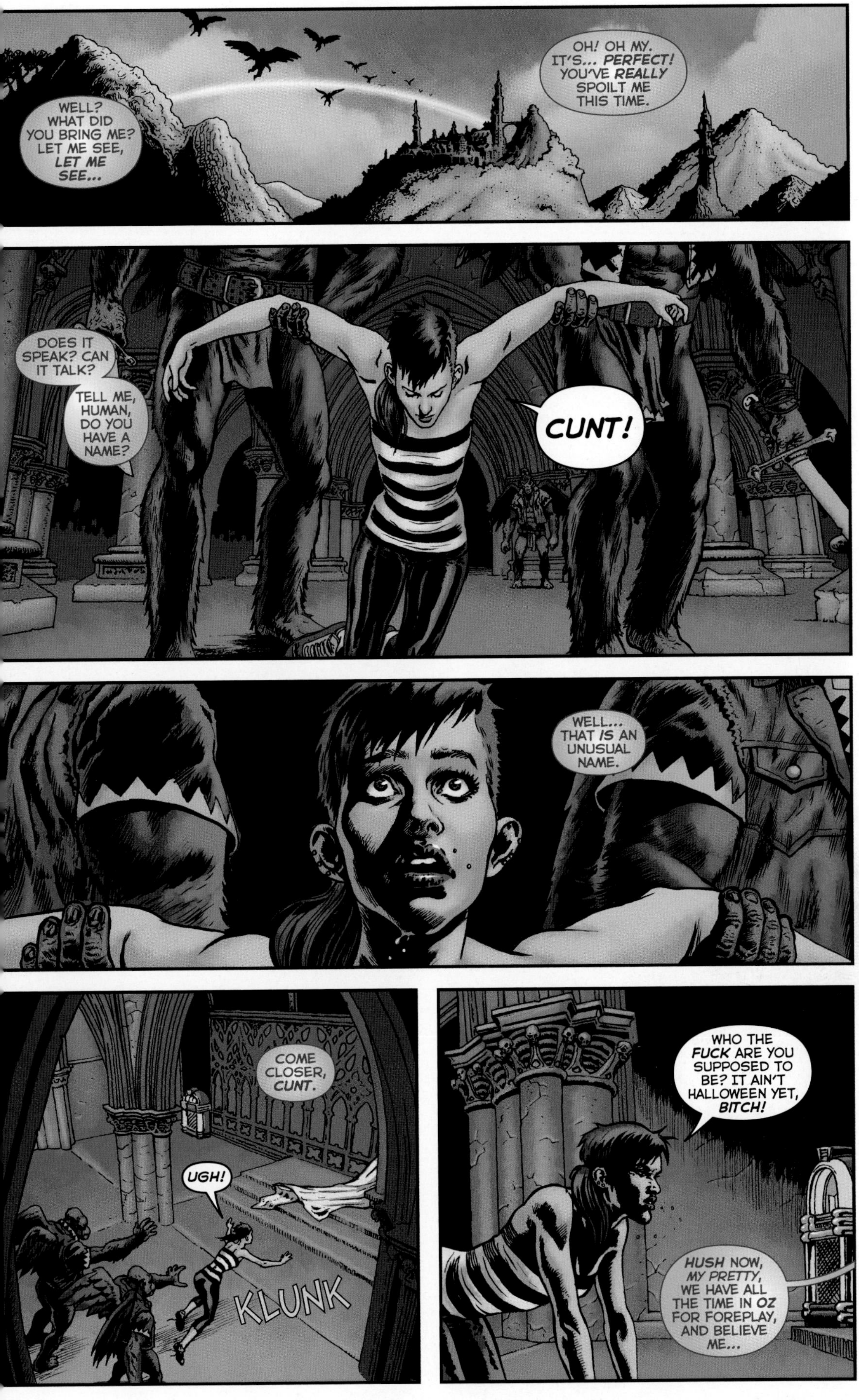
WELL? WHAT DID YOU BRING ME? LET ME SEE, LET ME SEE...
OH! OH MY. IT'S... PERFECT! YOU'VE REALLY SPOILT ME THIS TIME.
DOES IT SPEAK? CAN IT TALK?
TELL ME, HUMAN, DO YOU HAVE A NAME?
CUNT!
WELL... THAT IS AN UNUSUAL NAME.
COME CLOSER, CUNT.
UGH!
KLUNK
WHO THE FUCK ARE YOU SUPPOSED TO BE? IT AIN'T HALLOWEEN YET, BITCH!
HUSH NOW, MY PRETTY, WE HAVE ALL THE TIME IN OZ FOR FOREPLAY, AND BELIEVE ME...

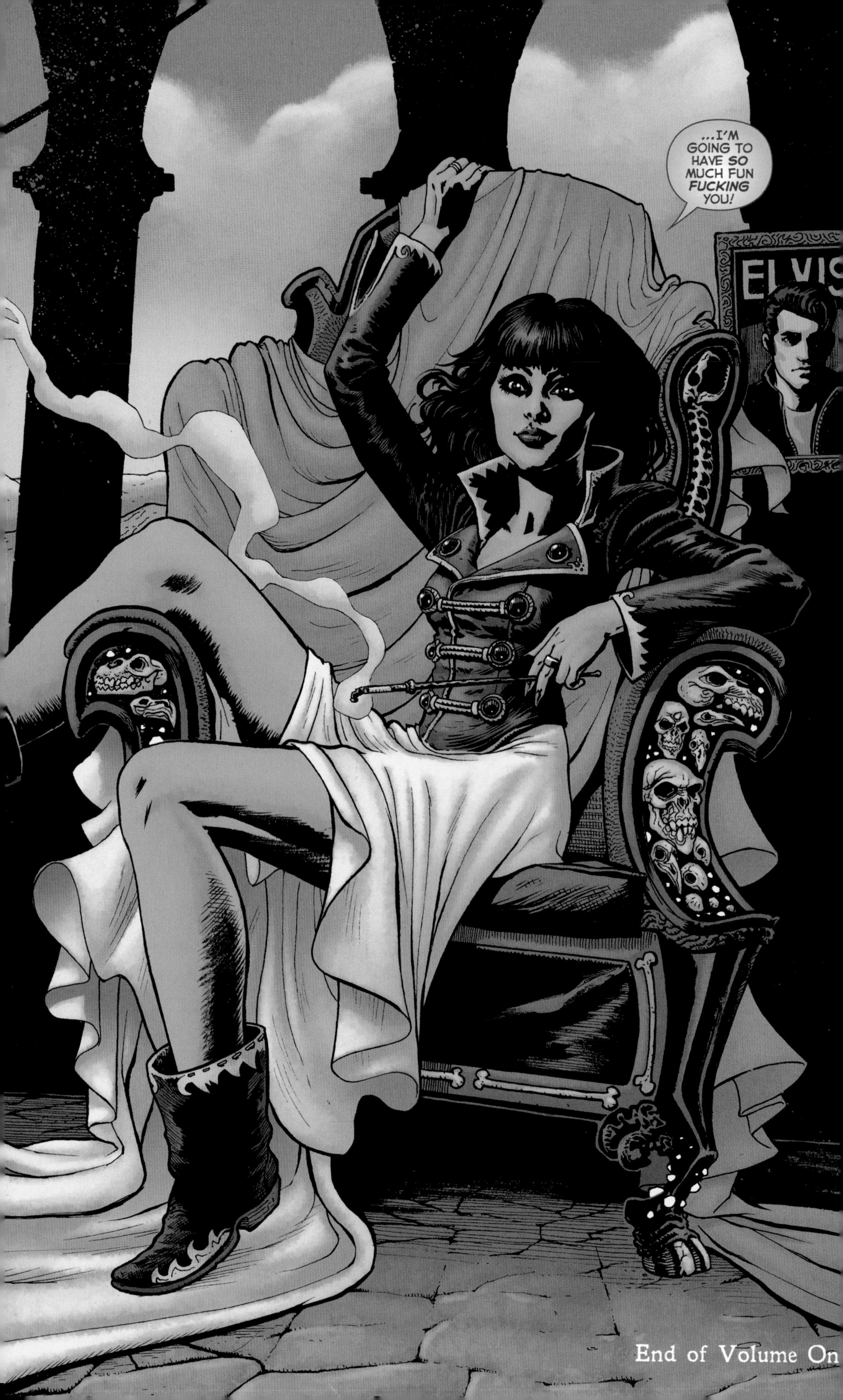
...I'M GOING TO HAVE SO MUCH FUN FUCKING YOU!
End of Volume On

NO PLACE LIKE HOME

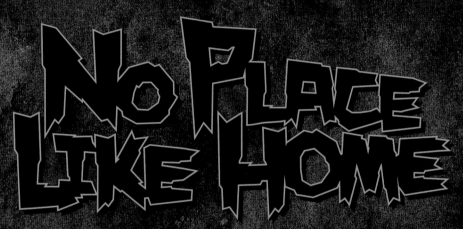

Art Gallery

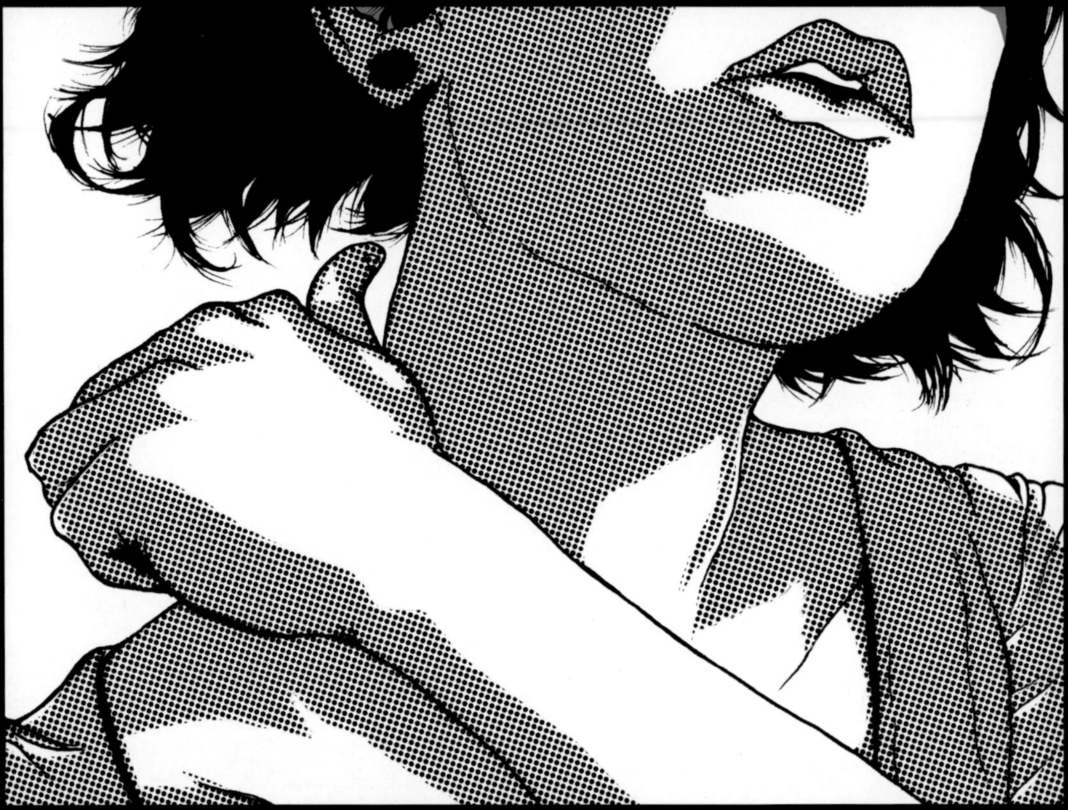

{HOME IS WHERE THE HEART IS}

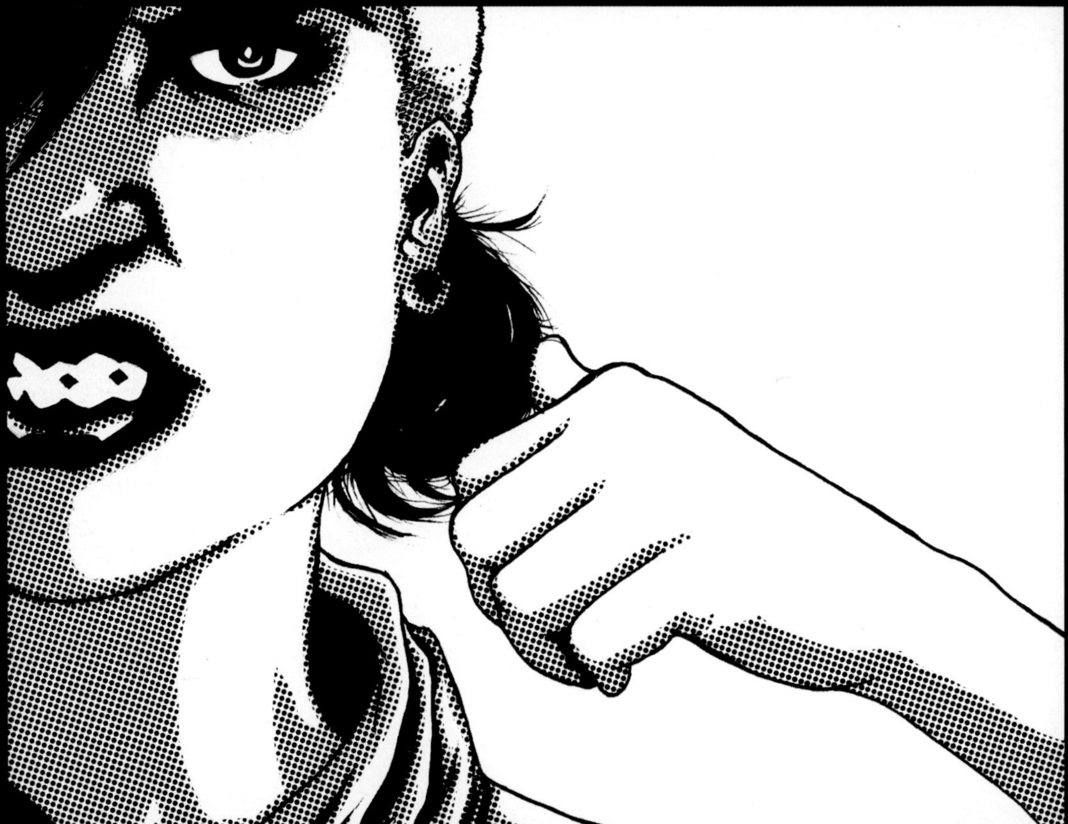

Jericho Vila

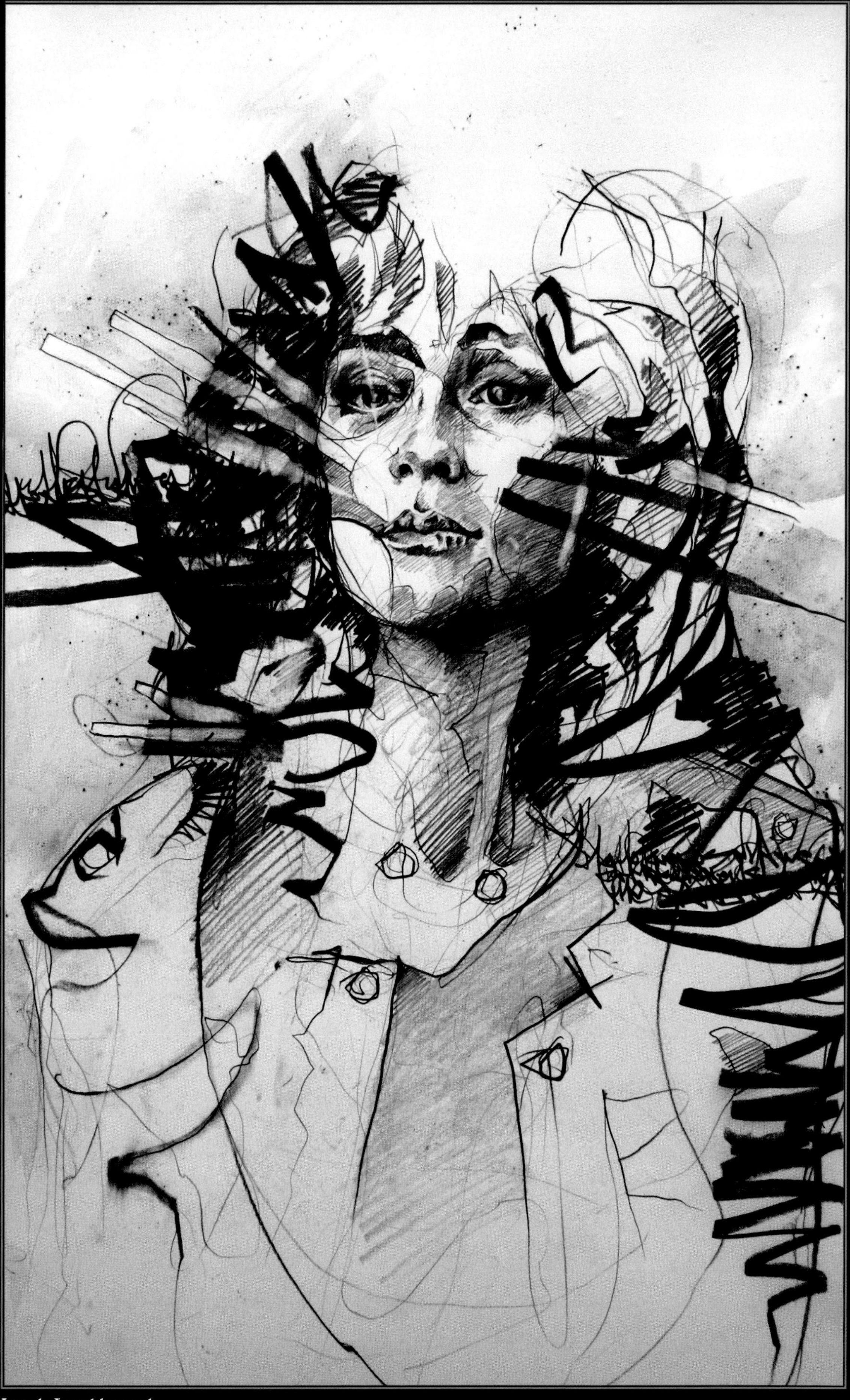

Joseph Loughborough

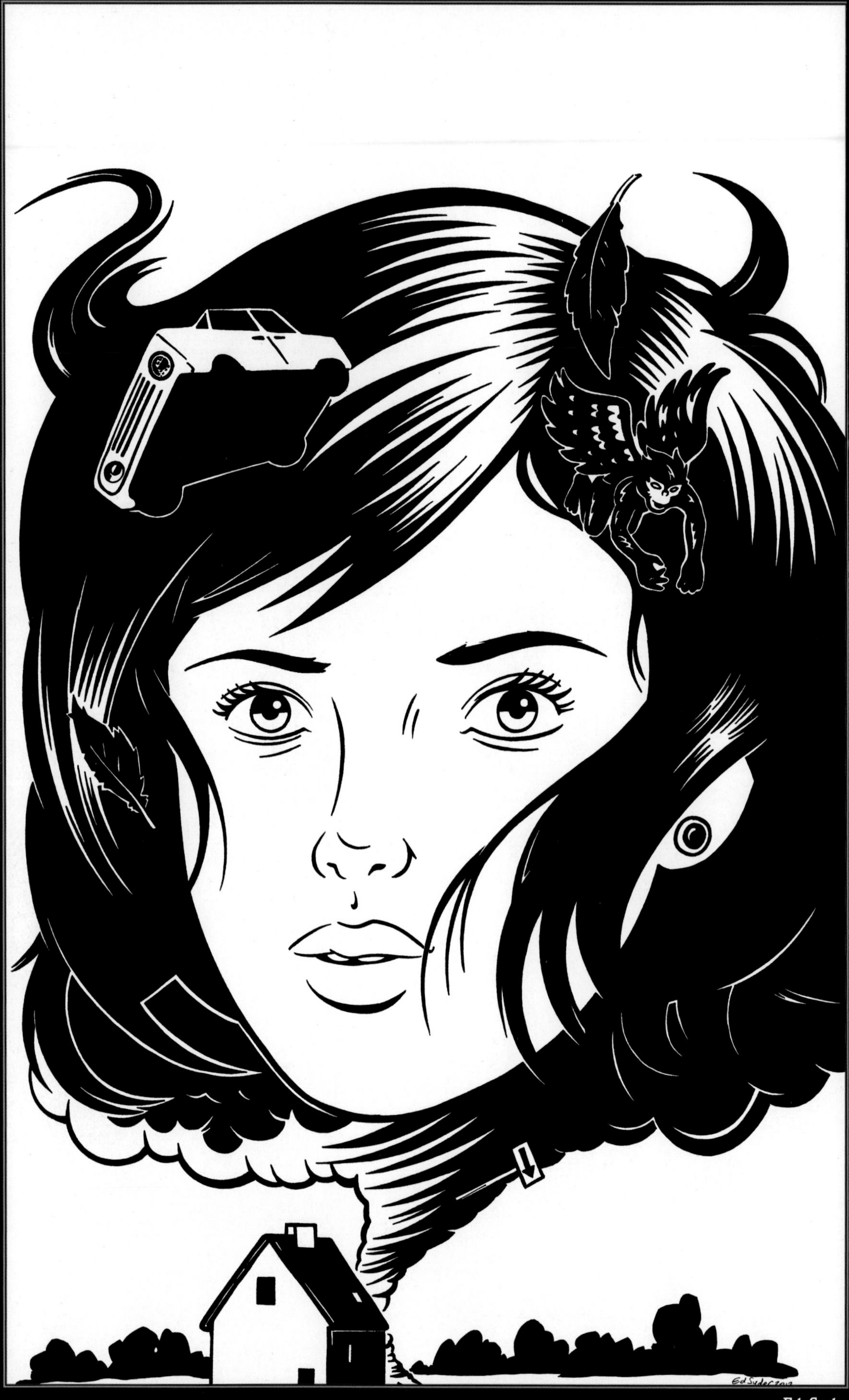
Ed Syder 2012

Ed Syder

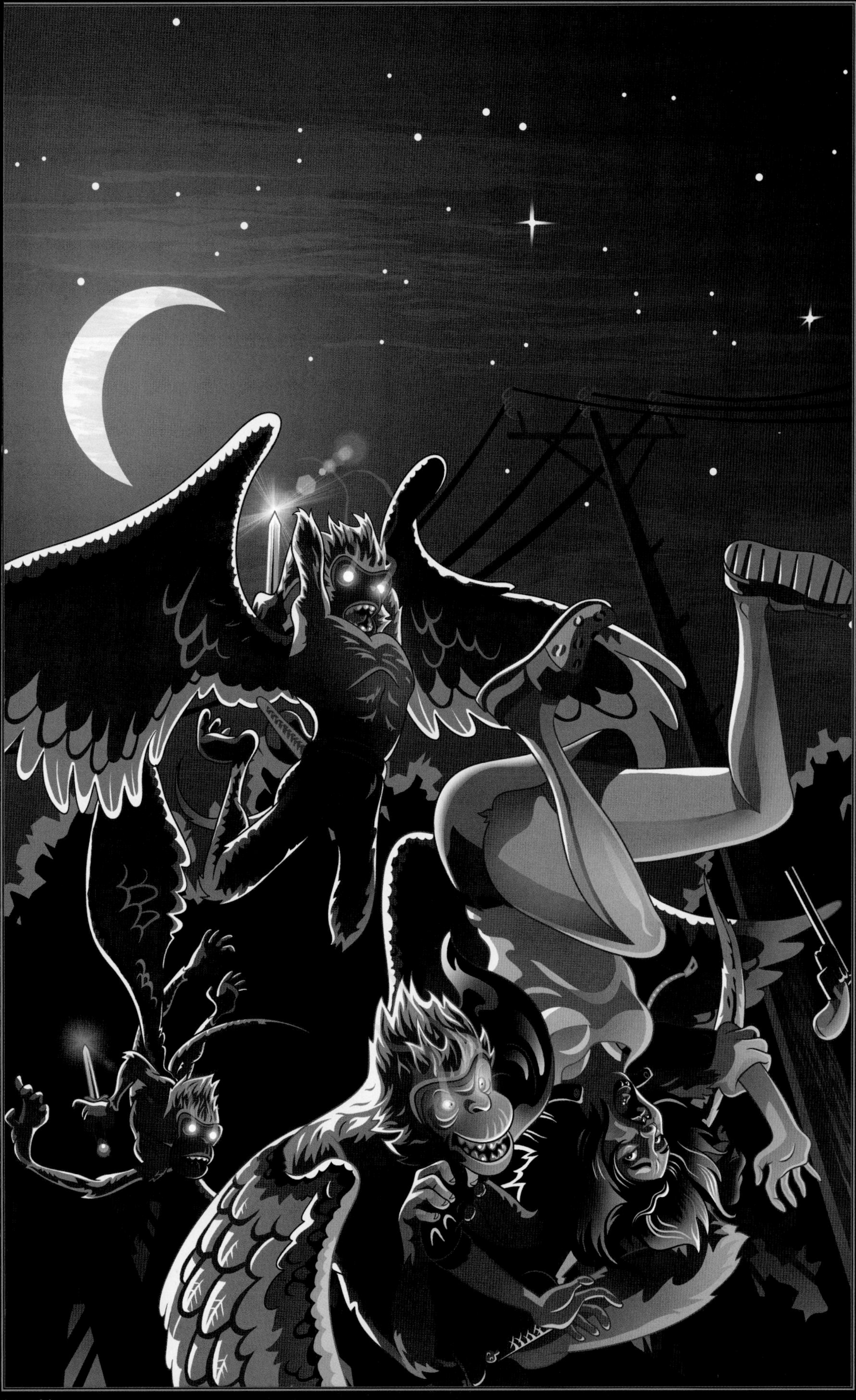
Paul Tinker

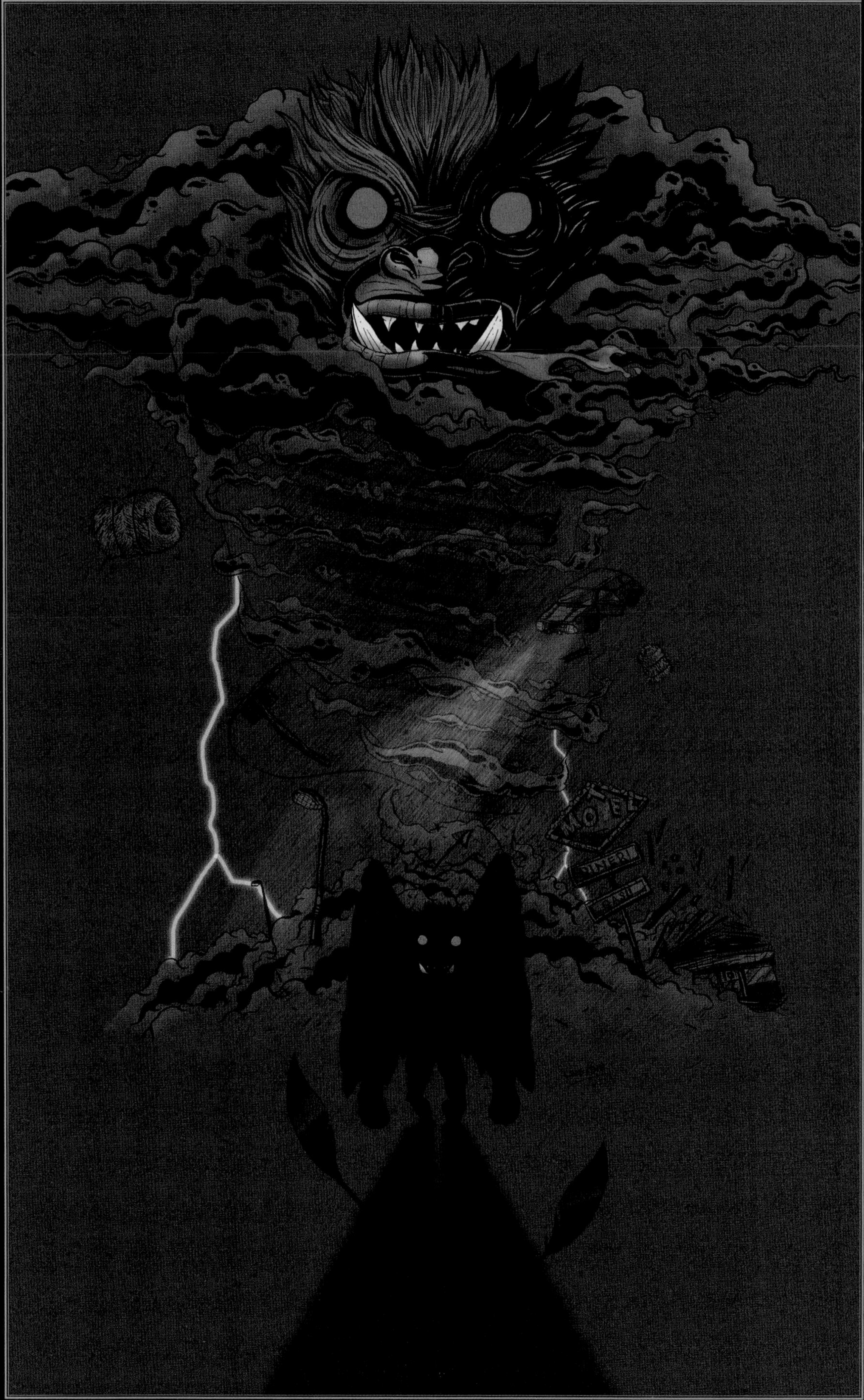
DINER
GAS

Paul Taylor

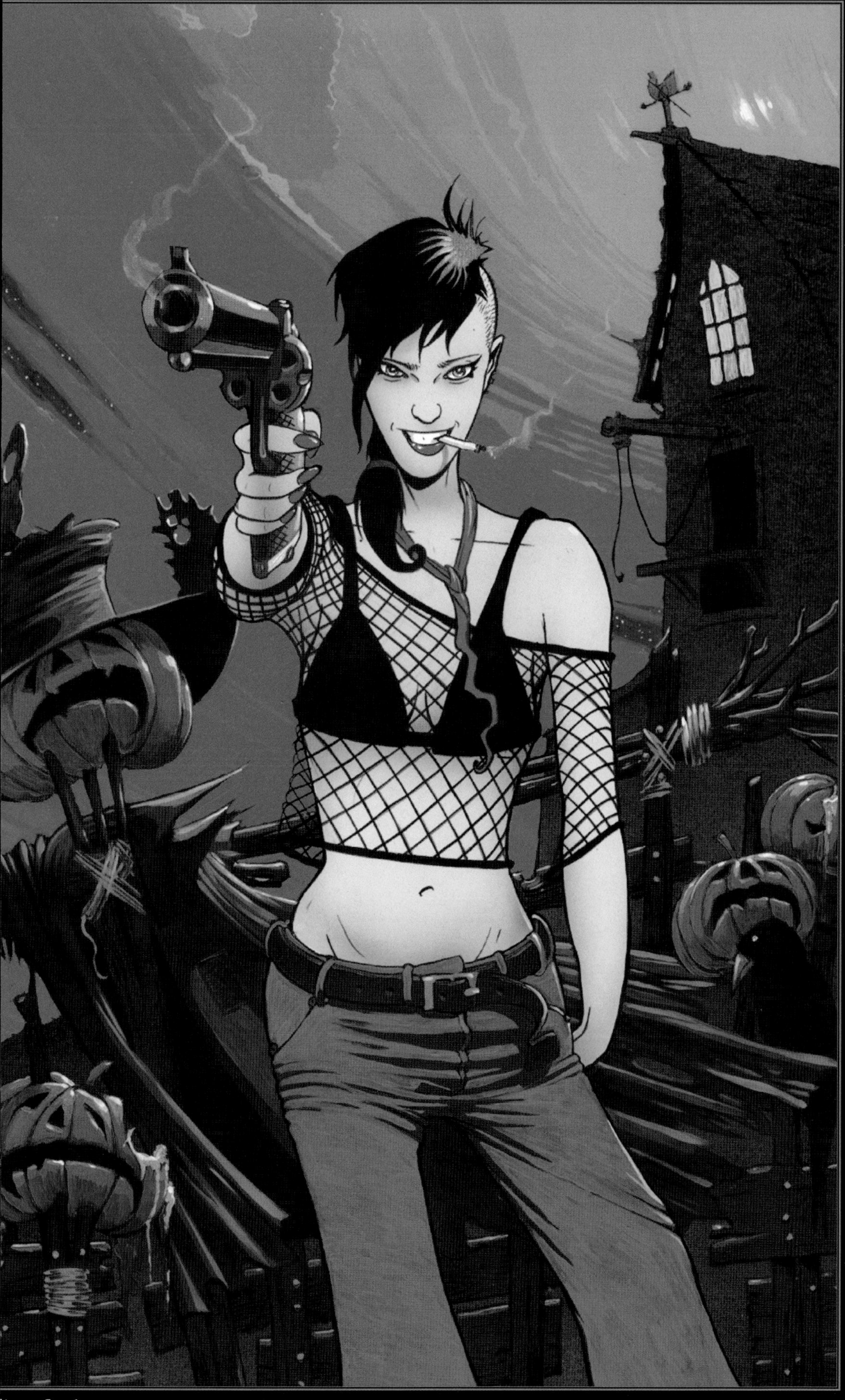

Simon Jacob

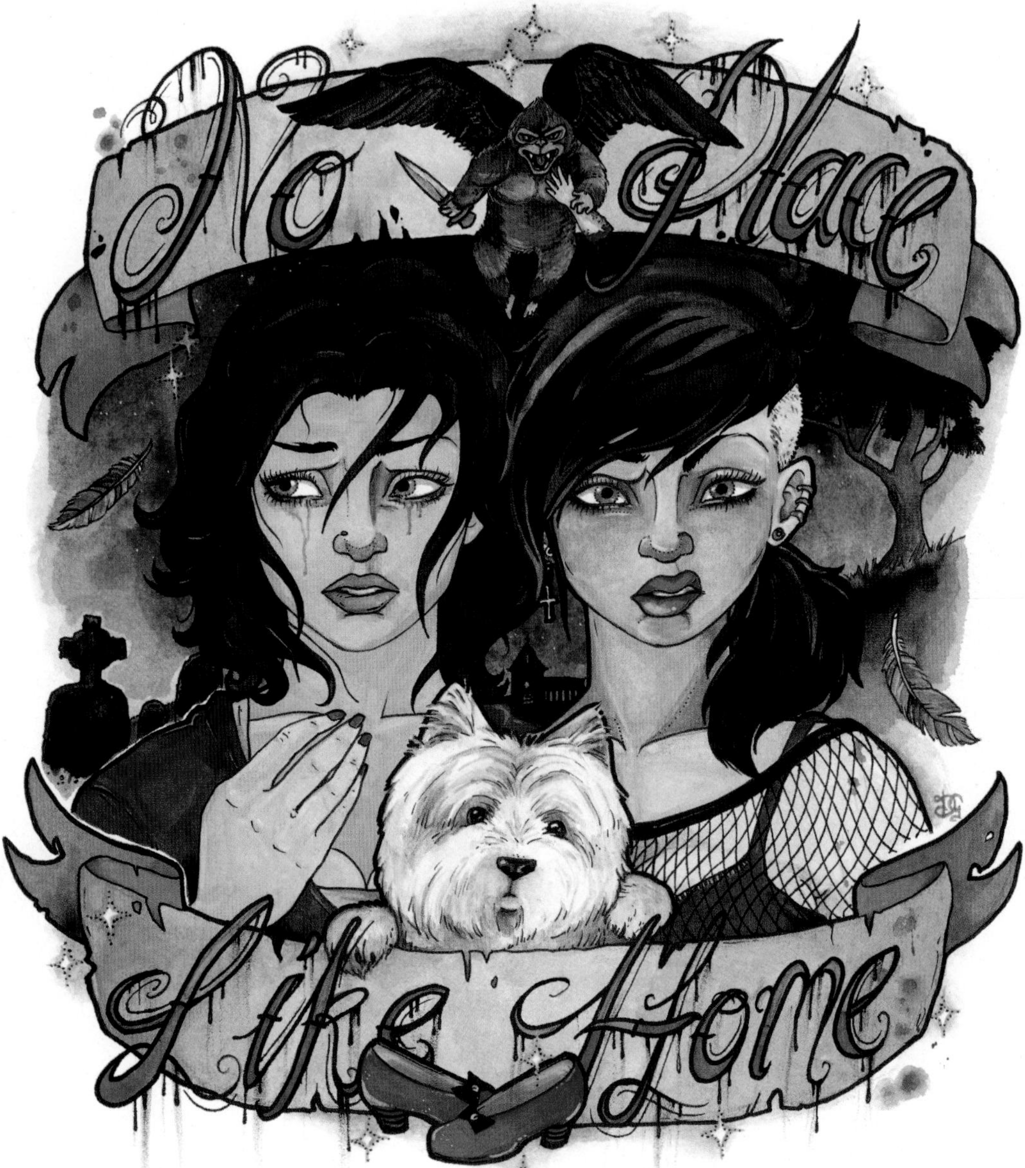
No Place
Like Home

Dani Gree

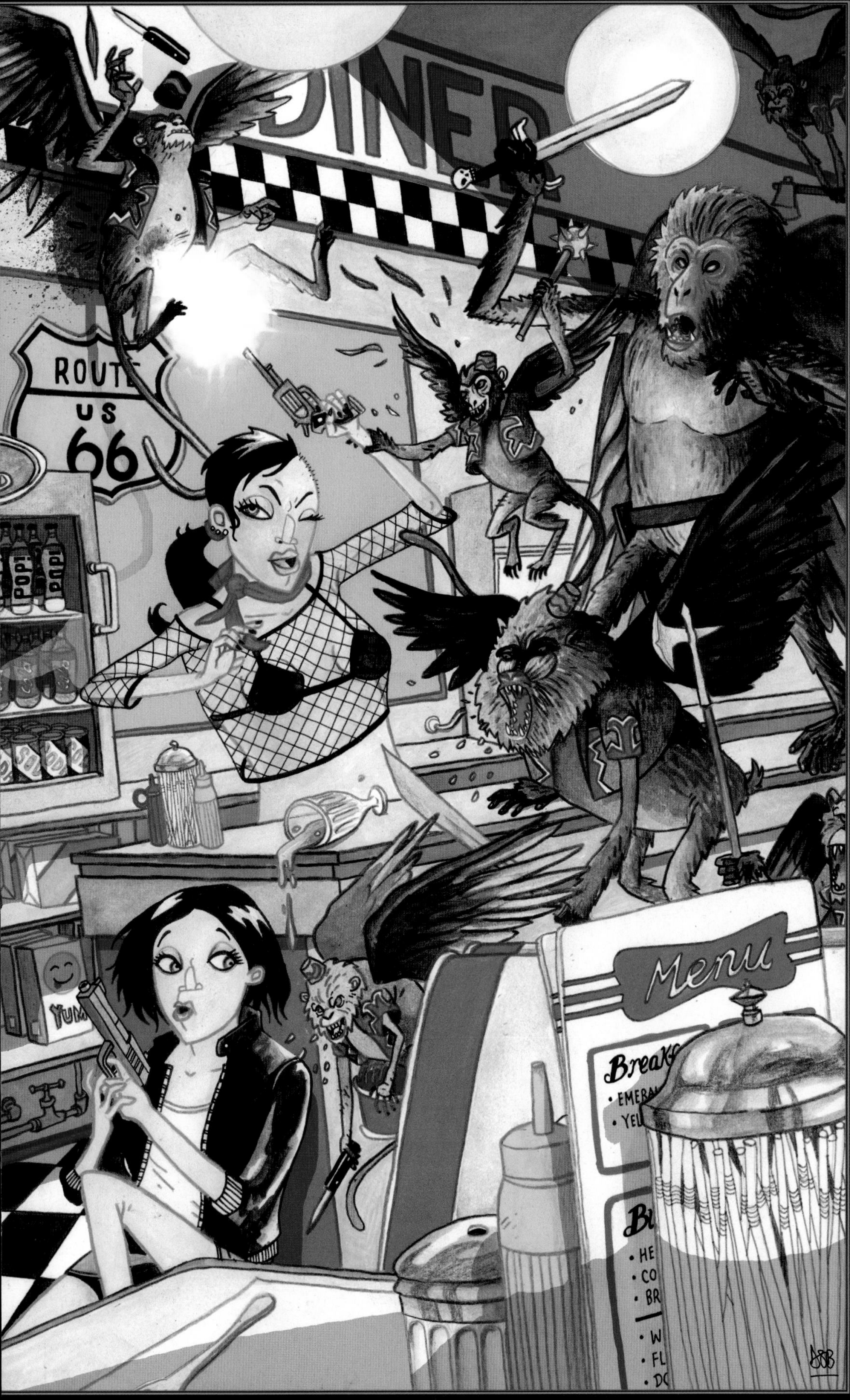
ROUTE
US
66
POP!
Menu

Dean Beattie

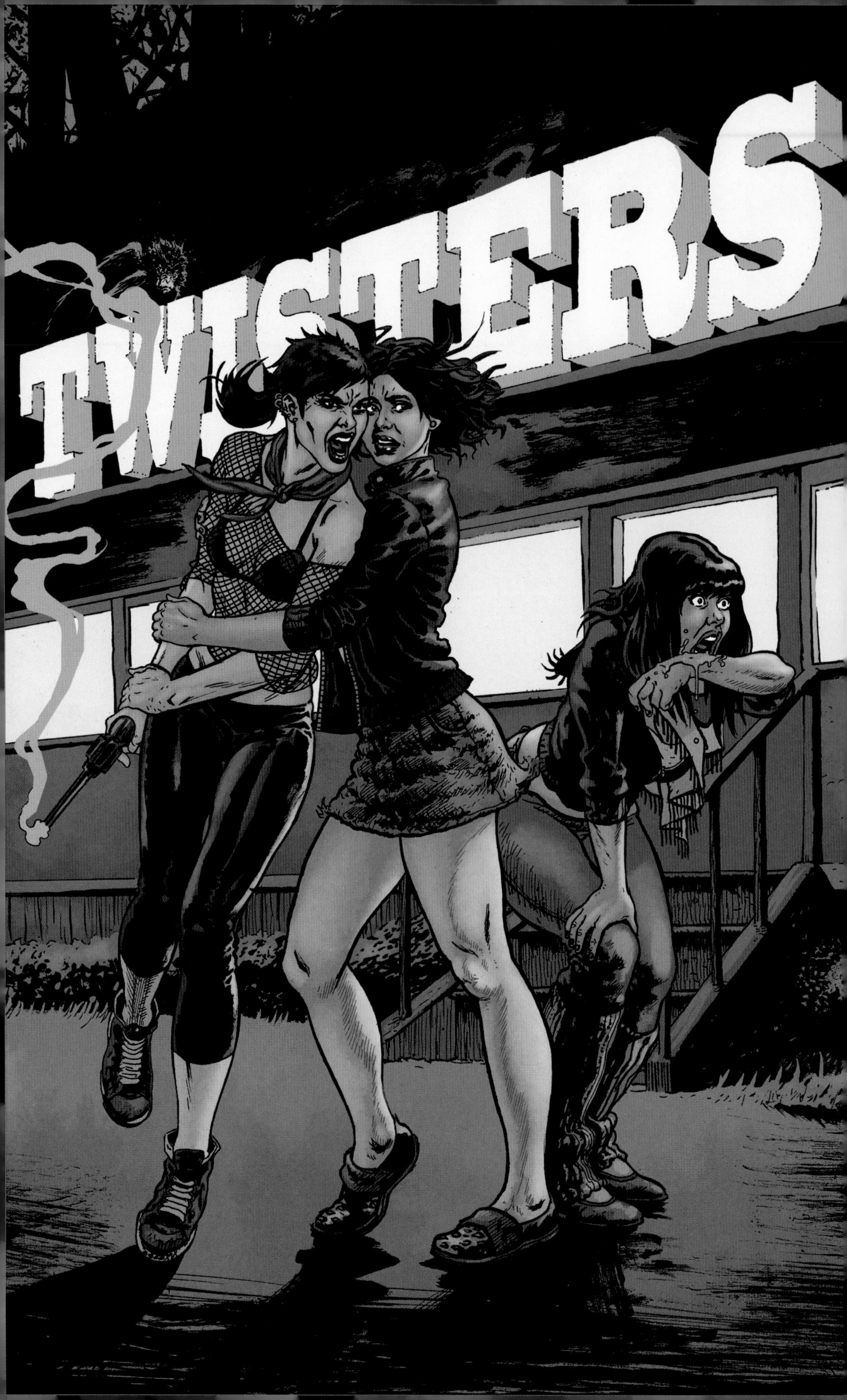
TWISTERS

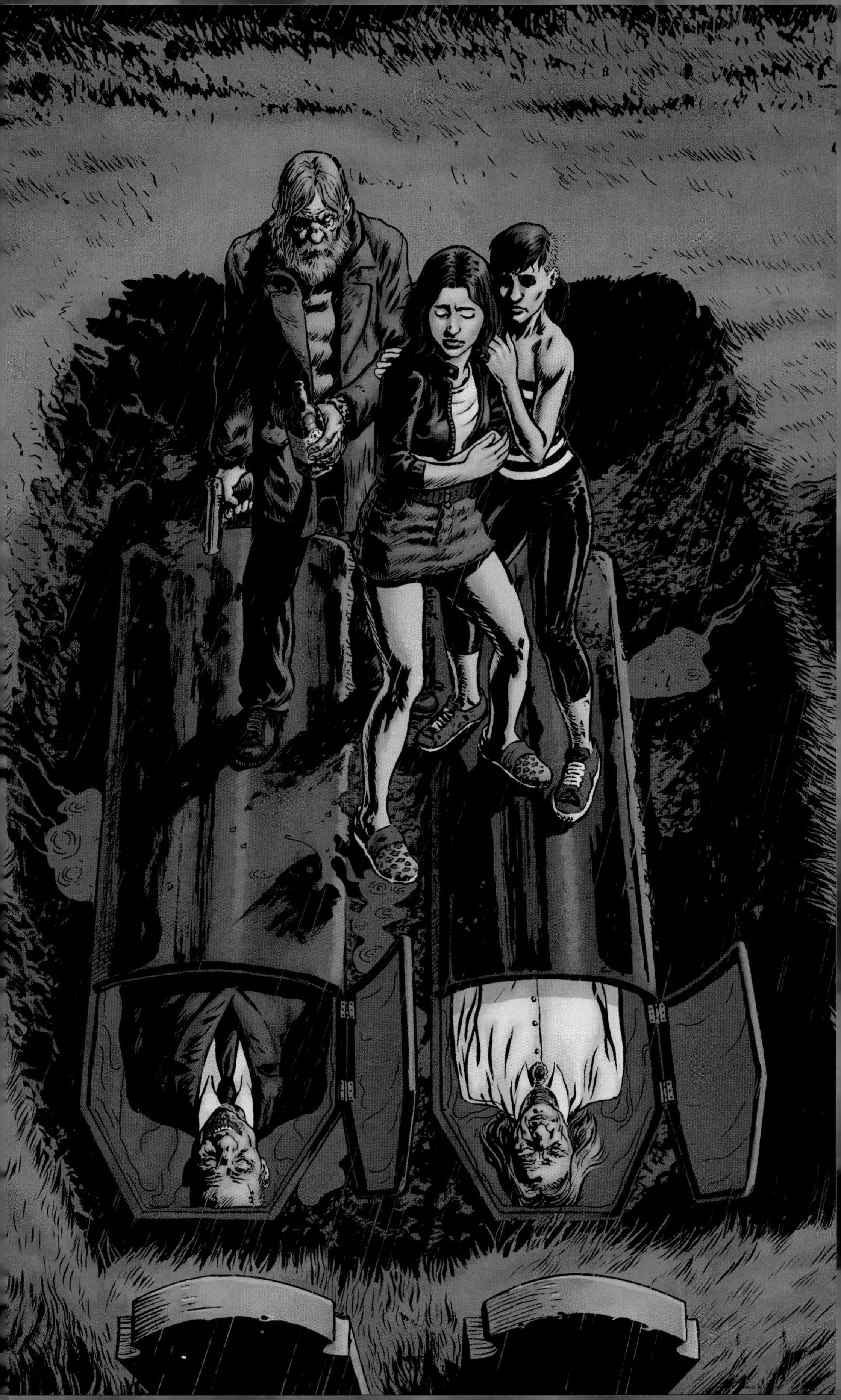

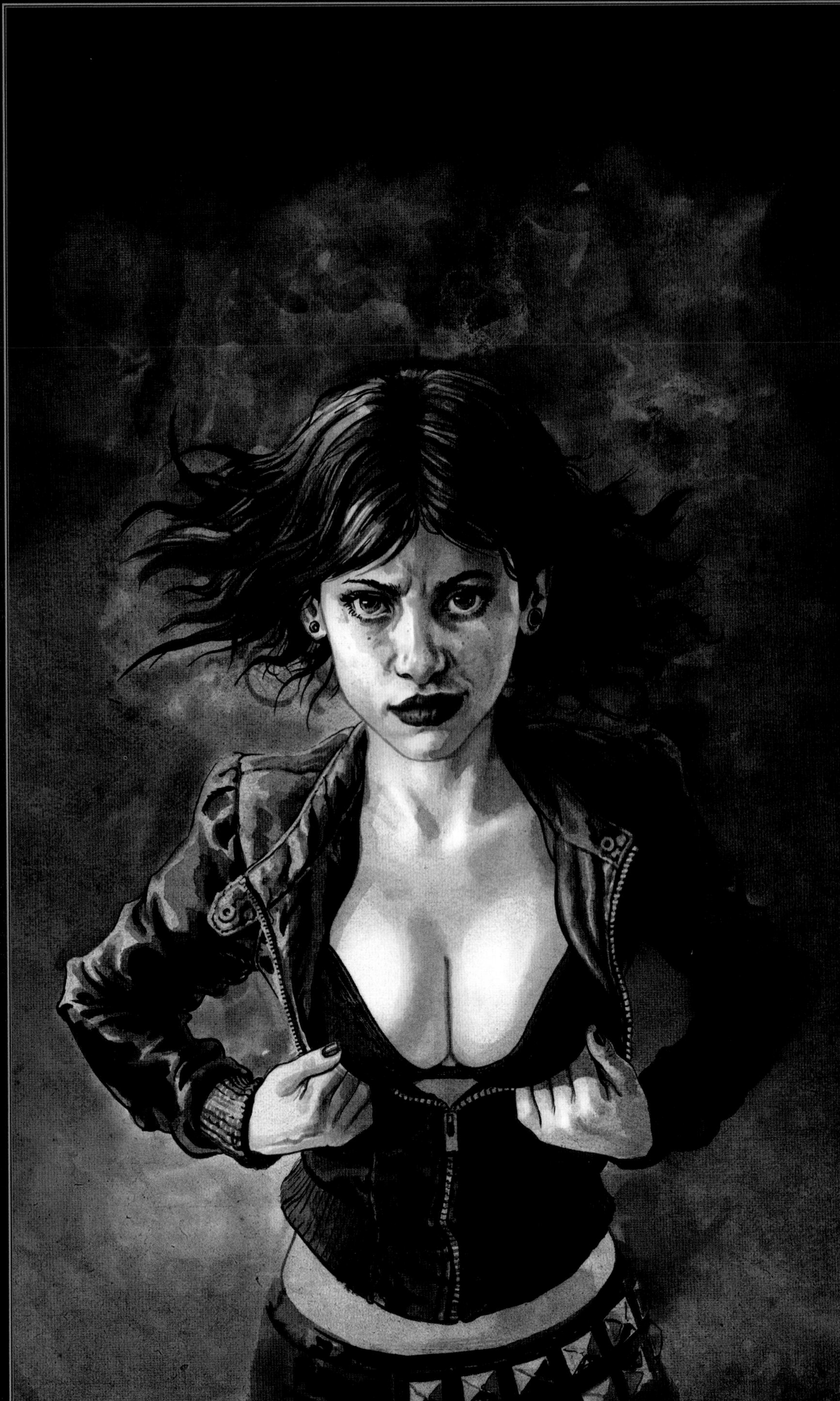

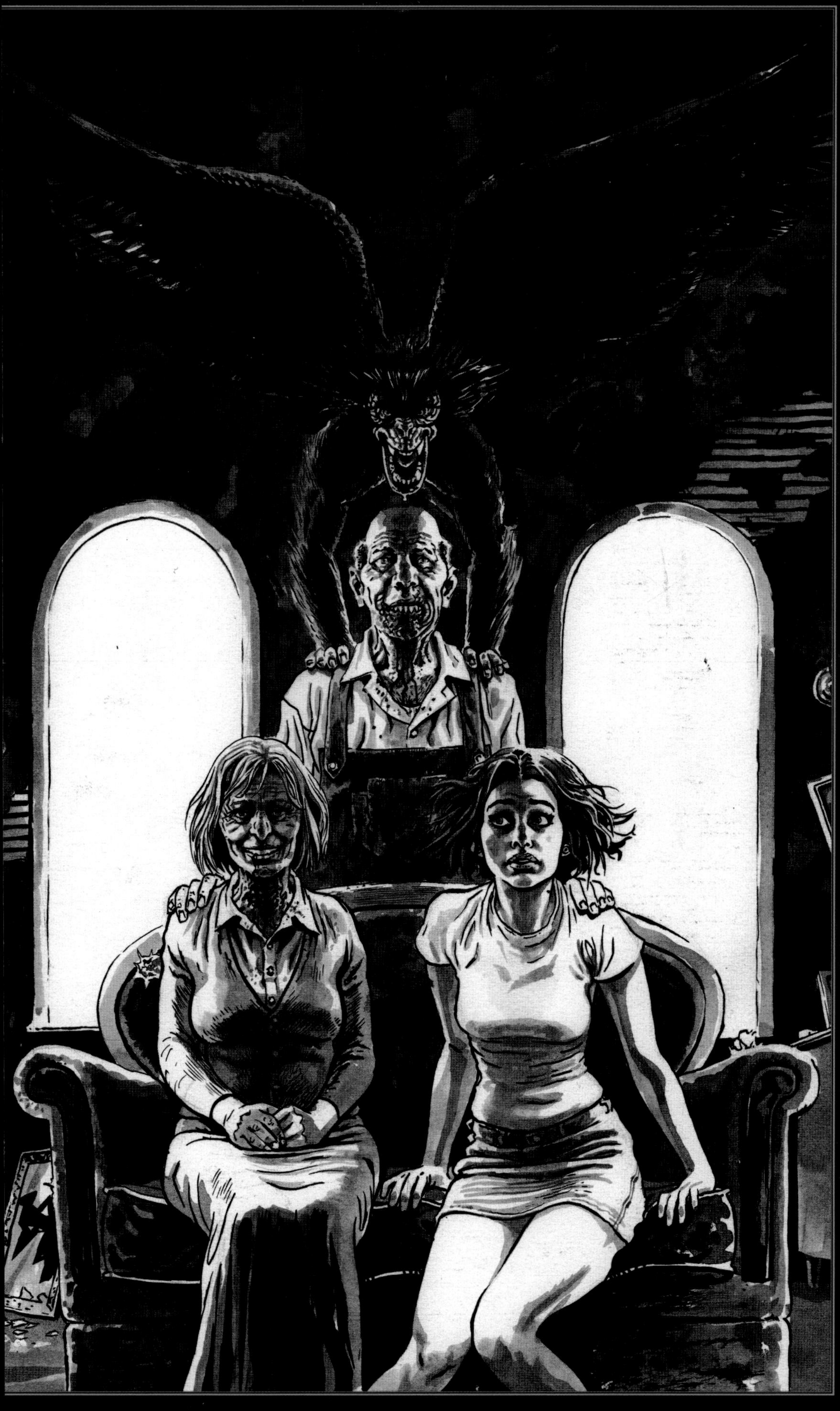

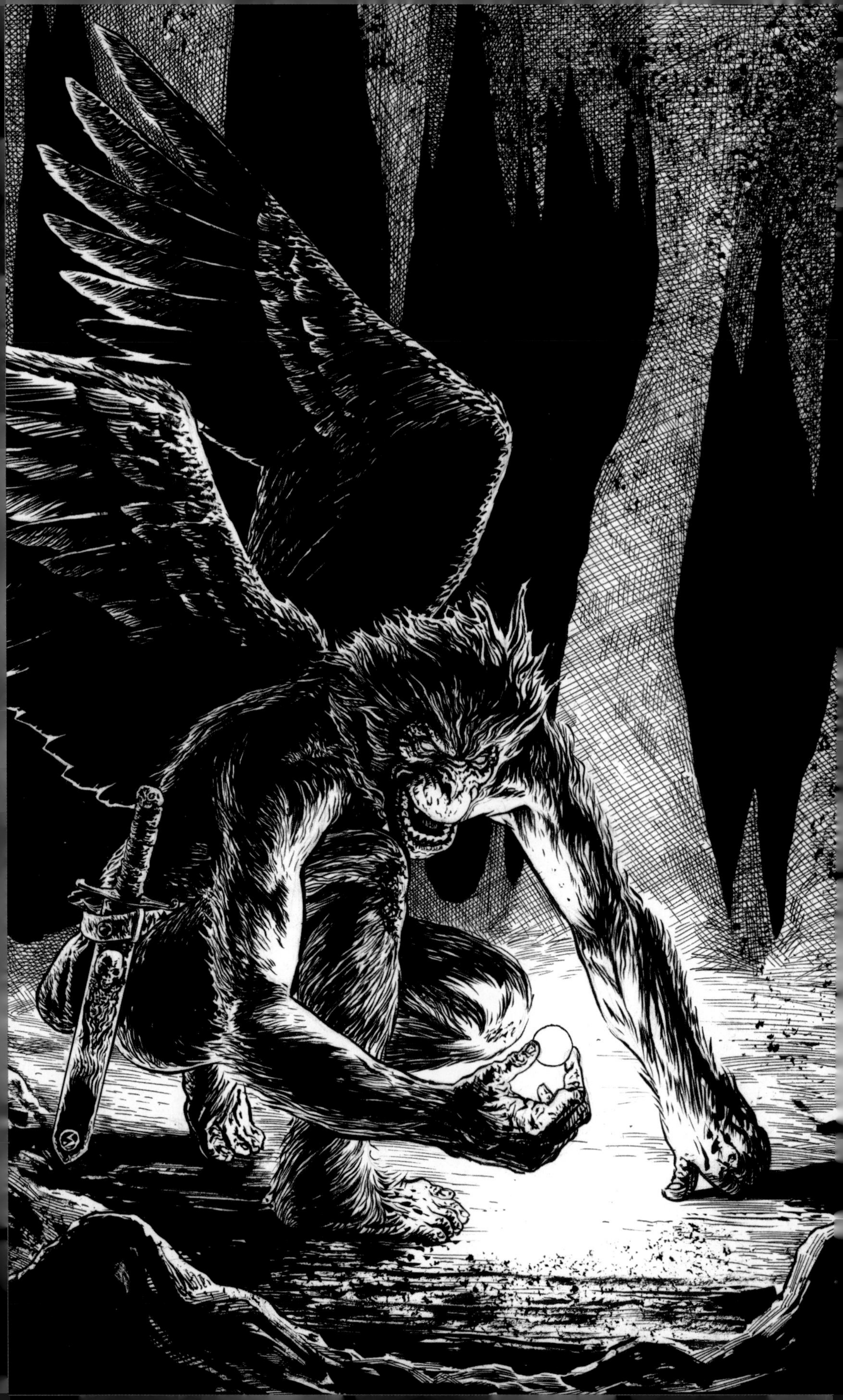

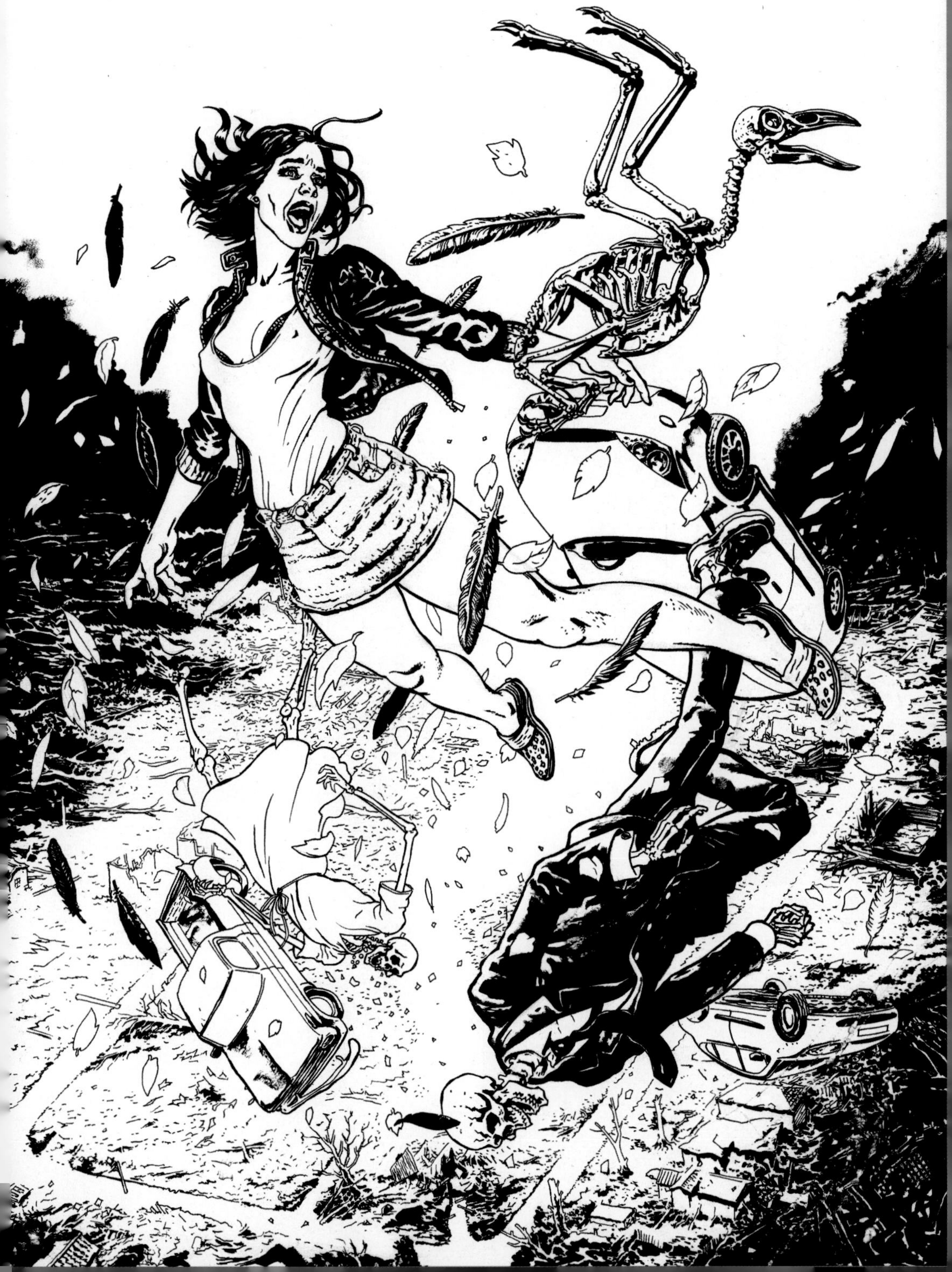

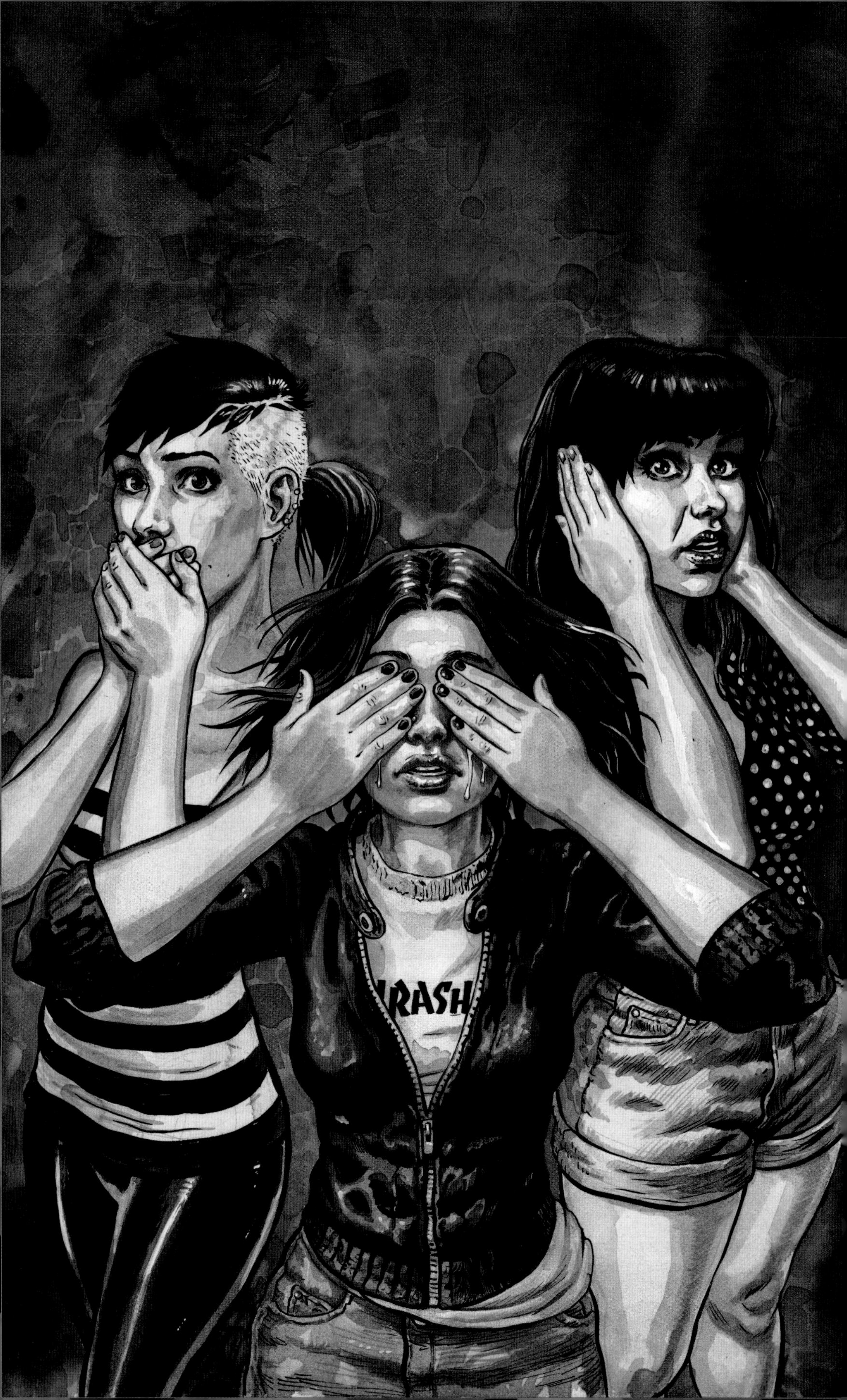

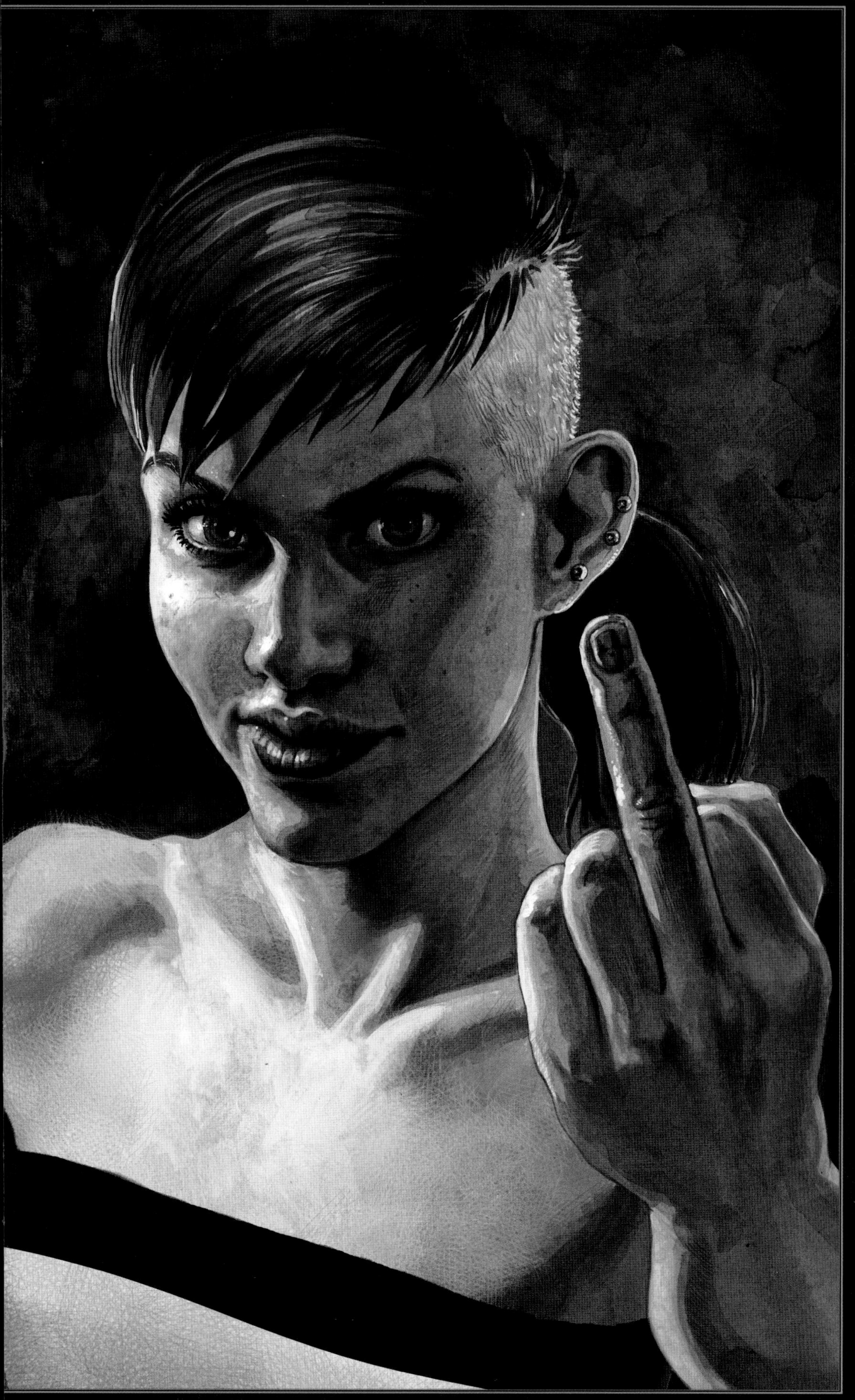